Quandaries of the Small-District Superintendency

Quandaries of the Small-District Superintendency

Edited by:
Gary Ivory
Adrienne E. Hyle
Rhonda McClellan
Michele Acker-Hocevar

palgrave
macmillan

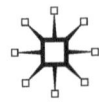

QUANDARIES OF THE SMALL-DISTRICT SUPERINTENDENCY
Copyright © Gary Ivory, Adrienne E. Hyle, Rhonda McClellan, Michele Acker-Hocevar 2015.

All rights reserved.

First published in 2015 by PALGRAVE MACMILLAN® in the United States—a division of St. Martin's Press LLC, 175 Fifth Avenue, New York, NY 10010.

Where this book is distributed in the UK, Europe and the rest of the world, this is by Palgrave Macmillan, a division of Macmillan Publishers Limited, registered in England, company number 785998, of Houndmills, Basingstoke, Hampshire RG21 6XS.

Palgrave Macmillan is the global academic imprint of the above companies and has companies and representatives throughout the world.

Palgrave® and Macmillan® are registered trademarks in the United States, the United Kingdom, Europe and other countries.

ISBN: 978-1-137-37014-3

Library of Congress Cataloging-in-Publication Data

Quandaries of the small-district superintendency / edited by Gary Ivory, Adrienne Hyle, Rhonda McClellan, Michele Acker-Hocevar
    pages cm
    Includes index.
    Summary: "Quandaries of the Small-District Superintendency teaches superintendents and superintendents-in-training how to develop critical frameworks for thinking through and addressing the problems and practices superintendents encounter daily. Focused on the particular needs of superintendents of districts of fewer than ten thousand students, the chapters invite students to examine the everyday practices of school leaders from different perspectives and to form a detailed and practical understanding of administration and leadership. The book draws equally on education administration and management practices and on social and educational theory, with the Interstate School Leaders Licensure Consortium standards for school leadership framing the whole in order to address all key aspects of superintendency. A thought-provoking consideration of the unsolvable quandaries every small-district superintendent faces, Quandaries of the Small-District Superintendency is a valuable touchstone for the issues that will be faced by current and future leaders alike"—Provided by publisher.
    ISBN 978-1-137-37014-3 (hardback)
    1. School districts—Unites States. 2. School superintendents—United States. 3. Educational leadership—United States. I. Ivory, Gary, 1947-
LB2817.3.Q36 2015
379.1'535—dc23
                                                2014028297

A catalogue record of the book is available from the British Library.

Design by Amnet.

First edition: January 2015

10 9 8 7 6 5 4 3 2 1

Transferred to Digital Printing in 2014

Contents

List of Figures   vii

1   Introduction   1
    Michele Acker-Hocevar, Adrienne E. Hyle, Gary Ivory, and Rhonda McClellan

2   Developing a Leadership Platform   15
    Gary Ivory

3   Pursuing a Vision on Which There Is Disagreement   19
    Sharon Gieselmann and William G. Ruff

4   District Superintendents as Instructional Leaders?   35
    Thomas L. Alsbury and Kathryn S. Whitaker

5   Decisions, Decisions, Decisions: Can Using Transformational Leadership and Mindfulness Theory Help You Make the Right Ones?   55
    Teena McDonald

6   Complexity Theory, Networking, and the Work of Small-District Superintendents   73
    Corrie Stone-Johnson

7   Generational Diversity and Feminist Epistemology for Building Inclusive, Democratic, Collaborative Community   91
    Debra Touchton and Michele Acker-Hocevar

8   Promoting the Success of Every Student with Integrity, with Fairness, and in an Ethical Manner: What If the Way Is Not Clear?   113
    Gary Ivory, Cristóbal Rodríguez, and Rhonda McClellan

9	Political Perspectives on Resource Allocation in Rural School Districts *Chad R. Lochmiller*	131
10	Choosing a Superintendent: A Decision Framework *Susan Printy*	153
11	The Self and Leader Expertise *Rhonda McClellan, Gary Ivory, and Adrienne E. Hyle*	179
	Appendix: Where Did We Get These Quandary Stories? *Gary Ivory and Michele Acker-Hocevar*	197

Notes on Contributors   201

Index   205

List of Figures

10.1	Competing values for organizational effectiveness	156
10.2	Excerpts from the 2013 Summerland School District Annual Report	159
10.3	CVF Worksheet A	174
10.4	CVF Worksheet B	175
11.1	Leader expertise development components and quality decision making	180

CHAPTER 1

INTRODUCTION

Michele Acker-Hocevar, Adrienne E. Hyle, Gary Ivory, and Rhonda McClellan

Thanks for selecting our book about superintendent leadership development. For those of us on the outside who look in at the world of district leadership, the daily work of the superintendent may appear deceptively simple. People need answers; superintendents provide them. People have problems; superintendents go about fixing those problems. Through the voices of practicing superintendents in this book, however, you will read in more detail about the challenges and complexities of their daily work. You will hear from them that there are no prescriptions for leadership and that no action is without a potential reaction. You will also hear from them that leaders often find themselves in a quandary—a difficult situation or a practical dilemma. A quandary is a crossroads of sorts. It is a situation in regard to which superintendents speak of weighing options and seeking multiple perspectives. They speak of having to step forward to make the best decision possible among competing perspectives.

Superintendents seem to us sometimes like sailors in stormy seas who cannot merely use their intellects to find the one safe, sure route amid the high, threatening waves. They must *negotiate* among the water, the wind, and the poor visibility, knowing the characteristics of their boats (both strengths and weaknesses) as well as their own skills and limitations and their experience with this particular kind of situation, concentrating at times on getting to their destinations and at other times simply on not drowning. The sailor cannot bring about a peaceful situation in order to find a sure route to his or her destination. He or she must work within the situation as it is. We think this is an apt metaphor for the small-district superintendency.

For those of you aspiring to be district leaders, or educational leaders at any level, we believe that this book will be helpful in your leadership preparation and development. We hope that the book will help you anticipate, confront, and navigate through many quandaries faced by today's superintendents. By presenting the many layers of an issue or the multiple ways an issue might be framed, we want to have you recognize the absence of an easy solution—this is what makes it a *true* quandary. In addition, we hope you will take one step closer to the superintendent's office by comprehending the value of your own leadership platform and seeing how you can navigate through these competing perspectives by understanding the importance of developing greater and more sophisticated approaches to assessing problems. The next chapter leads you through some steps for developing your leadership platform.

As a way to orient you to the tasks at hand in quandary negotiation, we divided this chapter into sections. The first sets the stage by presenting a brief history of the data upon which the book is based—the UCEA Voices project. The next section details what you can expect to encounter in each chapter.

The UCEA Voices 3 Project

The voices you are about to encounter in this book are real. In a project entitled "Voices from the Field: Phase 3" ("Voices 3"), researchers across the United States—members of the University Council for Educational Administration (UCEA) and the National Council of Professors of Educational Administration (NCPEA)—conducted 14 focus groups with superintendents. A focus group is an interview with a group of people (ideally four to ten) in which the interviewer asks questions and encourages a conversation among the participants. In the superintendent focus groups, the participants were asked to share their thoughts about doing what's best for students, adjusting their districts to No Child Left Behind mandates, and involving others in decision making.

We provide more specifics about the Voices 3 project in the appendix. We have found that the stories and explanations of these educational leaders reveal much about the nature of their work and the complex and thorny situations they encounter. We hope you find them helpful as well. They form the foundation of our work.

What to Expect in Each Chapter

The focus of this book is on quandaries of the small-district superintendency specifically and educational leadership generally. Given this focus, our authors have crafted each chapter to explore the negotiation of a quandary through theoretical frameworks or lenses that provide a better understanding of the professional guidelines that serve as a foundation for school district leadership. Quandary negotiation involves multiple strategies linked to the finding of middle ground, the recognition of parameters, and the give-and-take of solutions and perspectives. Each author works to help you understand the complexity of the quandary and the multiple ways in which the quandary could be understood, examined, and resolved. Interestingly, it is likely that no one answer, perspective, or direction will suffice.

Interstate School Leaders Licensure Consortium (ISLLC) Standards

The profession of school administration has a long history built on an extensive foundation of effective practice and research. From this foundation, a set of guidelines has emerged that details the capacities needed by today's school leaders both at the site and district levels. The Interstate School Leaders Licensure Consortium (ISLLC) standards provide "guidance to state policymakers as they work to improve education leadership preparation, licensure, evaluation, and professional development" (Council of Chief State School Officers [CCSSO], 2008a; see also CCSSO, 2008b). These standards are believed to depict the competencies of today's school leaders both at the site and district levels. According to these six standards, the capable school leader does the following:

Standard 1: Sets a widely shared vision for learning
Standard 2: Develops a school culture and instructional program conducive to student learning and staff professional growth
Standard 3: Ensures effective management of the organization, operation, and resources for a safe, efficient, and effective learning environment
Standard 4: Collaborates with families and community members, responding to diverse community interests and needs and mobilizing community resources
Standard 5: Acts with integrity, with fairness, and in an ethical manner
Standard 6: Understands, responds to, and interacts with the larger political, social, economic, legal, and cultural contexts

However, as comprehensive as these standards may be, the standards do not come with a manual for addressing the complexities inherent in achieving them. Each of the chapters in this book addresses a standard and a quandary linked to the standard and provides theoretical frames or lenses through which to view the quandary. The following is a list of the chapters organized by standard:

- **Standard 1** and the quandary of challenges and successes related to maintaining a vision on which there is disagreement is the focus of Chapter 3. The theoretical frameworks explored as lenses for viewing this quandary are those of Mary Parker Follett (1940) and Max Weber (1947).
- **Standard 2**, instructional leadership and the superintendent's role in that activity, is the focus of Chapter 4. Role theory (Katz and Kahn, 1966) and educational accountability (Leithwood, Aitken, and Jantzi, 2006; Argyris and Schön, 1978) serve as theoretical lenses through which to view this quandary.
- Chapters 5 and 6 are linked to the quandary of making major decisions that affect the academic, emotional, and physical safety of students, staff, and community members (**Standard 3**). In Chapter 5, transformational leadership (Burns, 1978; Heifetz, 1994) and mindfulness theory (Dhiman, 2009) help illuminate issues surrounding this quandary. In Chapter 6, complexity theory (Snyder, Acker-Hocevar, and Snyder, 2000) and networking (Printy, Marks, and Bowers, 2009; Stone-Johnson and Kew, 2013) are the lenses through which the learning organization quandary is viewed.
- Chapter 7 examines **Standard 4** and what collaborating with faculty and community members means in terms of responding to diverse community interests. The authors frame the quandary of diverse community interests in terms of generational theory (Strauss and Howe, 1991) and feminist epistemologies (Baumgardner and Richards, 2000; Rowe-Finkbeiner, 2004; Sommers, 1994).
- Chapter 8 focuses on **Standard 5** and the quandary of promoting the success of every student with integrity, with fairness, and in an ethical way. Normative and empirical approaches (Johnson, 1996) or theoretical frameworks are used in this chapter to illuminate the quandaries.
- Chapter 9 looks at **Standard 6** and resource allocation through the lens of a systems analysis model of politics (Easton, 1965; Wirt and Kirst, 1997).
- Chapter 10 focuses on the quandary of hiring a superintendent for a small, rural, but rapidly changing school district. This chapter spans

all six ISLLC standards. Competing Values Framework (CVF) is the lens through which the quandary is viewed (Cameron and Quinn, 1999).

Within each quandary chapter, you will be given a glimpse into superintendents' work through excerpts from the transcripts of the Voices 3 focus groups. Chapter authors will also introduce the theories to explore and/or address the quandary presented by the excerpts of the superintendents' voices. Your job will be to anticipate the various viewpoints and entertain multiple scenarios about how you might address the quandary. What responses and reactions might ensue under the different perspectives? You will be asked to navigate your way through the various opinions and recommendations by enlisting your leadership platform as a catalyst for this reflection. Discussion questions will provoke further thinking. The authors of the quandary chapters have listed resources to which you can go to learn more.

Quandaries

Each chapter uses excerpts from the Voices 3 transcripts in which practicing superintendents describe their work and the challenges they experience. We call these challenges *quandaries*. From their voices, we hear that school leadership is not simply putting prescribed solutions into action; rather, it is a constant encounter with quandaries that demand thinking, responding, and adjusting to the situations at hand. We have chosen the word "quandary" to describe your future life and work over two other popular words, "problem" and "dilemma." We think that "problem" connotes to most people something simple and short term. But problems in school leadership are seldom simple and often persist for years, decades, or longer. For example, as we write this, almost all states have been granted waivers to the No Child Left Behind Act (NCLB). Thus, an approach to district and school accountability that had come to be seen as onerous, cumbersome, and even counterproductive has been eliminated. Problem solved? No, because the calls for accountability will continue, and the different perspectives on what constitutes appropriate approaches to accountability are still out there. So, even though the NCLB "problem" has been solved, the accountability quandary persists, with Race to the Top waivers as one example.

Dilemma, in its strict definition, means you are stuck between two choices, both of which may have negative outcomes. For example, "Should I pay teachers on a standard scale, suggesting that only academic preparation and time on the job are valuable in this district? Or should I pay them according to market value and then be obliged to explain why a high school physics teacher is more valued by this district than a dual-language kindergarten teacher, or vice versa." Or, the two choices may both have positive outcomes: "Should I keep teachers in the classroom, maximizing instructional time, or send them to professional development, increasing their instructional effectiveness?" Murphy (2006) prompts aspiring school leaders to go beyond problem solving and instead to spend time "problematizing" their solution, that is, to consider what could or what did go wrong with a seemingly right or appropriate response.

"Quandaries" seem to us to describe better the complexity, persistence, and multifaceted nature of what educational leaders deal with, because quandaries can often be navigated successfully by leaders who think about opposing ideas; compare and contrast solutions from different frameworks and perspectives; and seek to break the patterns of mindlessness, to move to more creative and innovative solutions, and to include as many constituencies as possible. In fact, we will ask you to explore a presented quandary through a variety of perspectives. We provide more discussion of that below.

Quandary Negotiating

Why do we want you to think about quandaries? Certainly it is not to dissuade you from pursuing leadership in education. Education is of supreme importance to humankind, and we believe that education leadership is one of the noblest callings you can pursue. We want you to think about quandaries to promote your own growth as a leader and as a human, specifically in your ability to both frame and approach problems in fresh ways.

Simply said, we hope that this book of quandaries will help improve your grasp of the complexity of knowledge by posing and providing alternative frameworks for you to use to analyze and generate more innovative and creative approaches to quandary solving and decision making. The idea is that by posing different frameworks and perspectives for problem solving and decision making, we hope to help you to acquire more sophisticated knowledge sets and to see both the quandary and possible solutions in new ways.

To bring about the best education possible for each child, to help individual campus leaders rise to their own independent potential, and to help engage and persuade multiple constituencies, leaders must have a keen appreciation for the complexity of a situation and the people involved. This entails keeping an open mind, avoiding quick adoption of simple solutions, and considering varying perspectives and alternatives, in order to decide on and move forward with new approaches. By posing, comparing, and contrasting different ways of thinking about quandaries in education, we encourage you to develop the expertise required for *epistemic sophistication* (Day, Harrison, and Halpin, 2009, p. 88). This does not mean that you are so flexible that you just go with any idea propounded to you, but rather that through mindful action and quandary solving you look at a new idea and weigh it carefully, often looking for kernels of new thinking and action that may combine or transform ideas. Rejection of new ideas does not lead to epistemic sophistication, but neither does unquestioning acceptance. Rather, thoughtful leadership and quandary negotiation grows from critical thinking and carefully considered responses and analyses.

As a developing leader, you know that people cannot always do what someone else would have them do. In fact, when confronted with conflicting perspectives, you must realize that you cannot make all the people happy, all the time. So, how do leaders make their decisions? Whose voices count? What opinions matter? Given the many ways to go about doing something and the various opinions regarding what should be done, arriving at the "right" answer may even be impossible. To work your way through the quandary, we may ask you to select a specific perspective about the quandary and to pursue a solution from that viewpoint. What would resolution look like for someone holding that view?

We might further the argument by asking you to identify a contrasting perspective and a resolution from that view. We might pose to you, the leader, "What would you do?" In this process, we encourage you to consider alternate perspectives and approaches, to use theories as devices for dissecting and deciphering issues (issues sometimes behind the issue), and to go beyond the obvious solution—question your immediate response, boldly go where you may not have gone before. Think outside your own box.

Conceptual or Theoretical Frameworks

Contrasting perspectives may be presented in the form of conceptual or theoretical frames. It is your task to reflect on and listen to these various concepts or perspectives; learn from them. Attempt to find value in each. You may even want to read further about the theories or concepts. The chapter authors will guide you in this direction and suggest a few sources with which you can increase your knowledge and understanding of particular concepts or perspectives. Knowing more will help you anticipate reactions and guide your own action. It might help you to see where people come from ideologically and how they typically act. What scholars call theories or theoretical frameworks are collections of discussions, labels, and categories of human patterns. Any theory is primarily a description of two things: (1) which elements of a situation are most worth paying attention to and (2) how these elements relate to one another. Given certain elements, certain relationships are likely. And certain relationships are likely to predict certain actions or behaviors. Theories and theoretical frameworks for quandary negotiators function like tools for a carpenter or the various stitches for a quilter. Theories, if used reflectively, help leaders do their jobs better. Theories help leaders anticipate how people may respond to their decisions, and theories offer competing viewpoints. Simply said, theories function as guides for decision making by explaining typical responses and reactions and by ferreting out the different ways in which responses and reactions can be interpreted.

How Are Theories Used In Practice?
An a priori strategy might build from theory to action. For example, a leader might muse as follows: based upon a particular theory that I know, if I act in a way guided by this theory, the beliefs and actions of a group will likely be in support of my decisions. Why? Remember, theory predicts outcomes from sets of related concepts and actions. Consider Etzioni's (1975) compliance theory.

> According to compliance theory, organizations can be classified by the type of power they use to direct the behavior of their members and the type of involvement of the participants. In most organizations, types of power and involvement are related in three predictable combinations: coercive-alienative, utilitarian-calculative, and normative-moral. . . . Nevertheless, school officials who attempt to use types of power that are not appropriate for the environment can reduce organizational effectiveness. (Lunenberg, 2012, p. 1)

To use coercive power and expect moral involvement would be theoretically incongruent. If you want moral involvement, normative power is needed.

Yet, we know that theories can run counter to one another. Appropriate strategies from one theoretical framework may predict action, but viewing the situation through a different theoretical lens might predict or recommend a "wait and see" response. Thus, although I might frame my reaction by using one theory, viewing my action through another theory may result in a different set of decisions and actions. Using Etzioni's (1975) compliance theory again, if I decided to try to increase student academic performance by offering financial incentives to students for good grades, and grades did not improve, then what? An a posteriori analysis of the situation through Etzioni's theoretical lens would help me understand that I should not be surprised if students calculated whether or not the incentive was sufficient to justify altering their study time and habits. It is possible that analysis of the quandary and the decisions made would have been more appropriately understood through a different theoretical framework.

Theories Cannot Do It All
Theories can be accused of oversimplifying the world. Maxwell (2009) wrote, "No theory is a complete, accurate reflection of the complex realities we study; every theory is a lens for making sense of the world, and every theory both reveals some aspects of that reality, and distorts or conceals other aspects" (p. 5). So, are we contradicting ourselves now by urging you to be open to multiple perspectives but to attend to theories that oversimplify?

We see it this way: It is important to broaden your perspective beyond the issues on which you usually focus, but not to the extent that you are overwhelmed. A nineteenth-century psychologist, William James, noted that taking in all the details and issues will lead any human to "a blooming, buzzing confusion" (1890, p. 488). Confusion paralyzes us or renders us inept. So, we must simplify. Good theorists simplify more efficaciously, more systematically, and more thoughtfully than the rest of us. Furthermore, they accomplish the task in different ways. Not all simplify the same way, so even in simplifying, different theorists and perspectives can expand our ways of seeing quandaries.

Theorizing about human beings is more complicated than theorizing about the physical world. Because we humans put our own interpretations on events and because humans choose rationally and irrationally, it is not nearly so easy to predict or control what we will do. In any given situation, the soundest theory may not predict how a specific individual will behave. And it certainly may not enable us to control that individual. That may be why you hear people say things like, "I tried the theory, but it didn't work." So, theory can seem irrelevant to understanding humans.

The Benefits of Theories
But there are two important contributions that theories make to our work: First, they may *increase the odds* that we can predict and

control behavior, even if they do not enable us to predict and control every single instance of that behavior. Second, theories have academic respectability. As we said above, theories have been propounded by thoughtful, informed people and discussed and critiqued by other thoughtful, informed people in academia. Often, they have been tested against empirical evidence to assess the extent to which they are consistent with our experience of the world. They have earned some public credibility. Through careful consideration of theories, you can increase your epistemic sophistication and learn how they compare to your own views of the world.

We believe that the person who says, "I don't care about theory; I just go with what works," is misrepresenting, or perhaps misunderstanding, his or her situation. To define what it means to "work" and to recognize "what works," the person would have to have in his or her own head a specification for what to pay attention to and how to recognize "what works." *These are issues of theory.* That means the speaker has come up with his or her own theory. So, he or she is not skeptical of theory, just of academic theory. But, at the same time, such a person may be too confident in his or her own theory. In other words, he or she may lack epistemic sophistication. One way to develop epistemic sophistication is to carefully consider other people's theories. Reading about the different theories in this book should help you develop more perspectives on quandaries and make you a better navigator by helping you to view problems through multiple lenses.

In sum, each chapter includes the following:

- **A discussion linked to at least one of the ISLLC standards.**
- **A description of one or more quandaries faced by real school leaders in the first decade of the twenty-first century, given in their own words.** These leaders provide vivid and compelling views of the world in which you work or aspire to work. Your work as an educational leader will be largely dedicated to facing quandaries such as those our superintendents describe.
- **A variety of perspectives to use when negotiating quandaries.** Defining a problem incorrectly, or even just too narrowly, will hinder your ability to understand it and deal with it. Everyone has different ways of defining problems. Hearing out those different definitions may expand your own understanding of situations. But, it may also overwhelm you. The challenge is to listen well, to expand your perspectives, and to consider critically so you can weigh the validity of the different perspectives and their implicit preferences for approaching situations. We want to help you practice be-

ing simultaneously open-minded and critical. We offer a variety of different perspectives:
(a) Those of superintendents we interviewed
(b) Theoretical frames that offer insights into patterns of behavior and thinking and suggestions for leadership action
(c) Resources for additional study found within each chapter
(d) And, of course, the perspectives of the different chapter authors themselves. We hope you find rich opportunities to be both open-minded and critical, and epistemologically sophisticated.

- **Descriptions of a variety of behaviors to consider when negotiating quandaries.** We see leadership largely as requiring a repertoire of behaviors. You will read the words of superintendents describing how they dealt with quandaries in their lives and work, and you will be asked to consider ways you might deal with similar situations. You have to be open to the solutions and critical in considering them. The solutions can be as multifaceted as the quandary. The job never ends as long as you are a thinking, quandary-facing human. We want this book to help you along the path to doing the job well—and today that necessarily means enacting multiple approaches. This book can help you achieve the opposite of the situation described in Maslow's quip: "If the only tool you have is a hammer, [it is tempting] to treat everything as if it were a nail" (1966, pp. 15–16).
- **A number of academic theories, perspectives, and resources regarding education leadership.**

Here's a recap: The everyday work of superintendents is far more complex than perceived. Quandaries, for which there are no easy solutions, surface daily. Leaders must simply gather as many perspectives as possible, play out every scenario imaginable, and enlist theoretical frameworks to analyze even further—and then arrive at a decision. You might be thinking about now, "You have got to be kidding me. How am I to make a decision with all of these competing viewpoints—that offer no definitive correct answer?" Welcome to the quandaries of the small-district superintendency!

Organization of the Book

In this first chapter, we have introduced you to the UCEA superintendency voices project and to the role of this real-world, real-person data in setting the stage for superintendent quandaries and theoretical explorations. The ISLLC standards were also presented. In addition, in each chapter you will find Voices 3 excerpts (descriptions from practicing superintendents or compilations of descriptions), theoretical frameworks, discussion questions, and additional resources. A final chapter draws on research on expertise to suggest ways you can grow in your capacity to negotiate quandaries. An appendix provides more specifics about the UCEA Voices 3 project.

ACKNOWLEDGMENTS

Small-district superintendents are kept quite busy with their quandaries. So, we are grateful to all of them who, despite their busyness, participated in these focus groups. We have learned much from them. We thank all the UCEA and NCPEA members who had enough faith in the Voices 3 project to conduct focus groups across the United States. We appreciate the work of the quandary chapter authors, who accepted our guidance and wrote and revised in response to our growing understanding of what precisely we wanted from them for this book.

Finally, we thank the executive committee and the executive director, Michelle Young, of UCEA for their long-term support of the Voices projects. We acknowledge also the vision of Fran Kochan, Dan Duke, and Barbara Jackson, whose initiative gave birth to this whole line of research.

REFERENCES

Argyris, C., and Schön, D. (1978). *Organizational learning: A theory of action perspective.* Reading, MA: Addison-Wesley.

Baumgardner, J., and Richards, A. (2000). *Manifesta: Young women, feminism, and the future.* New York: Farrar, Straus and Giroux.

Burns, J. M. (1978). *Leadership.* New York: Harper and Row.

Cameron, K., and Quinn, R. (1999). *Diagnosing and changing organizational culture.* Reading, MA: Addison-Wesley.

Council of Chief State School Officers. (2008a). *Educational leadership policy standards: ISLLC 2008 as adopted by the National Policy Board for Educational Administration.* Retrieved from http://www.ccsso.org/Resources/Publications/Educational_Leadership_Policy_Standards_ISLLC_2008_as_Adopted_by_the_National_Policy_Board_for_Educational_Administration.html.

Council of Chief State School Officers. (2008b). *Educational leadership policy standards: 2008.* Retrieved from http://www.ccsso.org/Documents/2008/Educational_Leadership_Policy_Standards_2008.pdf.

Day, D. V., Harrison, M. M., and Halpin, S. M. (2009). *An integrative approach to leader development: Connecting adult development, identity, and expertise*. New York: Routledge.

Dhiman, S. (2009). Cultivating mindfulness: The Buddhist art of paying attention to attention. *Interbeing*, 2(2), 35–52.

Easton, D. (1965). *A systems analysis of political life*. Chicago: University of Chicago Press.

Etzioni, A. (1975). *Comparative analysis of complex organizations*. Chicago: Simon and Schuster.

Follett, M. P. (1940). *Dynamic administration: The collected papers of Mary Parker Follett*. H. C. Metcalf and L. Urwick (Eds.). New York: Harper and Brothers.

Heifetz, R. A. (1994). *Leadership without easy answers*. Cambridge, MA: Harvard University Press.

James, W. (1890). *Principles of psychology*. Cambridge, MA: Harvard University Press.

Johnson, P. F. (1996). Antipodes: Plato, Nietzsche, and the moral dimensions of leadership. In P. S. Temes (Ed.), *Teaching leadership: Essays in theory and practice* (pp. 13–44). New York: Peter Lang.

Katz, D., and Kahn, R. L. (1966). *The social psychology of organizations*. New York: John Wiley and Sons.

Leithwood, K., Aitken, R., and Jantzi, D. (2006). *Making schools smarter: Leading with evidence* (3rd ed.). Thousand Oaks, CA: Corwin.

Lunenberg, F. (2012). Compliance theory and organizational effectiveness. *International Journal of Scholarly Academic Intellectual Diversity*, 14(1), 1–4.

Maslow, A. H. (1966). *The psychology of science: A reconnaissance*. New York: Harper and Row.

Maxwell, J. A. (2009). Book review of *Theory and educational research: Toward critical social explanation*, in *Education Review: A Journal of Book Reviews*. Retrieved January 20, 2010, from http://edrev.asu.edu/reviews/rev882.pdf.

Murphy, J. (2006). *Preparing school leaders: Defining a research and action agenda*. Lanham, MD: Rowman and Littlefield Education.

Printy, S. M., Marks, H. M., and Bowers, A. J. (2009, September). Integrated leadership: How principals and teachers share transformational and instructional influence. *Journal of School Leadership*, 19(5), 504–533.

Rowe-Finkbeiner, K. (2004). *The F word: Feminism in jeopardy: Women, politics and the future*. Emeryville, CA: Avalon Publishing Group.

Snyder, K. J., Acker-Hocevar, M., and Snyder, K. (2000). *Living on the edge of chaos: Leading schools into the global age*. Milwaukee, WI: ASQ Quality Press.

Sommers, P. (1994). *Who stole feminism? How women have betrayed women*. New York: Simon and Schuster.

Stone-Johnson, C., and Kew, K. (2013). Systemic educational change: Applying social network theory to lateral learning among principals. In

R. Flessner, G. Miller, K. Patrizio, and J. Horwitz (Eds.), *Agency in teacher education: Reflection, communities and learning*. Lanham, MD: Rowman and Littlefield.

Strauss, W., and Howe, N. (1991). *Generations: The history of America's future, 1584 to 2069*. New York: William Morrow and Company.

Weber, M. (1947). *The theory of social and economic organization*. T. Parsons (Ed.). New York: Free Press.

Wirt, F. M., and Kirst, M. W. (1997). *The political dynamics of American education*. Berkeley, CA: McCutchan Publishing Corporation.

Chapter 2

Developing a Leadership Platform

Gary Ivory

Each of us has a leadership platform, either explicitly stated or implicitly held. It consists of our own statements of values and beliefs about education and educational leadership. A platform serves as a touchstone, a reminder of what we think is valuable and important to know and remember. It is an ethical compass of sorts, suggesting directions we might take and not regret later. We could also look at it as a bottom line for each of us, the ultimate values and assumptions to which we pledge allegiance. For some superintendents, the bottom line might be fiscal responsibility, and for others it might be student achievement. For still others, it might be expanding opportunities for students, creating a stable society, or treating associates decently; it could even be maintaining a promising career trajectory or seeking accolades for our work. Part of the leadership platform as well is considering how we should go about pursuing the bottom line. What are we willing to do and how much are we willing to do it? Finally, part of our platform is our list of assumptions about why certain actions will be effective or ineffective. What do we believe "works," and why do we believe that?

We have argued that leaders should seek and heed various perspectives. But those various perspectives will often contradict one another. Theories may offer a guide for decisions, but there are too many to be certain. Then what? What do you do when many opinions matter and seem right? What touchstone or guiding light can you use to navigate your way through? Have you ever heard a leader say, "At the end of the day, I knew I had to go home with myself"? Knowing your own values and visions for education can help you decide what action to take. In the previous chapter, we offered the metaphor of the sailor in stormy seas. A person moving into a leadership position without knowing what he or she believes as a leader is like a ship sailing without a rudder and perhaps without stars for guidance. Your leadership platform can serve as your rudder and your stars.

We propose that your leadership platform will assist you in navigating decisions. We acknowledge that we are presenting you with one of your most basic leadership quandaries by asking you to know when to heed alternate viewpoints and when to follow your own. While negotiating the swirl of contending perspectives around you, keep in mind your beliefs and values—what you want to do for students, teachers, principals, and communities. Your leadership platform will keep your feet on the ground so you can step forward.

One of the quandaries of leadership we have presented is deciding between being committed to your own values and beliefs versus being open to alternative perspectives. Both stances can be good ones for leaders; the puzzle is how to maintain both of them. We have put together this book of quandaries partly to help you learn about alternative perspectives. But we want you to begin by encapsulating as well as you can your own most basic values and beliefs about education, leadership, and organizations. So, let us walk through two exercises: (1) developing your educational platform and (2) composing your cultural autobiography.

Your Leadership Platform

Get a notebook or walk over to your computer keyboard. For the first exercise, jot down your own personal answers to the following eight items. Provide the most thoughtful answers you can, but do not self-monitor. That is, do not write what you think are the most socially acceptable answers. Write what you, in your heart of hearts, believe.

1. What is the purpose of education?
2. Since you probably will not be able to accomplish everything you want to in your career, what would you most like to accomplish? What do you want people to remember about you as an educator?
3. Make a list of reasons why students succeed or fail in school. Which reasons seem to you most compelling? Which seem to you to be most readily ameliorated by good leadership?
4. What conditions make adults effective in organizations? Which of those conditions can good leadership help bring about?

5. Think about experiences you have had where you engaged with people whose values and beliefs were different from yours. What happens when people with drastically different values and beliefs end up in the same organization? What things can leaders do to foster effectiveness and efficiency in people with widely different values and beliefs?
6. On which of your values and beliefs are you willing to compromise or negotiate? Why? On which are you not? Why not?
7. In light of your answers to the six items above, what kind of leader do you aspire to be? What will be your priorities? How will you aim to treat others in your organization? How can you grow and improve?
8. How do you deal with mental and emotional stress? What conditions make you feel defeated? How do you decide when to persist in promoting your own values and beliefs in the face of possible defeat? Are there ways to increase your own persistence?

Consider your answers "planks" in your educational leadership platform. Now, put them aside for the moment, but refer to them as you work through the chapters in this book. Feel free to add to, modify, emphasize, or even discard any of your answers in light of your consideration of the chapter material. Review them again and revise if necessary when you have finished. In your leadership role(s), use them in examining your work and how you might grow.

Your Cultural Autobiography

For the second exercise, we want you to examine the origins of your values and beliefs. This is a major step on the way to the greater *epistemic sophistication* (Day, Harrison, and Halpin, 2009) we discussed in Chapter 1. In the interest of helping you develop epistemic sophistication, we want you to compose a short cultural autobiography. We are indebted to Brown (2006) for suggesting this activity for students of educational leadership. She based it on the work of a number of other scholars. Follow these steps:

1. Name each country (if any) other than the United States that you identify as a place of origin.
2. Identify any ethnic/cultural/religious/political membership that is central to your family's definition of itself.
3. List any advice, even a motto, that seems to have been important to your family.

4. List values that seem to you important to your ethnic/cultural/religious/political/family membership. Rank these values according to importance.
5. If you are working with a group, describe your group's attitude toward others who have advice or a motto or values different from yours.

As you did for your leadership platform, put your answers in a safe place and refer to them as you work through the chapters in this book. Feel free to add to, modify, emphasize, or even discard any of your answers in light of your consideration of the chapter material. Review them again and revise if necessary when you have finished. In your leadership role(s), use them in examining your work and how you might grow.

Both of these exercises should get you thinking about your own values and beliefs, both to appreciate and to critique them. The rest of the book should expand your understanding of perspectives on education and on education leadership. May the material here and your deliberations with others help you use that understanding to make better decisions for all those connected with institutions you will lead, especially the students and families who look to benefit from your efforts and the members of the organization who need to be as effective as possible.

References

Brown, K. M. (2006). Leadership for social justice and equity: Evaluating a transformative framework and andragogy. *Educational Administration Quarterly*, 42, 700–745.

Day, D. V., Harrison, M. M., and Halpin, S. M. (2009). *An integrative approach to leader development: Connecting adult development, identity, and expertise.* New York: Routledge.

CHAPTER 3

Pursuing a Vision on Which There Is Disagreement

Sharon Gieselmann and William G. Ruff

As a superintendent, you will be charged with promoting the success of every student through a shared vision—a vision that you and the district's constituents agree upon. Standard 1 of the Interstate School Leaders Licensure Consortium (ISLLC) asserts this charge:

> An educational leader promotes the success of every student by facilitating the development, articulation, implementation, and stewardship of a *vision* [emphasis ours] of learning that is shared and supported by all stakeholders. (CCSSO, 2008, p. 14)

During your tenure as a school superintendent, your ability to formulate and shepherd the school district's vision to reflect a diversity of voices from stakeholders will bring both challenges and successes. The interrelatedness among stakeholders will at times be ambiguous, encompass underlying issues, and address differing trends. This interrelatedness will be a source of knowledge that shapes the continued refinement of your leadership platform. The competing demands offered by your school district, the local community, and state and federal education agencies will provide quandaries for you as a leader as well as provide grist for personal reflection. This chapter, "Pursuing a Vision on Which There Is Disagreement," examines how superintendents negotiate these competing demands. When quandaries arise during your superintendency, and there will be many because of stakeholder disagreement, how can you as a school leader best promote the success of every student along with the district's shared vision? Ponder this superintendent's comment as we move into a discussion of how this chapter is organized. Superintendent 51 said,

> Students must be your filter even when parents and community members disagree with your decisions. It's the classic problem of the superintendency. You are either going to be on the right side of the issue or the popular side. On a daily basis, you have to make a decision on everything that hits your table. And you're either going to be consistent one way [with a vision] or consistent the other way. But, if you waffle, your career is usually pretty short.

This chapter is organized as follows. First, we provide a brief description of the theoretical frameworks that we will use throughout the chapter. Then, readers will examine several quandaries related to pursuing a vision on which there is disagreement when superintendents talk about their challenges and successes related to maintaining a vision. Although the quandaries that school and school system leaders face today seem unique to the twenty-first century, many were faced by organizational leaders 70 to 80 years ago. To illustrate this point, we frame the quandaries discussed by superintendents participating in a series of post–No Child Left Behind focus groups using Mary Parker Follett's (1940) theory of management. We contrast her perspectives with the views of another management theorist, Max Weber (1947). As you reflect upon the quandaries and discussion questions posed, we invite you to analyze those presented while giving consideration to the theoretical frameworks offered. We hope you contemplate the possible avenues that you would pursue and their consequences in a school district. Finally, we will provide concluding remarks that include thoughts from contemporary scholars along with suggestions for using the ideas presented in the chapter to guide your practice as a school superintendent.

THEORETICAL FRAMEWORKS

In this chapter, we will explore the theoretical perspectives of Follett and Weber to further define how aspiring superintendents can consider the leadership challenges associated with pursuing a vision on which there is disagreement. These theories can help school administrators increase their effectiveness and hone their leadership skills.

Beginning in the late 1800s, as industrialization continued and organizations became larger, professional management of workers and the business environment became crucial for organizational success. Competition increased the need for standardization, productivity, and efficiency in the workplace, and this marked the beginnings of management theories. Max Weber developed a theory of bureaucracy that described a hierarchy within an organization that provides key players with positional power over a fixed jurisdiction to ensure that organizational tasks and goals are executed efficiently. Weber's theory was mainly operationally focused, and scant attention was given to the role of human interaction until Mary Parker Follett came along. Follett developed her approach to management on an assumptive base that was fundamentally different from those of her contemporaries. She described management as the art of getting things done through people (Staufer, 1998). As each of us balances task orientation and people orientation differently in our leadership styles across a variety of situations, an investigation of the different perspectives held by Weber and Follett can assist you as you develop your leadership platform and guide you as a practicing superintendent. Who were these insightful early twentieth-century individuals, and what can we learn from their theories?

Max Weber, a respected German social theorist, lived from 1864 to 1920. Weber believed that bureaucracies are the most efficient and precise structures for executing tasks and goal attainment and that organizational authority must rest with top level executives because of their specialized expertise, which ensures efficiency. Weber emphasized rationality; thus, the formal aspects of an organization, such as rules, procedures, and methods, were prominent in his thinking. This imposed formality and discipline depersonalized the organization because personal freedom inhibits an organization's efficiency. Yet, Weber also acknowledged that a fully rational organization becomes mechanistic but soulless. Human irrationality exists, and as a result leaders must instill faith in their followers. The leader's charisma instills this faith and kindles enthusiasm (Staufer, 1998).

Although more organic and egalitarian forms of organizational structures have emerged in the twenty-first century, such as Professional Learning Communities (DuFour, 2004; Hord and Sommers, 2008), schooling in the United States remains organized as a bureaucracy, with classrooms organized into schools and schools organized within districts. Many educational leaders rely on personal charisma to gain constituent support for an action plan or to navigate the politics of a given situation.

Schooling continues to be organized bureaucratically because this form of organization continues to be perceived as an efficient method for educating children. As an example of bureaucracy in action, districts often appoint assessment managers, who are then given the responsibility to ensure that testing is performed efficiently throughout the district. These district assessment managers ensure that school assessment coordinators are appointed in each school, train the school assessment coordinators, and direct their actions regarding testing procedures, routines, and practices. The school assessment coordinators are then tasked to train and direct the teachers of the school in how to conduct the tests. When teachers have questions, they seek the expertise of the school assessment coordinator, who seeks the expertise of the district assessment manager as needed. Thus, as we climb the levels of bureaucracy, expertise in testing procedures increases.

Another researcher Mary Parker Follett, was a management and political theorist who lived from 1868 to 1933; her ideas sharply contrasted with Weber's theories. She placed a strong emphasis on the practice whereby the community creates an interrelatedness among an organization's stakeholders, which provides for group and individual needs along with the inclusion and accountability of participants (Graham, 1995). Follett contributed the notion of a universal goal; this notion states that the goal of an organization is an integration of individual efforts into a synergistic whole. Consequently, she was one of the first management theorists to promote participatory decision making and a decentralized power base rather than a hierarchal structure.

Follett observed firsthand the strategies and viewpoints of competing factions within an organization, as often leaders were more concerned with power issues among one another than with the merits of the issues being discussed. Follett argued that stakeholders should seek an integrative approach rather than compromise, consensus, or an either-or approach. She believed that integration is the ability to obtain the best of both perceptions; by contrast, compromise and consensus lead to the lowest common denominator, and the either-or option simply rejects one idea in favor of the other. When two desires are integrated, a solution has been found in which both parties have found a place, and neither side had to sacrifice anything. Follett (1924) shared a very simple illustration of integrating viewpoints:

> In the Harvard Library one day, in one of the smaller rooms, someone wanted the window open, I wanted it shut. We opened the window in the next room where no one was sitting. This was not a compromise because there was no curtailing of desire; we both got what we really wanted. (p. 32)

Finally, Follett affirmed that an integration of ideas provides an appropriate resolution for a particular situation. However, she emphasized that there is no "best way" to accomplish or resolve anything because the proper approach to resolution or accomplishment depends on the situation at hand.

We can use the example of efficient testing procedures to compare the ideas of these two theorists. Each state has a set of administrative rules governing how accountability testing will be performed. These rules are published, and school districts or local education agencies (LEAs) within the state are expected to implement the rules appropriately within their respective jurisdictions. Officials at the state level recognize the need for each LEA to contextualize the rules, so the rules are written with a degree of ambiguity. This ambiguity provides district or LEA officials with the necessary space to contextualize the state's rules efficiently. This deliberate ambiguity is seen differently by Follett and Weber. Follett would see the deliberate ambiguity as an opportunity to engage and integrate differing perspectives in the LEA. Weber, by contrast, would view the deliberate ambiguity as proof that bureaucratically governed structures allow leaders at each level to interpret and enforce rules so as to efficiently obtain the goal within a dynamic context. Specifically, state officials have the duty to create rules that will facilitate efficient student testing, and LEA officials have the duty to interpret and implement those rules within their own jurisdictions so as to efficiently ensure that students are tested. For both Weber and Follett, efficiency is important, as is expertise in achieving efficiency. The difference is that Weber assumes that a shared perspective of efficiency exists—it is defined through the leader's interpretation of policy and procedures. Follett assumes not that a shared perspective of efficiency exists but instead that people must seek to integrate the different perspectives into a shared perspective. In weighing the two sets of assumptions, consider that state officials often hold conferences for LEA assessment officials. Are these conferences held to convey and clarify the state's assessment policy and procedures, or are these conferences held to mold the different perspectives into a shared perspective?

Pitting Perspectives against One Another

As you review the voices of superintendents and the quandaries presented, consider the competing viewpoints of Weber and Follett, along with your own ideas as developed in your leadership platform. The first quandary that we will explore relates to developing a community while pursuing a school district vision.

Quandaries of Developing Formal Organizations or Communities

How do superintendents negotiate the process of developing formal organizations or communities to promote the success of all students by facilitating the development, articulation, implementation, and stewardship of a *vision* of learning that is shared and supported by its stakeholders? To what extent do leaders, deliberately or not, make choices about defining schools as either formal organizations or communities (Lynch, 2012)? A leader who assumes that the school district is a formal organization will tend to take charge, facilitate rule-making to ensure that consistent standards are applied throughout the district, and assume that administrators are better able to make decisions because they are held accountable for success and failure. According to Weber (1947), the key players in an organization should have positional power over subordinates to ensure that organizational tasks and goals are achieved. He believed that stakeholder engagement and their full participation in organizational decisions offer few benefits, because organization leaders are the experts. Similarly, in the words of a superintendent recently promoted from being a high school principal, "Theoretically, I support the idea of free thinking students, but practically, I can't afford to have 2000 free-thinking teenagers at my school" (personal conversation with Rob Watson, school district superintendent, July 21, 2012).

Conversely, school leaders who define the district as a community are bound by more egalitarian values and beliefs, and thus self-managed teams and stakeholder input drive the organization. Follett sheds light on this view by encouraging stakeholders to participate in face-to-face encounters when developing the group. Her viewpoints and translation into practice differed from those of Weber, who endorsed organization leaders as the thinkers and workers as the doers (Urwick and Brech, 1949). Follett rejected the idea of leadership as the exclusive province of the trained elite, who impose their own vision on the organization. Her conception of engagement included viewing *all* stakeholders, including those at the district, building, and community levels, as thinkers *and* doers. She believed, in the end, that engagement is about getting constituents to share information regardless of the stance they take regarding issues or proposals (Follett, 1940). The partnership envisioned by Follett calls upon all involved in the organization to play a crucial role in identifying concerns and creating solutions, as it causes all to reflect upon the issues or ideas being addressed. Follett (1918) knew from experience that before a leader can help people reach agreement, he or she must elicit engagement.

"We must remember that most people are not for or against anything. The first object of getting people together is to make them respond somehow; to disagree as well as to agree with people brings you closer to them" (p. 212). She contends that differences are always grounded in an underlying similarity, and she believes that it is not opposition but indifference that separates human beings (Follett, 1940). The subsequent comments from superintendents describe the continual quandaries that demand a leader's thinking and attention. How might you lead when faced with similar challenges?

Some superintendents in the focus groups shared Follett's views on engagement, as they believed in involving their stakeholders in ways that allowed their voices to be heard. For example, Superintendent 29 stated,

> It's through discussion and dialog. . . . If you discuss an issue, then you dialog to establish the meaning of it. If we don't involve parents, students, community, businesses, and leaders in education about improving our district, then we really don't get to the heart of making the best decisions, in my opinion. It builds the ownership, the understanding, the support. It's through this dialog, that you create teamwork for the purpose of serving children and serving them well.

The effects of engagement in this particular situation led to increased ownership of and support for the issue via this decision-making process. Similar to Follett, this superintendent believed in the value of face-to-face encounters with stakeholders intended to obtain their responses. Their comments, positive, negative, or indifferent, were important to the district and helped secure positive support for the district's vision of serving children well. A contemporary leadership scholar, Bennis (2009), stated that

> great leaders and followers are always engaged in creative collaboration. We still tend to think of leaders, like artists, as solitary geniuses. In fact, the days when a single individual, however gifted, can solve our problems are long gone. The problems we face today, come at us so fast, and are so complex that we need a group of talented people to tackle them, led by gifted leaders, or teams of leaders. (p. xxii)

Conversely, another superintendent who utilized similar engagement processes had different results, even though stakeholders valued engagement in public education. Superintendent 30 indicated that the majority of individuals living in our country have attended public schools and that these people believe themselves to have a certain degree of "expertise," but this bias concerning what should occur or does exist in our schools and districts shouldn't supplant the expertise of professional educators.

> It's easy to get people involved in discussions. The hardest aspect of school administration is to deal with people who think they know, but they don't know . . . they have some sort of bias. Business is a good example, particularly in the past 10 to 15 years, because they want to have more influence on the kind of products they promote and what kind of employees they're going to have based upon what's happening in schools. We also get plenty of advice from people who have other things to gain, or other biases.

Follett would have leaders lead others to wise decisions via participatory decision making rather than impose their own ideas. Some superintendents in the focus groups shared Follett's views and encouraged the full participation of their stakeholders. For example, Superintendent 29 noted that creating an environment that facilitated involving all parents through forums provided stakeholders with an opportunity to fully participate, thereby building a sense of community within the district. However, Weber would suggest that superintendents have received specialized training; therefore, they are the experts. Thus, for followers of Weber's views, a top-down leadership approach possesses more merit than engagement and is warranted.

In congruence with Weber's thinking, another superintendent expressed concerns about full participation in school district decisions. Although this individual believed in empowering people on issues that directly impact them, Superintendent 50 stated that not all decisions can be shared. "If you live by the idea that every decision has to be shared and all the constituents must have input, you will never get anything done." In some situations, a more bureaucratic, authoritative framework as advocated by Weber might have a greater impact on decision making within the district because it is the most efficient structure for executing the task. More specifically, Superintendent 20 shared concerns about involving all constituents in decision making. He shared,

> Oh, yeah. Throw a school calendar out to 48 educators, teachers, and ask them to give you the input on the school calendar for the next year. I will never do that again. I will lay it in front of 'em and that's what they will work at and if they prefer [not] to work at that, they can find themselves another job. I got more static over the CALENDAR issue and the committees that I sent this to.

Superintendent 18 complained that "the calendar is the single most selfish thing that teachers do. They look at their families' schedules for the whole year . . . to see if the calendar will fit that."

As a leader, will you favor the beliefs of Follett or Weber when developing community in your school district? Landrieu (2011) stated that various reform efforts or innovations could place themselves along both dimensions, top-down and participatory. But, the challenge may be to discover a balance that works best for the organization and furthers attainment of the organization's vision. How might district circumstances or issues compel you to shift your leadership approach?

Quandaries of Integration

How do superintendents negotiate the concept of integrating ideas to promote the success of all students by facilitating the development, articulation, implementation, and stewardship of a *vision* of learning shared and supported by the school community? Is it important for superintendents to integrate ideas from stakeholders, or should they just use their own? Which ideas from stakeholders should a superintendent integrate?

Although Weber believed that a hierarchical approach within an organization whereby leaders give orders and subordinates follow orders is the best approach for ensuring that goals are executed consistently over time, Follett believed that integrative efforts provide the foundation for success regarding an organization's vision and do not include compromise, consensus, or an either-or approach. "Integration," Follett said, "requires a high order of intelligence, keen perception and discrimination, more than all, a brilliant inventiveness; it is easier for a trade union to fight than to suggest a better way of running the factory" (1940, p. 45). Several superintendents in the focus groups shared her views on integration. Superintendent 53 indicated that integration of ideas can be helpful when major district decisions are needed. For example, this superintendent stated,

> I could get this project [a building plan] together with a five-year plan over the weekend . . . and get it done . . . get input from my buildings and grounds and principals and it's a done deal. But, I'm very interested in community input. I invited every member of the community (giving them my phone number, my e-mail address and so on) to give me input on the things they've observed and seen in the district that they would like to see addressed. . . . And comments are coming from people, "Thank you for asking." When I sent the letter, I talked

to them about our school district, their children, and I didn't sign it, [identifying name] Superintendent of Schools, [district name]. I signed it [identifying first name] . . . I've taken an extra two weeks to integrate their ideas.

Counter to Follett's viewpoints are those of Weber, who would argue that superintendents should exercise their authority and execute a plan because of their expertise and positional responsibility, rather than endure the transaction costs of integrating diverse viewpoints. The urgency of the situation may warrant a straightforward command-and-control approach. A superintendent shared concerns about integration of viewpoints by stating, "I think there is a threshold where yes, you listen to the input and yes, I value what you have to say. But it is still a decision I need to make" (Superintendent 54). Additionally, Superintendent 52 indicated that integration of ideas is worthwhile, but "I go back to—you still need a leader. You still need someone to make that final decision of whether we can do this or we can't do this. . . . And that is our job." In spite of valuing integration of ideas through interaction with different constituencies, sometimes a leader must make successful school district decisions as the district leader. Lest anyone think that the leader who sees himself or herself as the expert and therefore should act authoritatively is a total anachronism, note this advice from DuFour (2007), a contemporary leadership scholar. He stated,

> If, however, all attempts to persuade educators to do the right work fail to persuade them to do it, leaders should exercise their authority to require the work be done. A professional is someone with expertise in a specialized field, an individual who has not only pursued advanced training to enter the field but who also is expected to remain current in its evolving knowledge base. (p. 42)

On the topic of school boards, some superintendents had difficulties with integration. For example, Superintendent 51 shared, "The care and 'feeding' of school boards is another thing that drains the energy of many superintendents and sometimes detracts from the job they need to do." In addition, lack of continuity in board membership can be a problem with integration because a trend in this particular state is reducing terms from five to three years. Superintendent 53 (New England and Mid-Atlantic) indicated,

> It's becoming a swinging door. . . . I'm not saying all board members are bad, but unfortunately we've got more of the "acid type" people that are invading boards and they are splitting boards 4/3, 5/2,

where we used to have maybe a 6/1. You could have that radical, but you could isolate him or her. Now you have no idea what you're dealing with on any given night because of who has gotten to [a board member] before the meeting.

Continuity in board membership can provide time to build strong connections between superintendents and board members. However, in this particular case, bringing together viewpoints, what Follett advocated, posed challenges. School board members, because of their term limits and resultant lack of knowledge regarding district policy, may leave the systematic study of best practices for the district to the superintendent because he or she will be better able to execute this task, just as prescribed in Weber's notions of bureaucracy. An unnumbered superintendent stated, "It was much easier 12 years ago with strategic planning or goal setting. There was more ability to bring people together in common accord." However, this superintendent shared that because of the increased diversity within her school district, individuals did not want to integrate ideas and think globally or systematically about the district. They would rather support what is best for their particular child at that particular moment; people moved toward an either-or approach. As a school superintendent, are your viewpoints more closely aligned with Weber's or Follett's? How will you negotiate the concept of integrating ideas to promote the success of all students in your district?

Opportunities for Introspection about Your Leadership Platform

As you compare and contrast your ideas with Follett's and Weber's, how will personal reflection about them shape your leadership platform? These competing ideas will be factors you encounter as you lead your respective districts. For example, engagement can provide for stakeholder dialogue and discussion, but personal and professional biases from constituents can pose challenges. In some cases, you may feel that engagement and participation among all stakeholders can aid the district in promoting a shared vision that contributes to student success, while in other cases you may not. Superintendent 51 described a situation where doing what was best for children was in direct conflict with the negotiated teacher contract as seen by union officials. He stated,

> Putting kids first often times means offending teachers' unions or whatever. . . . In our [union] contract we have a two-week vacation at Easter, but everyone else in the world has a split vacation now. So I asked the

union if they would allow me to split the vacation . . . because otherwise my kids would lose instruction at [names regional support centers for vocational and special education instruction]. . . . They said, "No, we want our two weeks." So I broke the contract; so now we're in a union dispute because . . . I'm not going to say to all my occupational education students, "You [now] can't have the instruction you need." . . . Yet, there are some other people that don't look at it that way. [In another district] they say "I don't want the hassle." [They] make the kids suck it up, because they didn't want to bother the union. . . . So doing what's best for kids means . . . that your life may not be that easy because adult agendas can take over in two seconds if you're not careful.

Reflect upon the efficiency of pressing for the instructional needs of the children (the task) versus the resistance offered by the union. Specifically, how can a leader most efficiently meet the instructional needs of children in an environment of resistance? In the above quote, Superintendent 51 is aligned with Weber's perspective. He sees the right decision simply and clearly, and those in the "other" district made the wrong decision by not challenging the resistance. On the other hand, from Follett's perspective, the need for reflection focuses on the challenges inherent in conflicting values. Specifically, should the leader prioritize being child centered over breaching an agreement with key stakeholders? Perhaps those in the "other" district are not wrong but rather place priority on not breaking an agreement with key stakeholders.

As you review and reflect upon the following discussion questions, compare and contrast the theoretical frameworks of Weber and Follett and your own perspectives. Strive to break the pattern of oversimplification, and work to move toward a more creative and pioneering solution.

- If we are to entertain differences of opinion, what happens to our own "nonnegotiables"?
- To what degree is the integration of all community ideas a social justice issue? As many of our communities grow increasingly diverse, how do superintendents facilitate the integration of voices into the daily practices of the school system?
- As you compare and contrast your ideas about formal organizations versus building community, consider the following: Will your ideas disrupt the status quo of the bureaucracy? Will they disrupt current trends?
- Does integration have a dark side? Does listening to stakeholders lead to procrastination? Does influence lead to manipulation by stakeholders?

- What are your thoughts on how to best communicate as a superintendent? Do you share Follett's theory more closely than Weber's, or vice versa? Explain.
- Weber advocated hierarchical structures within the organization whereby leaders are viewed as the experts. How could this framework, leaders as experts, increase productivity within an organization—for example, if stakeholders viewed superintendents as the experts? Is this situation plausible? Explain.
- How do administrators, faculty, staff, and community members become engaged so as to improve schools and school systems beyond the current level of operation and productivity? To what extent are Follett's ideas about engagement realistic? Explain.

Communities differ, with varied expectations for the role of the superintendent. How might a superintendent with a community-building mind-set fare in a community that expects the superintendent to be the expert and effectively direct all the affairs of schooling? Similarly, how would you meet the demands of such a community if you had spent years developing expertise in a particular area of district leadership, but your school principals and teachers demanded that ideas be run past them?

Conclusion

Contemporary leadership scholars and many practitioners write and speak about the importance of communicating the nonnegotiables. For example, Waters and Marzano (2006) described nonnegotiable district goals for student achievement and classroom instruction, while De Meyer (2011) stated that effective leadership in the current era requires collaboration, listening, influencing, and flexible adaptations. What will your nonnegotiables be as you, as a practicing superintendent, strive to pursue a school district vision while understanding that there will be disagreement from your stakeholders? To be successful, you will be required at times to stretch yourself beyond your preconceived capacities, those that can be extended or surpassed while you hold true to a framework or values. While focusing on this vision, continue to develop and transform your beliefs and practices, and aspire to achieve superior results regarding student learning and achievement while raising the bar for yourself as a school leader.

This chapter has offered multiple perspectives on creating a vision for school districts that can be supported by all of the district's stakeholders. The authors have made both practical and theoretical connections between practicing superintendents and the work of Mary Parker Follett and of Max Weber. As you continue to form your leadership platform, reflect upon the ideas of these individuals and upon the words of the superintendents we interviewed. Consider them, as well, in light of your leadership platform. As stated in ISLLC Standard 1, "An educational leader promotes the success of every student by facilitating the development, articulation, implementation, and stewardship of a *vision* [emphasis ours] of learning that is shared and supported by all stakeholders." This is one of your responsibilities as a school superintendent. This unification of meaning and purpose provides for mobilization of stakeholders and the support the district needs to accomplish any goals.

Additional Reading and Resources

Bennis, W. (2009). *On becoming a leader: A leadership classic.* Philadelphia: Basic Books.

Follett, M. P. (1918). *The new state: Group organization the solution of popular government.* New York: Longmans, Green and Company.

Sergiovanni, T. (1994). *Building community in schools.* San Francisco, CA: Jossey-Bass.

Tshannen-Moran, M. (2004). *Trust matters: Leadership for successful schools.* San Francisco, CA: Jossey-Bass.

References

Bennis, W. (2009). *On becoming a leader: A leadership classic.* Philadelphia: Basic Books.

Council of Chief State School Officers (CCSSO). (2008, April). *Educational leadership policy standards: ISLLC 2008.* Retrieved from http://www.ccsso.org/Documents/2008/Educational_Leadership_Policy_Standards_2008.pdf.

De Meyer, A. (2011). Collaborative leadership: New perspectives in leadership development. *European Business Review,* January–February, 35–40. Retrieved from http://www.europeanbusinessreview.com/?p=3316.

DuFour, R. (2004). What is a professional learning community? *Educational Leadership,* 61(8), 6–11.

DuFour, R. (2007). In praise of top-down leadership. *The School Administrator,* 64(10), 38–42.

Follett, M. P. (1918). *The new state: Group organization the solution of popular government.* New York: Longmans, Green and Company.

Follett, M. P. (1924). *Creative experience.* New York: Longmans, Green and Company.

Follett, M. P. (1940). *Dynamic administration: The collected papers of Mary Parker Follett.* H. C. Metcalf and L. Urwick (Eds.). New York: Harper and Brothers.

Graham, P. (Ed.). (1995). *Mary Parker Follett: Prophet of management.* Cambridge, MA: Harvard Business School Press.

Hord, S., and Sommers, W. (2008). *Leading professional learning communities: Voices from research and practice.* Thousand Oaks, CA: Corwin.

Landrieu, M. (2011). *Balance top-down and participatory approaches.* Retrieved from http://www.socialinnovation.ash.harvard.edu/innovators-toolkit/tools/balance-top-down-and-participatory-approaches.html.

Lynch, M. (2012). *A guide to effective school leadership theories.* New York: Routledge.

Staufer, D. (1998). What you can learn from 100 years of management science: A guide to emerging business practice. *Harvard Business Review,* reprint number U9801A.

Urwick, L., and Brech, E. (1949). *The making of scientific management,* vol. 3. London: Management Publications Trust.

Waters, J., and Marzano, R. (2006). *School district leadership that works: The effects of superintendent leadership on student achievement.* Denver, CO: McREL.

Weber, M. (1947). *The theory of social and economic organization.* T. Parsons (Ed.). New York: Free Press.

Chapter 4

District Superintendents as Instructional Leaders?

Thomas L. Alsbury and Kathryn S. Whitaker

This chapter explores the role of the superintendent as an instructional leader by first discussing the ways in which superintendents can and do influence instruction in their school districts. This is a particularly important goal given the call for school leaders to focus on instructional improvement in ISLLC Standard 2. Specifically, ISLLC Standard 2 challenges school leaders to promote the success of every student by advocating, nurturing, and sustaining a school culture and instructional program conducive to student learning and staff professional growth. This chapter presents quandaries encountered by superintendent respondents from the Voices 3 study (Acker-Hocevar, Ballenger, Place, and Ivory, 2012) who were attempting to serve as instructional leaders in a new No Child Left Behind environment. The chapter concludes with several perspectives based on role theory and organizational learning theory that shed light on quandaries superintendents face in leading.

Superintendent as Instructional Leader?

While the importance of principal instructional leadership has dominated the literature and practice in recent years, the instructional leadership role of superintendents has been largely ignored (Björk, 1993; Leithwood, 2005). Until recently, the district leadership's effects on students have been considered too indirect and complex to figure out (Leithwood, Seashore-Louis, Anderson, and Wahlstrom, 2004; Leithwood, 2005).

However, a few research studies have stressed the role of superintendents in the area of instructional leadership. Bridges (1982) and Cuban (1984) discovered that the success or failure of public schools has been directly linked to the influence of the superintendent, particularly in the instructional arena. Hart and Ogawa (1987) and other researchers suggest that superintendents could exert influence (albeit small and indirect) on academic performance (Björk, 1993; Crowson and Morris, 1990; Leithwood, 2005).

Recently, owing to strict federal accountability measures and the refocus on system-wide change (Depres, 2008; Fullan, 2006), we are seeing more emphasis on the role of the superintendent as instructional leader. Firestone and Shipps (2005) reported that a few research studies "suggest more potential for district instructional leadership than pessimists thought" (p. 92). The Bill and Melinda Gates Foundation issued a white paper (as cited in Archer, 2005) arguing that school success is more likely with a supporting district and system-wide guidance, and Archer (2005) indicated that superintendents are playing a more assertive role in shaping instruction. Indeed, Hightower, Knapp, Marsh, and McLaughlin (2002), Waters and Marzano (2006), and Leithwood (2005) confirm the influence of superintendents on instructional improvement and suggest explanations for how some superintendents have brought about gains in student achievement.

While the expectation for today's superintendent is to focus on curricular and instructional quality, particularly efforts to improve student achievement, pervasive daily management demands often conflict with this expectation (Archer, 2005; Glass, Björk, and Brunner, 2000; Schwahn and Spady, 1998; Short and Scribner, 2000). Moreover, superintendents face increasing conflict over pluralistic and polarizing community values and interests, including challenges regarding the purposes and goals of education (Keedy and Björk, 2001). Bredeson and Kose (2007) report that in the past decade, the majority of superintendents reported instructional improvement as their top priority, but they also indicated that the daily realities of their work had derailed their efforts toward this goal.

Superintendent Voices on Instructional Leadership

Various studies confirm that superintendents can make a difference in improving student achievement. However, many superintendents, despite their desire to lead instructional improvement, have trouble doing so. The question is, What are the quandaries facing superintendents that hinder them from enacting their desire to be instructional leaders? Superintendents in the Voices 3 study, expressed problems they faced when trying to define and carry out instructional leadership. Superintendents report the challenge of trying to satisfy both local *internal accountability demands* and federal or state *external accountability demands*, because they are not always aligned. To help you better understand how to address this challenge, we present several real-life quandaries below. Though each quandary addresses a specific concern, all share a common theme: how to negotiate the terrain between internal and external accountability demands within an unpredictable environment of educational reform. The quandaries are followed by descriptions of perspectives, based on role theory and organizational learning theory, that can help superintendents negotiate the quandary. We provide a series of discussion questions and exercises focused on the challenge of improving superintendent instructional leadership while navigating internal and external accountability demands.

Note that while the focus of this chapter is on external instructional accountability mandates in general, superintendent respondents understandably focused on the most influential mandate in place at the time of the focus-group interviews, the federal No Child Left Behind Act (NCLB). Though NCLB is not now the force in their lives that it was then, the issue of external instructional reform mandates persists, and so we believe there is still much to be learned from their comments on NCLB.

Quandary One: How do superintendents appreciate and grow from the positive aspects of external accountability mandates while simultaneously dealing with their challenges?

In the Voices 3 interviews, superintendents shared experiences regarding both the positive and the negative aspects of the external accountability mandate (NCLB). We present some of their comments here.

Positive Aspects of External Accountability Mandates

Superintendents in the Voices 3 study referenced external accountability mandates by focusing specifically on the potential benefits of NCLB. Superintendent 55 said, "I think public education is doing a better job today than [it was] ten years ago, and I think a lot of that can be tied to NCLB." Superintendent 72 noted, "It has raised our test scores. There's no question about it. We pay more attention to data." And Superintendent 2 told us, "NCLB has caused teachers to converse more about student performance. In regard to highly qualified, you have to hire quality teachers and that's a good thing."

Overall, superintendents acknowledged that an external mandate like NCLB can refocus a school district on instructional goals. Further, superintendents indicated that an external mandate can provide justification and support for a school leader's attempts to move the faculty's focus away from noninstructional concerns toward instruction. These goals include providing a more equitable education to reduce the achievement gap, achieving higher test performance, changing faculty conversations, and improving the quality of teachers.

Challenges of External Accountability Mandates

Superintendents, while confirming that NCLB forced schools to focus more on instructional improvements, indicated that external mandates can present challenges and may even be counterproductive for school district reform and improvement. Superintendent 2 noted the difficulty of finding highly qualified teachers. Superintendent 59 worried, "We have a lot of mandates and a lot of extra hours for staff. NCLB creates a lot of stress on staff and I think we are going to lose some quality folks because of that pressure and stress." A superintendent who was not numbered in the transcripts complained about moving from success to failure because of the increasing NCLB requirements:

> We did really well on the state test three years ago and a lot of us wondered whether we could maintain the scores and we haven't. We received this discouraging news from the state department that we are a step away from an academic watch. When you think you have good people and they are working hard, how do you raise awareness without coming across with a hammer and discouraging them?

While superintendents in the above conversations voiced negative opinions about state and federal intrusion, superintendents seemed to vacillate between support and disdain for externally mandated instructional accountability measures. They praised the impact of the mandate in regard to its focus on improving overall student achievement, using data to drive instruction, and enhancing achievement of all students. On the other hand, they deplored the use of academic tests as the sole indicators of success, useless paperwork, and increased stress and workloads for staff.

QUANDARY TWO: HOW DO SUPERINTENDENTS ACQUIRE AND ALIGN RESOURCES IN ORDER TO SATISFY NEW ACCOUNTABILITY REQUIREMENTS OF UNDERFUNDED EXTERNAL MANDATES?

Many superintendents recounted the difficulties of meeting all the requirements set forth in the eleven hundred pages of NCLB without the resources to do so. Superintendents spoke of NCLB as an "unfunded mandate." They spoke of conflicting requirements that posed difficulties in regard to the limited resources superintendents had at their disposal.

Waters and Marzano (2006) indicate that effective superintendents use resources to support targeted goals of instruction and student achievement. Take a look at comments from superintendents in regard to problems related to targeting and distributing fiscal and human resources while trying to meet local as well as state and federal accountability demands. Superintendent 29 expressed frustration:

> The issue is that once I identify the gaps in learning, I've got to have the resources and there's no money in here to provide other different resources that deal with . . . children that really need additional help and re-teaching? Not just simply failing a course and re-taking it. I'm talking about dealing with the gaps along the way.

Superintendent 32 described the obstacles to meeting another NCLB requirement:

> We can't get the teachers who are highly qualified out here. We can't pay them enough. There is no way. We cannot compete with the other districts. For us it is an on-going battle daily just to try to meet the minimum requirements for the Feds and still keep the focus on where it needs to be and that is on the kids.

Superintendent 31 echoed this frustration: "NCLB is an unfunded mandate and many parts are unrealistic. You find me a district that is not looking for a math teacher who is certified and qualified [according to the required NCLB definition of a "quality teacher"]." And Superintendent 34 decried the constraints on her flexibility: "I spend my extra pool of money to find a highly qualified math teacher. Then

I miss out having that extra classroom aide who might more directly meet the needs of kids [than the highly qualified math teacher]."

QUANDARY THREE: HOW DO SUPERINTENDENTS RESPOND TO LOCAL INTERNAL INTERESTS SO AS TO PROVIDE A HOLISTIC, WELL-ROUNDED EDUCATION WHILE STILL MEETING THE REQUIREMENTS OF A NARROW EXTERNAL ACCOUNTABILITY MANDATE?

Superintendents seem to struggle with balancing between local educational priorities and those from state and federal authorities. Past school district leaders were required to respond primarily to the needs and demands of their local communities. External mandates like NCLB can produce positive results in some areas (such as test scores) but negative results in other areas (such as diminishing the importance of art, music, and vocational preparation). Some superintendents questioned NCLB's focus on using only academic measures to determine school performance or evaluate overall student success. Superintendent 69 worried,

> Some [school districts] were doing some real high social things that the students really needed as well, that they had to pull back on. For instance, maybe music, art, you know, cultural things. . . . So you're no longer looking at [so] much of a well-rounded student any more, but rather how they're going to produce on a test or how they can do academically.

Superintendent 54 declared,

> I have to keep in mind that . . . we have a wonderful arts program and a music program that are just as important in developing children into productive democratic citizens as being proficient in English and Math. And that message tends to get lost with NCLB.

An unnumbered superintendent worried about the long-term effects of narrowing the curriculum:

> I am very concerned about what the federal and state governments have done to cut a mold for all kids. And, we're really focusing on education of the whole child and that's my driving force for what's best for kids. I try to maintain high quality arts and music programs and other programs besides just the core subject areas and what it comes down to

is a dilemma during the budget: where do you put your funds? So we're trying to do all kinds of creative choice things. Superintendents across the state are concerned about—you know, 10 years from now will we look back and say, "Gee what did we do back then?"

These quotes point to the quandaries superintendents face when trying to develop the whole child while simultaneously increasing student test scores in a few targeted academic subjects. The superintendents report feeling caught between the demands of their employer (the local community) and external accountability mandates. They expressed a desire to pursue both goals, yet they expressed frustration over how to balance often contradictory interests.

Most organizational leaders, including superintendents, struggle with limited resources (Honig, 2008). Misalignment between internal and external accountability and instructional goals complicates the problem by adding the challenge of where to focus resources. Given the staffing requirements of external accountability mandates, superintendents are making tough decisions, often ethical ones, as the instructional leaders in the district. Sometimes these staffing decisions may negatively impact the district's ability to meet local internal instructional demands while satisfying external accountability mandates.

THEORETICAL FRAMES

While you are contemplating the three quandaries presented above, it can be helpful to use theoretical constructs to frame the issues presented. Two theoretical frameworks that can help in unpacking the quandaries presented above are *role theory* and *organizational learning theory*. Bredeson and Kose (2007) employed role theory and Leithwood and Prestine (2002) used organizational learning theory to explore the challenges that superintendents face when they attempt to be instructional leaders while navigating local, state, and federal demands.

Role Theory

One way to understand how superintendents respond to sometimes conflicting demands is through role theory. Role theory is a construct or lens through which superintendents observe complex social and political demands within the context of their own local school districts. Katz and Kahn (1966) propose that local actors/stakeholders send to the superintendent clear messages about expectations and demands for the role of the superintendent. Thus, superintendents come to realize that internal stakeholders (e.g., school board members, principals, teachers, community members) influence and define their roles and actions.

But superintendents also learn that community stakeholders may want different purposes for education than are called for by state and local accountability systems. In a national survey of school board members, Hess and Meeks (2011) found that while local communities support improved student performance, they value a holistic educational experience over one focused on performance in isolated academic subjects like math or literacy. In this same report, board members asserted that the primary purpose of schooling is to develop a well-rounded, productive citizen, and not preparation for the university or the work force. Clearly, local community expectations and those of federal and state accountability mandates differ. This discrepancy in the characterizations of successful district performance makes it more difficult for superintendents to clearly identify their goals, which in turn define their role. This raises the following question: Is it the superintendent's role to work toward achieving the demands of the local community or those of state and national interests? Using this theoretical lens leads to the conclusion that at any given time the superintendent's task is to identify and fulfill a role that satisfies both internal stakeholders, who determine his or her continued employment, and external stakeholders, who control resources through accountability mandates.

Organizational Learning Theory

Organizational learning theory is another framework that can provide a lens with which to assess superintendents' work and determine how they should respond to instructional quandaries. Argyris and Schön (1978) noted that while teachers can gain knowledge and skills individually, organizational learning is when individuals learn to interact with one another in order to carry out shared tasks. When this occurs, it is said that the organization, as an entity, is "learning." As such, organizational learning has also been characterized as collective learning, and it is offered as one approach that can lead to enhanced student learning (Marks, Seashore-Louis, and Printy, 2000; Silins, Mulford, Zarins, and Bishop, 2000). According to several studies (Argyris and Schön, 1978; Leithwood, Aitken, and Jantzi, 2006; Leithwood, Seashore-Louis, Anderson, and Wahlstrom, 2004), school district characteristics associated with increased organizational learning are linked to improved student academic performance.

Organizational Learning Characteristics

Organizational learning theory as described by Honig (2008) specifies that district leaders can engage in a series of instructional leadership processes linked to improved district-wide performance. The organizational learning characteristics most relevant to the quandaries raised by the superintendents in this study include (1) valuing and legitimizing improvement, (2) supporting engagement in joint work, (3) making sense, (4) dealing with contextuality and prior knowledge, and (5) attending to both single-loop and double-loop learning. For the superintendent who desires to lead instruction, each of these five concepts can be illuminating. Each also brings with it its own quandaries. Let us consider each one in greater depth.

Valuing and Legitimizing Improvement

Organizational learning theory recognizes the importance of developing a culture of continuous improvement within school organizations, but it emphasizes the negative effects of labeling schools as "low performers" and using accountability pressures to drive change (O'Day, 2002). Organizational learning underscores the importance of valuing and legitimizing improvement among all schools. The NCLB requirement to designate schools according to whether the school reached particular standards, resulted in schools being labeled as a "school of improvement" or a "failing school" even though they may have demonstrated significant academic improvement. Rather than providing encouragement through valuing and legitimizing growth, district leaders are forced to convey this negative reinforcement, which organizational learning theory links to a declining motivation to continue improving performance (March, 1994).

Superintendents in this study seemed to recognize this as a quandary when reflecting upon the simultaneous positive and negative aspects of external reform mandates. Superintendents are faced with the decision to focus on negative accountability motivators rather than to value and legitimize all improvement as supported by organizational learning theory.

Supporting Engagement in Joint Work

Superintendents are faced with the incongruous expectations of accountability and curriculum mandates that support the use of collaborative decision making (e.g., professional learning communities) while simultaneously espousing the adoption of standardized curricular content (e.g., Common Core State Standards) and assessment (e.g., Smarter Balanced Assessment System). Organizational learning theory would support a superintendent focus on internal organizational capacity building through allowing internal stakeholders to develop curricula, processes, and evaluations tailored to the unique needs of the district and community. This process supports a legitimate desire for internal stakeholders to act as meaningful participants in improving instruction. Honig (2008) indicates that external mandates can come into conflict with the development of authentic internal processes. Standardized external reform mandates generally lack fluency in the norms and language of the school culture. However, external mandates may enable superintendents and other leaders to push for needed reforms in the face of local desires to maintain the status quo (Kew, Ivory, Muñiz, and Quiz, 2012).

Sense-Making

Sense-making can be described as a process in which data and knowledge are interpreted; meaning is constructed; and actors determine whether the evidence is meaningful and actionable. Because there is generally too much evidence to which superintendents must respond (March, 1994), they must assign value to particular data that most directly suggest what they should do. Organizational learning theory emphasizes that sense-making is necessarily shaped by individuals within each organization. However, individuals tend to notice evidence that is relatively easy to understand and that can be processed into actions that they believe are easy to implement. Thus, individuals in a school organization tend to focus on data that confirm their competency and that fit into prior understanding (Levitt and March, 1988; March, 1994).

In addition, sense-making is dependent upon an individual's past experiences (March, 1994), so internal stakeholder collaborative decision-making teams are apt to rely on prior knowledge and experience (Levitt and March, 1988). Reliance on prior knowledge helps to unite individuals within the organization and to provide what is termed coherence (Fullan, 2001). However, overreliance on prior knowledge supports the status quo and produces resistance to new knowledge and change (Levinthal and March, 1993).

Conversely, organizations overly eager to add more and more external knowledge may become excessively reliant on new knowledge and may thus disregard prior knowledge (Levitt and March, 1988). This tends to result in the rapid adoption and poor implementation of multiple new programs or processes—overwhelming school faculty, spreading resources thin, and creating fragmentation, all outcomes of what Fullan (2001) calls "projectitis" (p. 105).

Organizational learning theory supports superintendents that encourage school stakeholders to seek out new knowledge and grapple with data in order to discover and create new processes for instructional improvement. This process of discovery builds capacity for organizational learning. However, too much data or new knowledge can simply become overwhelming. Therefore, directing teachers to particular data arguably reduces confusion and ensures their ability to manage the new knowledge and incorporate it into existing processes (Feldman, 2000). This is how individuals make sense of new knowledge and reinforce internal ties that enhance organizational learning. The quandary for the superintendent is to balance that acquisition of new knowledge while protecting against an excessive amount or diversity of new learning (Feldman, 2000).

Contextuality and Prior Knowledge

Critical to the use of organizational learning theory as a framework for instructional leadership quandaries is the concept of contextuality. Cohen and Levinthal (1990) indicated that an organization's capacity to learn or "ability . . . to recognize the value of new information, assimilate it, and apply it . . . is largely a function of the firm's level of prior knowledge" (p. 128). Thus, if it is true that each school has a unique combination and level of knowledge, a standardized approach to instructional reform as espoused through many of the external mandates we have seen is utterly opposed to the concept of organizational learning. Indeed, organizational learning theory would advocate context-sensitive solutions for improving instruction. In addition, reform is thought to increase organizational capacity to learn only if the new knowledge and reform initiatives are apprehended through an iterative process by each group of internal and external stakeholders.

On the other hand, organizational learning theory speaks to the need for a school district to develop a common language and a common set of norms and processes in order to better apply shared prior knowledge and enhance coherence. It could be argued that standardized external mandates actually help develop normative culture, language, and processes. Superintendent comments in this study seem to recognize that NCLB provided shared goals that benefited schools by diminishing fragmented reform initiative, often driven by self-serving local politics.

Superintendents ultimately must find a balance between mandating external programs of "best practice" versus reinforcing the development of local contextualized reforms. The former approach can provide the appearance of being "cutting edge" and of using processes proved in other school districts. The latter increases the likelihood of faculty buy-in and improves implementation fidelity (Leithwood, 2000).

Single-Loop and Double-Loop Learning

Another critical element in organizational learning theory is the concept of single-loop and double-loop learning. Argyris and Schön (1978) noted that single-loop learning is performed when organizations make corrections that allow the organization to continue existing policies and objectives. Conversely, they claimed that double-loop learning occurs when an organization modifies its underlying norms, policies, and objectives. In double-loop learning, school faculties engage in contextualized and creative assessments that question existing norms and processes. Hauke (1997) noted that double-loop learning is exemplified by organizations that collectively and deliberatively engage in experimentation. Fiol and Lyles (1985) refer to this as higher-level learning, and Leithwood and Prestine (2002) suggest that this approach to reform is supported by organizational learning theory and linked to sustainable instructional improvement. Driver (2002) suggests that both single-loop and double-loop learning are necessary in a learning organization. Hoy and Miskel (2006) noted that in an educational world in constant change, double-loop learning is critical.

Indeed, Honig (2008) reports that district superintendents often fall into what organizational learning theorists call a "success trap" or "failure trap" (Levitt and March, 1988). Specifically, studies found that superintendents in successful districts tended to rely too heavily on evidence that confirms the success of organizational goals. Further, they tended to interpret new data as confirming their current actions, even when this evidence was thought by researchers to challenge existing activities.

In the same manner, district superintendents who perceived that their districts were failing tended to limit search strategies and to allow attention only to evidence that they believed would help them move closer to predetermined performance goals. Indeed, O'Day (2002) found that superintendents responded to external high-stakes accountability mandates by restricting reform strategies to those promising superficial but immediate improvements. These district leaders sought to limit organizational flexibility and thus diminished organizational learning. The result was a focus on single-loop learning as opposed to deeper and more sustainable double-loop learning. Superintendents in the Voices 3 study seemed to recognize that external mandates forced them into a need to produce quick results and thus curtail the development of organizational capacity focused on long-term double-loop learning as supported by organizational learning theory.

The theoretical frameworks of role theory and organizational learning theory both highlight the interplay between internal and external influences and how the superintendent balances those influences in order to address instructional leadership issues. Superintendents improve leader effectiveness when balancing the positive aspects of external accountability mandates while simultaneously dealing with their challenges (Quandary #1), acquire and align resources to meet new accountability requirements of underfunded external accountability mandates (Quandary #2), and focus on local internal interests to provide a holistic, well-rounded education while still meeting the requirements of external accountability mandates (Quandary #3).

Perspectives on Instructional Quandaries

In all of the quandaries presented above, superintendents are grappling not with whether they have a role as an instructional leader but with how to negotiate a balanced response between internal and external accountability forces. Arguably, no single superintendent response can fit every scenario, and thus a leadership platform that provides flexibility is the most effective. One such leadership platform is transition leadership (Goldring, Crowson, Laird, and Berk, 2003), which corresponds to a leadership style that is fluid in response to shifting internal and external accountability forces. Superintendents need to embrace a leadership style that allows them to adjust their behaviors according to shifting internal and external accountability demands. According to role theory, superintendents need to balance their role in management and public relations with the role of instructional leader. When applying organizational learning theory, superintendents need to balance the need for locally developed reform efforts (which tend to build organizational learning capacity) with external innovation, which compels districts to test their locally developed views of their successes and failures against views projected from the larger society (e.g., from state and federal accountability systems).

Superintendents have faced difficulties with state and federal mandates to increase student achievement, and we can study how district leaders grapple with these mandates as they strive to both ensure reflection on reform efforts and attend to district and school priorities (Leithwood, Seashore-Louis, Anderson, and Wahlstrom, 2004). Leithwood and Prestine (2002) identified three sets of leadership practices that respond to this challenge:

1. Capturing the attention of school personnel through using formative and summative student assessments aligned to standards
2. Building capacity through professional development by developing strong, in-house, systematically aligned instructional improvement products and processes
3. Pushing the implications of state policies into schools and classrooms through fostering widespread participation of school and district staff in concentrated efforts to implement the changes

Embodied in the first and third leadership practices noted above is the notion that leaders will not be effective in successfully implementing reform efforts in schools without participation from a broad stakeholder contingent that includes staff and community. This has led to a call for district leaders to engage in collaborative decision-making approaches, which are a primary construct in organizational learning theory.

Discussion Questions

Respond to these questions in light of role theory, organizational learning theory, the comments from the Voices 3 superintendents, your leadership platform, and your own experiences with and insights into education leadership.

1. Suggest guiding principles that superintendents might find helpful in navigating between internal and external accountability mandates that may conflict with one another.
2. What are some merits of local control of public education? What are some merits of state and federal control? How might a superintendent lead a district toward improved instruction by leveraging multiple influences? In what way(s) might external calls for changes in district operations work against internal desires to maintain certain ways of operating, and vice versa?

Quandary #1

1. What behaviors would you engage in as an instructional leader in order to use external accountability mandates to encourage school improvement?

2. What positive and negative results could come from leveraging external accountability measures? How can you minimize the negative effects?
3. How could you leverage an external accountability measure while still building the positive learning culture of a district?

Quandary #2

1. How would you allocate resources to balance local internal interests with external accountability demands? Give examples.
   a. How might changes in external accountability mandates change your hiring practices?
   b. A rudimentary familiarity with teaching reveals that students vary from one to another and from one day and situation to the next. Teachers need to recognize these variations and respond to them. How would you balance this realization with external (or internal) pressures to use standardized curricula, practices shown by research to foster learning, and even scripted lessons?
   c. What would you cut if you had to reduce staff in your district? What grade level or subject area would you cut? How would you balance local internal demands to maintain "pet" programs with the demands of external accountability mandates for improved test scores?

Quandary #3

1. As an instructional leader, how would you set priorities to balance the curriculum between academic subjects requiring testing and those that are not tested but which local stakeholders view as important?
2. Do you think it is appropriate to require all students to take four years of mathematics in high school while making it optional for them to take applied and personal enrichment courses like communications, family living, and physical education? Defend your answer.
3. How would you balance internal and external accountability forces? For example, parents define success in school broadly while external reform demands measure success and failure using math- and literacy-focused academic tests.
4. Do you think the most important purpose of schooling is to produce good citizens, to train for more productive workers, or to prepare for college through emphasizing academics over other kinds

of learning? Do you think all three can be accomplished simultaneously? How would you balance these three aspects of education as an instructional leader?

CONCLUSION

The goal of this chapter is to help superintendents and aspiring superintendents move toward the role of instructional leader and navigate conflicting forces such as external accountability demands and internal demands that conflict with the external ones.

Superintendents may want to enhance their instructional leadership, but they must balance the benefits of external mandates with their negative aspects. However, achieving both accountability goals and the development of organizational capacity for continual learning requires time, support, and the capacity to transition from one role to another in support of the long-term goal of student learning.

ADDITIONAL READING AND RESOURCES

If you would like to read further about the role of the superintendent in balancing external and internal demands, consider these works, which provide practical guidance on district reform and renewal within the constructs of organizational learning theory and role theory.

Björk, L. G., and Kowalski, T. J. (2005). *The contemporary superintendent: Preparation, practice, and development.* Thousand Oaks, CA: Corwin.

This book provides a scholarly and objective analysis of the issues with which superintendents must deal. Of particular relevance to our work is Petersen and Barnett's chapter on the superintendent as instructional leader.

Cambron-McCabe, N., Cunningham, L. L., Harvey, J., and Koff, R. H. (2005). *The superintendent's fieldbook: A guide for leaders of learning.* Thousand Oaks, CA: Corwin.

Drawing on the experiences of nearly two hundred superintendents over the past ten years, this book offers guidance on navigating the external and internal demands of the position. The book describes such challenges as budgets, standards and assessment, changing demographics, and public engagement.

Cooper, B. S., and Fusarelli, L. D. (Eds.). (2004). *The promises and perils facing today's school superintendent.* Lanham, MD: Scarecrow.

Cooper and Fusarelli address many different challenges of the superintendency, including relationships with internal and external stakeholders, the federal accountability shift from process to outcome measures, and the role of the superintendent as instructional leader.

Depres, B. (Ed.). (2008). *Systems thinkers in action: A field guide for effective change leadership in education*. Lanham, MD: Rowman and Littlefield.

This book provides current examples of systematic thinking and action relating to district-wide educational reform. The book explores specific reform theory relevant to district leaders in light of systemic and organizational learning theory.

Leithwood, K., Aitken, R., and Jantzi, D. (2006). *Making schools smarter: Leading with evidence* (3rd ed.). Thousand Oaks, CA: Corwin.

This book applies organizational learning theory to the demands on superintendents to lead reform efforts. This practical guide includes tools to assist the superintendent in achieving accountability goals through building organizational capacity for self-motivated improvement via district-level professional learning communities.

Thomas, J. Y. (2001). *The public school superintendency in the 21st century: The quest to define effective leadership*. Washington, DC: Department of Education, Center for Research on the Education of Students Placed at Risk (CRESPAR). (ERIC Document Reproduction Service No. ED 460 219).

This report examines research on public school leadership effectiveness, focusing specifically on the superintendent. It begins with a discussion of the historical mission to define leadership effectiveness, followed by a review of existing research on effective school districts and superintendents. The report then details the challenges that superintendents face in effectively managing a school system, including stability, the politicization of the profession, and relations between the superintendent and school boards.

REFERENCES

Acker-Hocevar, M., Ballenger, J. N., Place, A. W., and Ivory, G. (Eds.). (2012). *Snapshots of school leadership in the 21st century: Perils and promises of leading for social justice, school improvement, and democratic community*. Charlotte, NC: Information Age.

Archer, J. (2005, September 14). Theory of action: The idea that schools can improve on their own gives way to a focus on effective school leadership. *Education Week*, S3–S5.

Argyris, C., and Schön, D. (1978). *Organizational learning: A theory of action perspective*. Reading, MA: Addison-Wesley.

Björk, L. G. (1993). Effective schools—effective superintendents: The emerging instructional leadership role. *Journal of School Leadership*, 3, 246–259.

Bredeson, P. V., and Kose, B. V. (2007). Responding to the education reform agenda: A study of superintendents' instructional leadership. *Educational Policy Analysis Archives*, 15(5), 1–26.
Bridges, E. (1982). Research on the school administrator: The state-of-the-art, 1967–1980. *Educational Administration Quarterly*, 18(3), 12–33.
Cohen, W. M., and Levinthal, D. A. (1990). Absorptive capacity: A new perspective on learning and innovation. *Administrative Science Quarterly*, 35, 128–152.
Crowson, R., and Morris, V. (1990, April). The superintendency and school leadership. Paper presented at the Annual Meeting of the American Educational Research Association, Boston.
Cuban, L. (1984). Transforming the frog into a prince: Effective schools research and practice at the district level. *Harvard Education Review*, 54(2), 129–151.
Depres, B. (Ed.). (2008). *Systems thinkers in action: A field guide for effective change leadership in education*. Lanham, MD: Rowman and Littlefield.
Driver, M. (2002). Learning and leadership in organizations: Toward complementary communities of practice. *Management Learning*, 33(1), 99–126.
Feldman, M. S. (2000). Organizational routines as a source of continuous change. *Organization Science*, 11(6), 611–629.
Fiol, C., and Lyles, M. (1985). Organizational learning. *Academy of Management Review*, 10, 803–813.
Firestone, W. A., and Shipps, D. (2005). How do leaders interpret conflicting accountabilities to improve student learning? In W. Firestone and C. Riehl (Eds.), *A new agenda for research in educational leadership* (pp. 81–100). New York: Teachers College Press.
Fullan, M. (2001). *Leading in a culture of change*. San Francisco, CA: Jossey-Bass.
Fullan, M. (2006). *Turnaround leadership*. San Francisco, CA: Jossey-Bass.
Glass, T., Björk, L., and Brunner, C. (2000). *The study of the American school superintendency: A look at the superintendent of education in the new millennium*. Arlington, VA: American Association of School Administrators.
Goldring, E., Crowson, R., Laird, D., and Berk, R. (2003). Transition leadership in a shifting policy environment. *Educational Evaluation and Policy Analysis*, 25(4), 473–488.
Hart, A. W., and Ogawa, R. T. (1987). The influence of superintendents on the academic achievement of school districts. *Journal of Educational Administration*, 25(1), 72–84.
Hauke, M. (1997). Leadership and learning in organizations. Unpublished PhD dissertation. Tuscaloosa: University of Alabama.
Hess, F. M., and Meeks, O. (2011). School boards circa 2010: Governance in the accountability era. A report published by the National School Board Association, the Thomas B. Fordham Institute, and the Iowa School Boards Foundation. Retrieved on August 17, 2012, from http://www.nsba.org/Board-Leadership/Surveys/School-Boards-Circa-2010.

Hightower, A., Knapp, M. S., Marsh, J. A., and McLaughlin, M. W. (2002). *School districts and institutional renewal.* New York: Teachers College Press.

Honig, M. I. (2008). District central offices as learning organizations: How sociocultural and organizational learning theories elaborate district central office administrators' participation in teaching and learning improvement efforts. *American Journal of Education,* 114(4), 627–664.

Hoy, W., and Miskel, C. (2006). *Contemporary issues in educational policy and school outcomes. A volume in research and theory in educational administration.* Greenwich, CT: Information Age.

Katz, D., and Kahn, R. L. (1966). *The social psychology of organizations.* New York: John Wiley and Sons.

Keedy, J., and Björk, L. (2001). The superintendent, local boards, and the political arena. *The AASA Professor,* 24(4), 2–5.

Kew, K., Ivory, G., Muñiz, M., and Quiz, F. (2012). No Child Left Behind as school reform: Intended and unintended consequences. In M. Acker-Hocevar, J. N. Ballenger, A. W. Place, and G. Ivory (Eds.), *Snapshots of school leadership in the 21st century: Perils and promises of leading for social justice, school improvement, and democratic community* (pp. 13–30). Charlotte, NC: Information Age.

Leithwood, K. (2000). What we have learned about schools as intelligent systems. *Advances in Research and Theories of School Management and Educational Policy,* 4, 315–330. Stanford, CT: JAI Press.

Leithwood, K. (2005). *Educational leadership: A review of the research.* Philadelphia: Mid-Atlantic Regional Educational Laboratory.

Leithwood, K., Aitken, R., and Jantzi, D. (2006). *Making schools smarter: Leading with evidence* (3rd ed.). Thousand Oaks, CA: Corwin.

Leithwood, K., and Prestine, N. (2002). Unpacking the challenges of leadership at the school and district level. In J. Murphy (Ed.), *The educational leadership challenge: Redefining leadership for the 21st century* (pp. 42–64). Chicago: National Society for the Study of Education.

Leithwood, K., Seashore-Louis, K., Anderson, S., and Wahlstrom, K. (2004). *How leadership influences student learning.* Minneapolis: University of Minnesota, Center for Applied Research and Educational Improvement.

Levinthal, D. A., and March, J. G. (1993). The myopia of learning. *Strategic Management Journal,* 14, 5–112.

Levitt, B., and March, J. G. (1988). Organizational learning. *American Review of Sociology,* 14, 319–340.

March, J. G. (1994). *A primer on decision making.* New York: Free Press.

Marks, H., Seashore-Louis, K., and Printy, S. (2000). The capacity for organizational learning: Implications for pedagogical quality and student achievement. In K. Leithwood (Ed.), *Understanding schools as intelligent systems* (pp. 293–314). Stanford, CT: JAI Press.

O'Day, J. A. (2002). Complexity, accountability, and school improvement. *Harvard Educational Review,* 72(3), 1–31.

Schwahn, C., and Spady, W. (1998). *Total leaders: Applying the best future-focused change strategies to education.* Arlington, VA: American Association of School Administrators.

Short, P., and Scribner, J. (2000). *Case studies of the superintendency.* Lanham, MD: Scarecrow.

Silins, H., Mulford, B., Zarins, S., and Bishop, P. (2000). Leadership for organizational learning in Australian secondary schools. *Advances in Research and Theories of School Management and Educational Policy,* 4, 267–291.

Waters, J. T., and Marzano, R. J. (2006). *School district leadership that works: The effect of superintendent leadership on student achievement.* Denver, CO: Mid-Continent Research for Education and Learning.

Chapter 5

Decisions, Decisions, Decisions: Can Using Transformational Leadership and Mindfulness Theory Help You Make the Right Ones?

Teena McDonald

As a superintendent, you make major decisions daily that affect the academic, emotional, and physical safety of students, staff, and community members. How you make those decisions could be a matter of life and death. Take the perennial decision that all superintendents in the northern states make throughout the winter: to put the school buses on the road or to cancel school when inclement weather is predicted. This seemingly straightforward decision can be a very difficult quandary for superintendents, and there is no textbook to look to for answers. If you call school off and the nasty ice storm does not materialize, you have hundreds of angry parents who had to scramble for day care, and students and staff must make up a day at the end of the school year. If you do not call off school and a bus slides into the ditch and students are injured, you have another quandary. In each case, your decision-making skills may be questioned. Decision making is a critical aspect of leadership, and how you as a leader both make decisions and allow others to be involved in making decisions can be a key factor in the success of your tenure in a school district.

This chapter will allow you to think about mindfulness theory and how it can be used in conjunction with transformational leadership to help you embody most effectively the skill set described by ISLLC Standard 3 and effectively make decisions. The standard exhorts education leaders to promote the success of every student by ensuring management of the organization, operation, and resources for a safe, efficient, and effective learning environment. You will be taken through a scenario, using the inclement weather quandary from the introduction, where you see an example of how using mindfulness as a transformational leader can help you make a decision. You will then be asked to look at several quandaries, taken from the Voices 3 data, that superintendents faced and to answer questions.

The history of leadership theory has swung from being male dominated and trait specific to transformational leadership studies common to educational leadership indicating that both men and women can be good leaders using this theoretical base. By embracing both transformational leadership theory and mindfulness, leaders can be even more effective. Mindfulness takes the interaction beyond others to the leader being present in the now and listening carefully to his or her inner wisdom before making decisions.

Transformational Leadership Theory

Burns (1978) introduced the concept of transformational leadership, describing it not as a set of specific behaviors but rather as a process by which "leaders and followers raise one another to higher levels of morality and motivation" (p. 20). In order to raise leaders and followers to higher levels of consciousness, an adjustment is required in beliefs, values, and attitudes. According to Daft (1999), transformational leadership is characterized by the ability to bring about significant change. Heifitz (1994) further defined transformational leadership as adaptive leadership. Heifitz believes that adaptive leadership consists of the learning required to address conflicts in the values people hold or to diminish the gap between the values people stand for and the reality they face. Specific characteristics of adaptive leaders include the ability to help a group set priorities and clarify values and beliefs, resolve conflicts among stakeholders, maintain a level of tension that mobilizes people, and help stakeholders understand the need to change and how to have a systematic change process.

Daft (1999) shares four significant leadership components of transformational leadership:

1. Transformational leadership develops followers into leaders. Followers are given greater freedom to control their own behavior. The transformational leader motivates followers to take initiative and solve problems and helps people look at things in new ways. This is consistent with much of the work being done now in school systems, where teacher leaders are asked to help make transformational change in the classrooms, and teacher leaders are being given more authority to make those important changes.
2. Transformational leadership elevates followers' concerns from lower-level physical needs (such as safety and security) to higher-level psychological needs (such as self-esteem and self-actualization). Transformational leaders pay attention to each individual's need for growth and development, while at the same time showing concern for each individual.
3. Transformational leadership inspires followers to go beyond their own self-interest for the good of the group. Transformational leaders motivate people to do more than originally expected. Transformational leadership motivates people not to follow the leader personally but to believe in the need for change and be willing to make personal sacrifices for the greater purpose.
4. Finally, transformational leadership paints a vision of a desired future state and communicates it in a way that makes the pain of change worth the effort. It is a vision that launches people into action and engages the commitment of followers.

Recent studies by Eagly, from Northwestern University, indicate that women are more likely than men to use leadership styles that studies have shown to produce better worker performance and effectiveness in today's world. Eagly (2002) shares that women are more likely to be transformational leaders, strengthening organizations by inspiring followers' commitment and creativity. She, along with Johannesen-Schmidt and van Engen (2003), strengthened the credibility of the initial study by conducting a meta-analysis of 45 studies of transformational, transactional, and laissez-faire leadership styles, finding that women are more transformational in their leadership style than their male counterparts. Eagly (2002) goes on to say that a transformational leadership style may be especially well adapted to women because this way of leading is relatively androgynous and has some nurturing, feminine aspects. Eagly, Johannesen-Schmidt, and van Engen (2003) also noted that women engaged in more of the contingent reward behaviors that are a component of transactional leadership. They state, "By combining the transformational leadership as well as the contingent reward aspects of transactional leadership may provide a particularly congenial context for women's enactment of competent leadership." Finally, Eagly (2002) indicates that women's past socialization may give them more ability to lead by teaching—that is, by developing and nurturing workers' abilities and inspiring them to be outstanding contributors.

Transformational leaders promote change. In the education setting, oftentimes superintendents must also reflect the balance of being a good manager while at the same time promoting change as a transformational leader. Marzano, Waters, and McNulty (2005) specifically conducted meta-analyses based on school and district-level leadership. Interestingly enough, they found that behaviors associated with leadership at the district level are not always associated with an increase in average student achievement. For example, in the wake of school shootings, many district leaders are being mandated by public sentiment to focus resources on tightening security rather than on measures focused around student achievement. This is called the "differential impact" of leadership. They found that a superintendent can focus the attention and resources of the district on many goals, depending on the needs that the superintendent and the board find most important at the time. By focusing a district on goals that are unlikely to impact achievement, a seemingly strong superintendent can have a minimally positive or even a negative effect on student performance. They referred to the second explanation for the differential impact of district-level leadership as the order of magnitude of change. They found that the superintendent must accurately estimate the order of magnitude of change that goals imply for stakeholders. Instructional leaders are on a continuum based on their knowledge, skill set, and willingness to embrace change. This meta-analysis indicates that leaders need to know how to anticipate needs, motivate colleagues, and be very aware of the situation and the organization.

Senge (1990) and Bolman and Deal (2003) both performed leadership research based on how the organization can be framed and decoded. Bolman and Deal (2003) developed frames and metaphors of organizations and share how leaders must use these multiple frames to be more effective leaders with a greater understanding of their organization. The four frames are the structural, human resources, political, and symbolic frames, with corresponding metaphors of factory/machine, family, jungle, and carnival/temple/theater. Interestingly enough, Bolman and Deal quote Langer (1989), one of the early mindfulness theory researchers, by describing her view of "mindlessness" as what makes the great chasm of leadership and organizational shortfalls diminish.

Mindfulness Theory

So how does mindfulness theory interrelate with transformational leadership theory? Dhiman (2009) shares that mindfulness has tremendous potential to enhance workplace well-being through improved communications, efficient meetings, optimum performances, better decisions, and greater understanding. Professionals practicing mindfulness can result in an increase in competence and ethical behavior (Thomas, Schermerhorn, and Dienhart, 2004) and an increase in memory, creativity, and positive mental state (Langer, 2000). Brody and Coulter (2002), in their article about preparing business school graduates for the twenty-first-century workplace, share that mindfulness helps an individual process and make better use of information outside of contexts in which it was initially learned. Mindful leaders are able to respond to the needs of others, assess the level of supports needed, and better gauge the appropriate level of change that must be managed.

Further exploration of leader mindfulness reveals that definitions borrow heavily from work by Langer (1989) and colleagues—in which mindfulness is defined as the process of drawing novel distinctions. It is a simple definition with deep undertones, "including (1) a greater sensitivity to one's environment, (2) more openness to new information, (3) the creation of new categories for structuring perception, and (4) enhanced awareness of multiple perspectives in problem solving" (Langer and Moldoveanu, 2000, p. 2). The conceptualization of mindfulness also borrows from Eastern philosophy (Weick and Putnam, 2006). Bare attention and awareness are other terms used to convey the approach to understanding existence through experience posited in this tradition (Beck, 1993; Epstein, 1995). Kabat-Zinn (2003), in providing a definition of attention, wrote that it is "not the same as thought. It lies beyond thinking. . . . [Attention] is more like a vessel which can hold and contain our thinking, helping us to see and know our thoughts as thoughts" (p. 93).

There remains ongoing debate about the essential nature and definition of mindfulness, but "it is most commonly defined as the state of being attentive to and aware of what is taking place in the present" (Brown and Ryan, 2003, p. 822), the direct opposite of "multitasking." Bishop (2003) adds to this definition an orientation that embraces curiosity, questioning, or interest in the immediate experience.[1]

Mindfulness can help superintendents as they lead and make difficult decisions. Weick and Sutcliffe (2001) note that successful highly reliable organizations use determined efforts to act mindfully in managing the unexpected. Weick and Sutcliffe (2006) have labeled the components of highly reliable organizations as (1) preoccupation with failure, (2) sensitivity to operations, (3) commitment to resilience, (4) reluctance to simplify, and (5) deference to expertise.

In being preoccupied with failure, a leader and organization note that the unexpected may give off only weak signals of trouble. A normal tendency would be to respond to weak signals with a weak response. Mindfulness requires the counterintuitive approach of strong responses to weak signals. For example, in the educational system, when leaders ignore minor student learning difficulties, this can lead to a catastrophic downward spiral for those students whose seemingly insignificant difficulties were not addressed when only weak signals were given. If instead the leader were to highlight small errors or discrepancies as a part of ongoing activities and put pyramids of interventions in place early on by developing effective response-to-intervention programs, his or her preoccupation with failure would increase the reliability of student success. Some schools and districts are lulled into a sense of complacency when schools are making adequate yearly progress; leaders forget to continue to be preoccupied with failure, and they do not mine the data for the weak signals, which could become bigger student achievement issues at a later time.

Leaders who show sensitivity to operations pay attention to "real-time" information. Two examples, later in this paragraph, give examples of superintendents who pay attention to real-time information and exhibit situational awareness. They are in-the-moment thinkers, rather than leaders who think ahead or relive the past. They provide stakeholders with detailed real-time information on what is happening so everyone has the big picture. They figure out how to widely disseminate operational measures of performance, and they take the time to get out of the office and have face-to-face interactions with key players. If there are small disruptions in operations, they give their undivided attention to the early identification of problems so that action can be taken before the problems become substantial. For example, although the district enrolls over twenty-eight thousand students, the superintendent of Spokane public schools, Dr. Shelley Redinger (2013), takes every Thursday morning through the entire school year to be in a different school and in different classrooms. This is an example of how even a large urban school superintendent is keeping those face-to-face interactions as a priority. Dr. Nancy Coogan (2013), superintendent of Tukwila School District in Washington State, shared a time when a principal and staff noted a gas smell in the building. When the principal called the district office maintenance personnel, the person at the central office said that the sensors indicated no problems and that students should remain in class. The principal was sensitive to operations and made the call to evacuate students and staff anyway, overriding the central office recommendation. In this case, Nancy will tell you it was the right decision, and that is because she empowers her principals to be continuously aware that they are "on the front line" and must mindfully make the right decisions, based on sensitivity to operations. In large-district operations, when a leader shows sensitivity to operations, he or she encourages administrators and staff members to pay attention to real-time information.

The next component of highly reliable organizations is a commitment to resilience. Leaders return to normal functioning after unusual circumstances are over. They are able to cope with surprise and develop ways to improvise. Resilient leaders support their staff and give them authority to "work outside the box" to fix problems. This support also suggests the need to have administrators regularly observe teachers and coach them to higher levels of performance. This ensures great teaching and leading through evaluation and accountability.

Reluctance to simplify interpretations is a principle whereby the leader and an organization notice more and ignore less, by taking nothing for granted. A key component of mindful leaders is their ability to draw novel distinctions and notice things in the "here and now." They have a mindful awareness of situations and staff members around them. They have a system of checks and balances in place and welcome skeptical voices. Simplifying information produces blind spots, so highly reliable leaders and organizations work against that by elaborating their simplifications. This is important in a school system in regard to looking at data and assessment. Unless the leader and the educational team develop data-driven systems that look at both the big picture and, more importantly, the microlevel data, areas of weakness can be missed. Think of this like a fishing pole with varying sizes of eyelets that the fishing line passes through. Many leaders stop at the big eyelet when looking at data and don't thread the data line completely down to the narrower focus of individual student data.

Finally, highly reliable organizations and leaders show deference to expertise. Mindful leaders take the time to listen, without multitasking, giving everyone in the organization the "authority" to share their expertise. During normal operations, there is a chain of command,

and staff members demonstrate deference to authority. However, it is often the case that staff members who work closest with the situation at hand see problems arising first. They might consider themselves to be of low rank, partly invisible, and certainly not authorized to make changes. What highly reliable leaders have mastered is the ability to alter their typical patterns of chain of command in order to make decisions quickly and accurately as unexpected problems occur. They allow these voices to be heard. For example, if a bus driver who has lived in the area for 25 years tells the superintendent that when east winds blow at a certain speed and the humidity and temperature are at a certain level, freezing rain is likely to occur, the superintendent takes that expertise into his or her decision making when deciding to close schools. The key is that the bus driver needs to feel valued and safe in sharing his or her expertise.

Using the example of the weather quandary I gave at the beginning of the chapter, let us walk through using the mindfulness components of a highly reliable organization and through being mindful, as a guide that will encourage you to look at the quandaries later through this frame.

1. Preoccupation with failure: Know that the decision you make will impact staff, students, and their families. Call attention to mistakes; if someone was not trained to put on chains or drive on slick roads, figure out how that failure occurred and make plans so it doesn't happen again. Look at worst-case scenarios, for example, if school was canceled and no big storm arrives, or if school was not canceled and a bus wrecks. Avoid complacency and unawareness of possible dangers.
2. Sensitivity to operations: As you look at all aspects, find out how other districts in the area are responding to the weather. Be continuously aware of those on "the front line"—Are the drivers experienced? Have they been trained on how to put on chains? Is everyone ready to deal with the weather if school is not canceled? Gather all the information possible and be data heavy before proceeding. However, know that this type of decision is time sensitive. Do not procrastinate on making the decision once you have all the data.
3. Commitment to resilience: Know that no matter which choice you make, someone will be unhappy. Have the ability to "bounce back" and cope with surprise. Be prepared with a positive sound bite for the situation, no matter which way you decide. Learn from your mistakes and proceed forward.
4. Reluctance to simplify: Notice more and ignore less. Acknowledge the reality of surprise by taking nothing for granted—run all of the

"what ifs" through your mind as you look at the situation. Just because one of the news stations predicts freezing rain does not mean the National Weather Service will have the same prediction. Make sure there are checks and balances in place. Have contingency plans if emergency snow routes prove to be too difficult for the driver. Accept and respect inquiry. If you are mindful, you respect differences of opinion. Listen to opinions other than just your own and those of people inclined to agree with you.

5. Deference to expertise: Look at the National Weather Service in addition to the TV stations' forecasts. Talk to the transportation supervisors and get their opinions after being out on the roads. Develop a protocol that includes allowing the county road department supervisor to work in conjunction with you to provide knowledge on plowing. Listen to your bus drivers who know the area roads and conditions. If a competent, knowledgeable bus driver who has lived in the area for 50 years tells you that when east winds come up the valley there can still be freezing rain even when it is 36 degrees, listen to that driver.

Ultimately, the decision is yours. By using the above steps and by developing mindful awareness of the situation, taking the time to pause and breathe, and then mindfully addressing the situation, you may find that this framework can help you make a decision that you and your stakeholders are happy with.

As you know, most quandaries revolve around decisions that need to be made. As we look at the Voices data, think about using transformational leadership through a mindfulness lens to make decisions related to the quandaries shared by superintendents. Superintendent 11 shares the following in the Voices 3 data:

> Rural superintendents—what you do is make decisions. And, you make hundreds and hundreds of decisions every single day. And, if you lose sight of the fact that the child needs to be the center of those decisions—how is it going to impact the child?—you can quickly be off to the wrong direction in a hurry. And, there are plenty of folks who want to take you off and lead you in the wrong direction. Whether it's a school board member or board of supervisors or a parent or someone who thinks they have the best of intentions. But in the long run, it could be wrong for or detrimental to the child. So, that's the challenge of the superintendency. Making those instantaneous decisions when you're standing in two feet of water and looking at a sewer line. Or, you're looking at textbook adoption materials. It's always about what impact it has on children.

SCENARIO 1

Read the following discussion between Superintendent 18 and Superintendent 19, both superintendents from small districts, as they discuss decision making:

> *Superintendent 19:* I was in a situation as a principal, where we had a superintendent; and I absolutely loved the man; he was great. He gave me my building. He walked away, he let me run it. There [were] no problems about it at all. When I was hired there was a committee of 12 people that were part of that committee to make that decision. The perspective in that district—and I was there six years—the perspective in that district was this man cannot make a decision. He put the committee together every time to make a decision, so he didn't have to take the heat for it. And he was a great guy, and he was a good man and he had a lot of knowledge, but pretty soon, all that stirring and fussing and mixing within the faculty, it came out that he couldn't make a decision, so he put it off, so he didn't have to take the heat.
>
> *Superintendent 18:* I remember when I was—I don't know how long you've been here. Were you here when [name] was here? . . . He was a superintendent here when I started. Very autocratic, y'know, it was kind of [name's] way or the highway. And when he left, it was like the board went to the other extreme.
>
> *Superintendent 19:* Right.
>
> *Superintendent 18:* And for however long [name] was here, maybe five or six, seven years. Those principals'd go to [name]: "Whattaya wanna do?" He'd tell 'em; they'd go back. And when the new guy came in, it was interesting. He'd say, "Okay, go back to your school. You decide, give me some choices," and those principals could not do that. A few could, but for the most part, the principals hated that guy because he would not make a decision, but it wasn't really his decision to make. It was that building level principal's decision and that was the kind of the direction that a lot of management skills were going, y'know, site-based management, things like that. "Talk to your teachers, find out what you guys can do with this," and those guys could not handle that.

Questions:

1. Analyze how you balance your leadership style to allow adequate input while still giving enough support to principals when making difficult decisions. How do you allow important input but still maintain your ability and authority to make decisions without seeming autocratic?

2. What types of decisions should you make yourself, and in which decisions should you involve others?
3. How can you use the mindfulness components of a highly reliable organization to help you make decisions?
4. How could you, as a leader, inspire others to use mindfulness components to help them make effective decisions?

Scenario 2

Some decisions involve controversy, and some are very emotional for stakeholders. The moderator, speaking with the group of small-district superintendents, asks them, "Since you've been under diverse leadership styles and decision making environments, . . . can you tell us of a great disappointment that you've seen or experienced?" Superintendent 20 responded energetically:

> Oh, yeah. Throw a school calendar out to 48 educators—teachers—and ask them to give you the input on the school calendar for the next year. I will never do that again. I will lay it in front of 'em and that's what they will work at and if they prefer [not] to work at that, they can find themselves another job. I got more static over the CALENDAR issue and the committees that I sent this to . . .
> *Superintendent 18*: The calendar's the single-most-selfish thing that teachers do. They look at their families' schedules for the whole year . . .
> *Superintendent 20*: Oh yeah!
> *Superintendent 18*: To see if the calendar will fit that.
> *Superintendent 20*: So, I think committees take the pressure off . . . leaders, somewhat. The bottom line comes down to the administrator, but I think committees [take] the pressure off of them somewhat. And I think that's a difference in leadership. Some people don't mind the pressure; some people want a little of it taken off. No, that's up to my counselor, my principal and myself.

Questions:

1. Earlier, we said that mindful leaders show deference to expertise and that transformational leadership elevates followers' concerns from lower-level physical needs (such as safety and security) to higher-level psychological needs (such as self-esteem and self-actualization). Analyze this quandary of the school calendar in terms of self-esteem and self-actualization. What might be ways of dealing with the school calendar other than the either-or choices these superintendents seem to see?

2. Using the mindfulness framework shared in this chapter, propose a solution to the problem of gaining consensus on the calendar issue. Design responses related to each of the five characteristics of a highly reliable organization: preoccupation with failure, sensitivity to operations, commitment to resilience, reluctance to simplify, and deference to expertise.

SCENARIO 3

For many decisions, superintendents use their adopted policy guidelines to help them with day-to-day work. What becomes quickly apparent to administrators is how often policy does not guide a critical decision.

Superintendent 20 shares the following:

> Probably the one thing that I've realized is that everything is not black and white. Everything is not in policy. Everything is not mandated, and you have to make decisions pretty much daily on things that are not black and white. You have to enter that gray area and you have to make decisions on what's best for your students. And that, I think we've gotta do what's right. I think that's the bottom line. It may not be in black and white but at least you can go home and know you've done what's right, for the majority of the students.

The moderator asks superintendents if something guides them in their decisions. Superintendent 20 replies,

> What's best for them, what's beneficial to them. And that's the way I get out of a lot of problems. I'll have an irate parent sitting in front of me about their student and I'll say, "With you working and [me] working towards what's best for that student, we're gonna come [to] the right conclusion here." And they'll usually say okay. Not what they want, not what I want, but what's best for that student. And they'll usually get out of it a pretty good [decision].

The moderator asks for further explanation. Superintendent 18 interjects,

> I think just sometimes, we call it "Talking a different language." In my mind there's a certain situation should be handled a certain way, but you know when that parent's coming in you know there's no way you're gonna convince them of that. I had one this morning where

they have a tee shirt for the after-prom party and on the back it said—it was an underwater theme for the whole prom and the back of the shirt said—something about "The boat rockin', so don't come knockin'." Well, I know what that means, y'know, and that girl who did that design knows what that means, but there were a group of parents who had no idea what that meant.

"That's not what that means!"

That's exactly what that means. Yeah, and this girl's mom came in this morning all fired up because we wouldn't even take it to the vote of the kids or the parents or whatever.

I said, "I'm not gonna put that on the back of a tee shirt and have some 'Sweetwater Public Schools' on there," y' know, and advertise that we're rockin' boats, so—c'mon.

"Well, why not? That just means dance, rockin'."

"Ma'am, that's not what that means."

Y'know, and she just did not get it, and she thought that was perfectly okay.

And I said, "That's not perfectly okay."

"I'll take it to the board."

"You're more than welcome to do that, ma'am." Sometimes they just don't get it.

Questions:

1. As you reflect on your leadership platform you started working on in Chapter 2, what guides your decision making?
2. Do you ever have to go against "what is right" as you make a decision?
3. How could mindfulness help you when you have a difficult decision that will not make a stakeholder happy?

Scenario 4

ISLLC Standard 3 is about ensuring management of the organization, operation, and resources for a safe, efficient, and effective learning environment. You recall that Marzano, Waters, and McNulty's (2005) meta-analysis of leadership found that a superintendent can focus the attention and resources of the district on many goals. We discussed how sometimes resources have to be focused on things other than student achievement, like safety. By focusing a district on goals that are unlikely to impact achievement, a seemingly strong superintendent can have a minimally positive or even negative effect on student performance.

Listen to the voices of rural superintendents as they deal with the quandary of deciding how to best use resources. Superintendent 22 states,

> Well to me, it means that you're trying to make decisions and help your board make decisions that are the best for all students. I was thinking about that the other day. . . . This is my second superintendency, and I was thinking about what I have really spent my time on the last two years in the district. And it really—most of the time, as much as I really hate to say it, I have not had the opportunity to spend my time thinking about what is best for students. If I'm really honest, it seems like I have spent the majority of my time in my particular situation working with the board trying to help the board to understand things, trying to help the board to see the bigger picture, and not having the luxury of focusing on kids. And I don't—maybe I'm just a little jaded right at this point in my career, but I don't see any way in our district where decisions are truly made based on what's best for kids. I don't see board members looking at the big picture and seeing that they have to make a decision because it's the best thing to do for kids. I think that they get sidetracked by agendas. They get sidetracked by different community groups that get their attention, and they really struggle with that so much. And I have a young board too; it's not a veteran board who's been at it for a long time, so a lot of turnovers that are always—I'm always going to be having board members that are learning what their role is. But I also see the same thing with all the staff, and I think that's kind of unfortunate. I think sometimes teachers and principals—principals get very building minded—which is good, they're out to support their building. And teachers are out to protect their classroom, to get what they need for their kids. So I think that sometimes they lose sight of why decisions are made for the good of the whole and for the good of all kids, not just this one group of kids, or not just this one building. So I don't know, maybe my situation is unique, but I just—we're working toward that, but I don't feel like it's happening.

Superintendent 25 acknowledged,

> One of the things I've experienced—well first of all, it's a small district of 320 students versus the size that you have, and I think that some of it is built [into] the larger districts, the more buildings that you have, the more layers, the farther removed your board and you tend to be from where it's impacting. The downside to that in a district—of being so close to it—is that you handle so many things, that you feel that you're still mostly a principal sometimes, and would like to spend more time with those others. But as far as impacting students, besides the personnel, what I've found in my experience in a couple districts has to do with following somebody whose priorities weren't looking at the curriculum

and keeping textbook adoptions up to date and things like that. So in a couple districts I've been able to—just by how you channel the monies—how you focus some things, it makes a big difference in materials that teachers have to work with, and again getting good teachers.

Questions:

1. How can your decision-making process, guided by the theoretical frameworks in this chapter, help you make sure you are focusing on an effective learning environment while still making sure that safety and district efficiency are adequately covered?
2. How do you address the quandary of competing interests in districts with declining resources?

Conclusion

Leadership has many definitions. The *World English Dictionary* defines it as the "ability to guide, direct, or influence people." Burns (1978) says, "The ultimate test of practical leadership is the realization of intended, real change that meets people's enduring needs" (p. 461). Fullan (2002) describes education leaders as people who combine

> a strong sense of moral purpose, an understanding of the dynamics of change, an emotional intelligence as they build relationships, a commitment to developing and sharing new knowledge, and a capacity for coherence making. (p. 2)

Many researchers currently affirm that leadership is now understood as being about the process of influencing people to adopt particular values by working collaboratively, building trust, engaging in emotional work, and regulating stress. The study of leadership cannot, in Burns's (1978) opinion, be synthesized into one theory of historical causation. Instead, he believed that leadership studies and theories should contribute to developing theories of causation that are more sophisticated. Burns (1978) further states,

> As leadership comes properly to be seen as a process of leaders engaging and mobilizing the human needs and aspirations of followers, women will more readily be recognized as leaders and men will change their own leadership styles. (p. 50)

Pellicer (1999) shares that "we don't become leaders until we can trust ourselves enough to listen to our inner voices and know for certain that those voices will guide us in making the decisions we instinctively know are right for us as leaders" (p. 121). Bennis (1992) notes,

> No leader sets out to be a leader. People set out to live their lives, expressing themselves fully. When that expression is of value they become leaders. The point is to become yourself, to use yourself completely—all your skills, gifts, and energies—in order to make your vision manifest. You must withhold nothing. Become the person you started out to be, and enjoy the process of becoming. (pp. 111–112)

NOTE

1. Sections of this chapter that relate to mindfulness are adapted from "Mcdonald, T., and Gates,G. (2014). Mindfulness in Educational Leadership. In Gates, G. (Ed.), *Mindfulness for educational practice: a path to resilence for challenging work* (pp. 59–80). Charlotte, NC: Information Age Publishing, Inc.

ADDITIONAL READING

Bolman, L. G., and Deal, T. E. (2003). *Reframing organizations: Artistry, choice, and leadership*. San Francisco, CA: Jossey-Bass.

Burns, J. M. (1978). *Leadership*. New York: Harper and Row.

Carroll, M. (2007). *The mindful leader*. Boston: Trumpeter Books.

Gunaratana, B. H. (2011). *Mindfulness in plain English*. Somerville, MA: Wisdom.

Hanh, T. N. (1991). *Peace is every step: The path of mindfulness in everyday life*. New York: Bantam Books.

Heifetz, R. A. (1994). *Leadership without easy answers*. Cambridge, MA: Harvard University Press.

Langer, E. (1989). *Mindfulness*. Reading, MA: Addison-Wesley.

Langer, E. (1997). *The power of mindful learning*. Reading, MA: Addison-Wesley.

Marzano, R. J., Waters, T., and McNulty, B. A. (2005). *School leadership that works*. Alexandria, VA: Association for Supervision and Curriculum Development.

Olson, K., and Brown, V. (2012 July). Developing mindfulness in school leaders. *Education Week*, etrieved from http://www.edweek.org/ew/articles/2012/06/29/36olson.

Pellicer, L. O. (1999). *Caring enough to lead: Schools and the sacred trust*. Thousand Oaks, CA: Corwin.

Senge, P. (1990). *The fifth discipline: The art and practice of the learning organization*. New York: Doubleday.

Stahl, B., and Goldstein, E. (2010). *A mindfulness-based stress reduction workbook*. Oakland, CA: New Harbinger.

REFERENCES

Bennis, W. (1992). *Leaders on leadership: Interviews with top executives.* Boston: Harvard Business School Publications.

Bishop, S. (2003). Clarifying the construct of mindfulness in the context of emotion regulation and the process of change in therapy. *Clinical Psychology: Science and Practice*, 11, 255–262.

Bolman, L. G., and Deal, T. E. (2003). *Reframing organizations: Artistry, choice, and leadership.* San Francisco, CA: Jossey-Bass.

Brody, R., and Coulter, J. M. (2002). Preparing business school graduates for the 21st century workplace. *College Student Journal*, 36(7), 222–233.

Brown, K. W., and Ryan, R. M. (2003). The benefits of being present: Mindfulness and its role in psychological well-being. *Journal of Personality and Social Psychology*, 84, 822–848.

Burns, J. M. (1978). *Leadership.* New York: Harper and Row.

Coogan, N. Personal communication, October 2013.

Daft, R. L. (1999). *Organization theory and design.* Cincinnati, OH: South-Western College Publishing.

Dhiman, S. (2009). Cultivating mindfulness: The Buddhist art of paying attention to attention. *Interbeing*, 2(2), 35–52.

Eagly, A. (2002). Role congruity theory of prejudice toward female leaders. *Psychological Review*, 109(3), 573–598.

Eagly, A., Johannesen-Schmidt, M. C., and van Engen, M. (2003). Transformational, transactional, and laissez-faire leadership styles: A meta-analysis comparing women and men. *Psychological Bulletin*, 129(4), 569–591. doi:10.1037/0033-2909.129.4.569.

Epstein, M. (1995). *Thoughts without a thinker.* New York: Basic Books.

Fullan, M. (2002). Leadership and sustainability. *Principal Leadership*, 3(4), 1–7.

Heifetz, R. A. (1994). *Leadership without easy answers.* Cambridge, MA: Harvard University Press.

Kabat-Zinn, J. (2003). Mindfulness-based interventions in context: Past, present, and future. *Clinical Psychology: Science and Practice*, 10(2), 144–156. doi:10.1093/clipsy.bpg016.

Langer, E. (1989). *Mindfulness.* Reading, MA: Addison-Wesley.

Langer, E. (2000). Mindful learning. *Current Directions in Psychological Science*, 9(6), 220–223. doi:10.1111/1467-8721.00099.

Langer, E., and Moldoveanu, M. (2000). The construct of mindfulness. *Journal of Social Issues*, 56(1), 1–9. doi:10.1111/0022-4537.00148.

Thomas, T., Schermerhorn, J., Jr., and Dienhart, J. (2004). Strategic leadership of ethical behavior in business. *Academy of Management Executives*, 18(2), 56–66. doi:10.5465/AME.2004.13837425.

Weick, K., and Putnam, T. (2006). Organizing for mindfulness: Eastern wisdom and Western knowledge. *Journal of Management Inquiry*, 15, 275–287. doi:10.1177/1056492606291202.

Weick, K., and Sutcliffe, K. (2001). *Managing the unexpected.* San Francisco, CA: Jossey-Bass.

CHAPTER 6

COMPLEXITY THEORY, NETWORKING, AND THE WORK OF SMALL-DISTRICT SUPERINTENDENTS

Corrie Stone-Johnson

As a principal in small districts, I was always at the board table with the board members, so I got a knowledge of the networking and the way boards work and all those kinds of decisions, and just the little things you can say or the little things that you do that make such an impact on kids. But then from the superintendency end—again it's not one specific thing—it's a series of things that just by very small movements or very small suggestions, all of a sudden out of that grows so much positive in things you can do. It's not just at the board table, but it's at the correspondence that comes across your desk, the offers that are out there, and it's that linker. And you realize that you're the only person there that's doing that, and if it would not be for you making that phone call to this or latching on to that, all of a sudden a whole series of things set in motion would never be.

As a future or practicing administrator, you are undoubtedly committed to ISLLC Standard 3, which states that an education leader should promote "the success of every student by ensuring management of the organization, operation, and resources for a safe, efficient, and effective learning environment." But what does such an environment look like? And how can you possibly ensure management of it when, in a time of dwindling human resources, your work feels like it is 24 hours a day, seven days a week, and it seems that there are never enough people to help? In such times, you might believe that managing an organization relies upon trying to control as many elements as you can. Supervising people, handling emergencies as they pop up, and running interference between parents and the district are par for the course in your daily life.

As described in the opening quotation, it is also clear that what gets "set in motion" is unpredictable and therefore almost impossible to plan for. More important, though, setting things in motion requires decisions, and adding these decisions to an already full plate may seem to act in conflict with the very type of efficient organization that is the supposed goal. This situation presents a quandary: How do you work toward efficiency and a smooth-running organization when being the most effective leader possible may require stepping away from or deemphasizing these very goals? Taking this assumption one more step leads to the following question: Does being a leader who can handle and thrive in complexity work against meeting Standard 3?

New paradigms of leadership suggest that a goal of efficiency, as specified in ISLLC Standard 3, may be an important first step, but it is ultimately not enough to sustain an organization. Sustainability, as defined by Fullan (2005), is "the capacity of a system to engage in the complexities of continuous improvement consistent with deep values of human purpose" (p. ix). Thus, while the barrage of pressures that a small-district superintendent faces may create a sense of anxiety, there is a good deal of research that suggests that rather than attempting to minimize pressures, a key facet of leadership is "containing anxiety" (Zellermayer and Margolin, 2005, p. 1279) and helping the organization to use it productively. It is at this "edge of chaos" that natural systems "are most alive, vital, responsive and creative" (Snyder, Acker-Hocevar, and Snyder, 2000, p. 68).

Research on educational leadership has begun to better comprehend how organizations, and by extension how organizational leaders, succeed and lead in unpredictable environments. This chapter uses two theoretical approaches from the research—complexity theory and networked leadership—to examine this topic and to try to gain understanding about the quandary identified earlier: What should a small-district leader prioritize when the work is around the clock? Both theoretical approaches suggest that key to successful leadership is developing and sustaining connections both within the organization and beyond.

The first approach, complexity theory, focuses on the interaction between knowledge, identity, and participation in communities (Zellermayer and Margolin, 2005) and provides a lens through which to understand how organizations respond to external pressures. The second, networked leadership, focuses on collective problem solving (rather than attempting to lead alone) and offers a vehicle for understanding how work might be reorganized. These approaches are intended not to solve the challenge but rather to refocus thinking and bring a fresh perspective on how the myriad pressures of a 24-hour-a-day, seven-day-a-week job can be a source of organizational energy rather than a challenge. These theories also suggest that while ISLLC Standard 3 is a starting point for strong leadership, alone it is not enough. To contextualize these more theoretical approaches, I also bring in the voices of practicing small-district superintendents. These individuals highlight the on-the-ground reality of their work.

THE WORK OF SUPERINTENDENTS

A defining feature of the work of superintendents is the sheer volume of effort required to do the job well. A growing body of research suggests that this work has a problematic impact: turnover is high; 39 percent of superintendents have reported intending to retire within the next five years, and the average tenure of superintendents is between five and six years (Glass and Franceschini, 2007; Jazzar and Kimball, 2004). Often the suggestion is to distribute leadership (Spillane, Camburn, Lewis, and Pareja, 2007; Spillane, Halverson, and Diamond, 2001), but superintendents describe a marked sense of isolation in their work, such that potential connections and the capacity to distribute leadership in a meaningful way are difficult to develop. Professionally, many superintendents feel that the intense workload keeps them in their districts rather than out networking with peers (Hatch and Roegman, 2012). Socially, superintendents describe an inability to socialize related to the fear of being judged for their behavior (Jazzar and Kimball, 2004) or accused of favoritism (Orr, 2006). This lack of connection has important implications for leaders' ability to think about how they might manage the numerous tasks they are assigned as well as how they might distribute them.

To begin to understand the work of small-district superintendents and the challenges they face as they attempt to uphold the principles of ISLLC Standard 3, let us turn to the words and perspectives of people who actually hold the position. The interviews all began with small talk, asking participants how they enjoy their free time. This question gave the interviewers and participants a good, hearty laugh—what free time? Several joked that they had no free time, but behind their words was a nugget of truth. The job of superintendent in a small district is more than full time—if "full time" means a 40-hour week.

It encompasses time in and out of school and conversations that take place not only in the office but also in the community. Indeed, Superintendent 16, new on the job, took a work call in the hospital:

> Well, I think one of the most shocking things that happened to me was when I first became superintendent and I had some minor surgery and I was called out from my sick bed to go to a town council meeting to be asked why the chiller broke down in the middle of the night in the high school!

It is undoubtedly true that a superintendent's work is never really done. There are sports events to attend, board meetings, assemblies, plays, and art shows. But there is also something more. Many superintendents report a tension between simply keeping the district running smoothly, as ISLLC Standard 3 calls for, and truly *leading* the district. Superintendent 13 describes this tension:

> I think sometimes we talk about visions, and we all share a common vision, but there's so many other things pulling at you, sometimes it's easy to not [be] able to tell what your vision is or even think about it on any given day or week depending on what happens with the board or with the boiler or when a pipe breaks. And, you know, two weeks ago, I'm standing in 3 inches of water on a Monday morning in a school building trying to mop it up. There wasn't a whole lot of visioning going on there and I wasn't thinking about how we're going to educate kids, I was thinking, "How are we going to get all of this water up!" In a small school, the custodian doesn't come in until 3:00, so you know, you have to wear so many hats that sometimes it distracts you from your vision.

Similarly, Superintendent 31 says, "You spend so much time dealing with what you really didn't get into the profession to deal with and it's draining. It is physically and mentally draining." These concerns make leadership that goes beyond organizational maintenance seem quite difficult, as at times such concerns feel, to these leaders, more pressing than more important but less urgent concerns.

Beyond the generally high workload of superintendents, the work of small-district leaders also presents a set of unique challenges that differ from those faced by leaders of larger districts. Superintendent 19 works in a district with 365 students and has been in the job for five years. She says,

> If the biscuits are bad at breakfast, they call you. If a kid is not being successful in class, they call you—the whole gamut, from the time it opens in the morning, 'til the time it shuts down at night, you have to

know. You have to know what's goin' on. You have to know how to handle it. You have to know how to get in contact with people who can handle it in that situation, and you have to—I've had little old ladies sittin' on my sofa at home because "we just couldn't talk to you on the phone, and just couldn't come to the school." It's that whole thing of a small school system.

Superintendent 31 discusses this challenge further, commenting, "When you give 100% or actually more than that, you give your life in full, your whole career, 16–18 hour days, it never ends. You want it to be the best it can be." Superintendent 17 works in a district with nine hundred students and has been in the job for four years. He says,

> I can't count the number of times that I've been awoken at 2 o'clock in the morning by the sheriff's department because the alarm is going off in the elementary school and the principal isn't answering his cell phone. But, we are expected to be out in front on every issue and we become a lightning rod for an array of issues that, you know, if you're not keeping a close watch on it, you reach a tipping point where everybody in the community believes, "Oh, my goodness, the superintendent really is responsible for everything that's been wrong in the school division."

An outsider might suggest that the work could be shared. However, the superintendents in this study point out that they are expected to work all the time while others are able to pass when they want or need to. Superintendent 22 highlights this challenge. She notes,

> And people expect you to give it up. They will think absolutely nothing about not attending a meeting because "Grandma's in town," or not attending a board meeting because "my kid's got a football game." But by God, you can spend every day Monday through Friday in that school or at an activity until 10 or 11:00 at night, and if the Booster Club wants you to do something on Saturday morning and you say, "No, I can't do it because it's my turn to take care of my mom" or whatever, well, you're not very cooperative; you don't want to help; you don't support the Booster Club.

Many superintendents also feel unprepared for the work. Even with extensive backgrounds in teaching and school leadership, Superintendent 18 says,

> I think this is one of those kind of jobs, too, that when you're a teacher, you kind of, as you teach, you're prepared to become assistant principal or principal because you see the day-to-day workings of a building. As a superintendent, there's no training there.

Further, Superintendent 18 comments, "I mean, the training that you get to be superintendent is on the job training, and talk about having to be an expert in so many—especially in a small school—ohmigod!" Superintendent 20 says, "I think we're the most unprepared people, when we take a job, that we could possibly be." Particularly vexing are the financial and political aspects of the job, largely unfamiliar to even the most expert of educators. Superintendent 19 says,

> And you're not gonna have a clue because you've never had any experience with that. You don't even know what's out there. You don't know what those federal programs are. You don't have any idea of where the money comes from, how it gets there and what you can do with it. And that's the first thing you're responsible for, is all the financials, all the financial stuff. And the legislation, the legislative part, y'know, how involved you get in that.

Thus, even though a small-district superintendent might not feel trained for the job, he or she also knows that the teachers, parents, and other stakeholders are not likely to be able to provide input, especially in areas such as finance and policy; this further diminishes their ability to draw upon the support of the larger school community.

Finally, small-district superintendents describe a feeling of remove from the workings of the school at a building level. Because there is so much to do, even though the buildings may be physically close to one another, the moments to be at the schools are rare. Superintendent 72 describes this feeling:

> As a principal, going back to that time in my life, you really got some positive feedback from staff and students at that time. Kids like to be disciplined. They want an ordered ship. And they don't want to be picked on going down the hallway and stuff. I think you had more connection. And you can see more positive things. People thanking you. You're in that hallway every day. You're talking with teachers and doing things. Now as superintendent, boy, it's few and far between then. You know, that contact. And the way it's set up, it's more difficult as superintendent. You're definitely more isolated.

Similarly, Superintendent 18 noted,

> I don't feel outstanding the same way now as a superintendent as I did as a teacher. I think part of that is because I'm further away from students. I try to get back as much as I can but that bugs me. . . . But the same outstanding feelings I had as a teacher, I very rarely have as a superintendent.

Thus, a quandary of the work of small-district superintendents is that they work around the clock, seemingly attempting to maintain order in a context that feels continuously out of order. Because of the time-consuming nature of the work, the small number of people with whom to share the work, and the general lack of preparation for the challenges such work presents, it is difficult for them to move beyond putting out fires toward a broader sense of leadership. Further compounding the quandary is a sense that because they are so busy with their work they rarely get out to the schools to connect with people, even though they understand that doing so would enhance their work. How can small-district leaders move beyond this challenging condition? The two potential theoretical frameworks I introduced above provide a window into this question. Both of these frameworks rely upon understanding organizations—here, school districts—as complex adaptive systems.

Complex Adaptive Systems

Until fairly recently, understandings of leadership and management employed a "closed" systems thinking approach. Such systems exist in isolation from their environment (Bertalanffy, 1968) and operate under the assumptions of "rationality, authority, unitary goal structure and self-contained dynamics" (Marion, 2002, p. 108). If a system is closed to its environment, "the original condition really determines the end state of the organization" (Snyder, Acker-Hocevar, and Snyder, 2000, p. 47). As an example, Snyder et al. say that closed systems thinking would assume that a school in a poor community could not do much to diminish the effects of poverty on the students or community. More recent forms of systems thinking, however, move beyond the assumption of rationality and self-containment and perceive the environment as a source of energy rather than as a challenge to be managed. These "open" systems are responsive to their environments and are able to strengthen both themselves and ultimately the environment in which they exist through constant adaptation. While leaders of closed systems focus on "the pursuit of productivity," leaders of open systems work to "juggle multiple pressures" (Marion, 2002, p. 86). In this view, successful organizations are not those that seek to maintain balance or control—stasis—but rather those that are constantly emerging, always responding to issues while at the same time continuously furthering the vision. These dynamic organizations are understood as complex adaptive systems.

Complex adaptive systems include "a diversity of agents [that] . . . interact with each other, mutually affect each other, and in doing so generate novel, emergent behavior for the system as a whole" (Lewin, 1999, p. 198). This notion of emergent behavior can be seen in the opening quote of this chapter, in which the superintendent refers to the "series of things that just by very small movements or very small suggestions, all of a sudden out of that grows so much positive in things you can do." Zellermayer and Margolin (2005) suggest that leadership is not simply "looking to influence the participants directly" but seeking "to foster the conditions that enable the participants to face their current difficulties as well as an unexpected future" (p. 1277). These conditions include relationships, "particularly patterns of interaction that emerge among elements in a complex adaptive system" (McQuillan, 2008, p. 1773). The challenges posed by the complex nature of districts, and particularly small districts, lend themselves well to the use of both complexity theory and networked leadership as lenses with which to make sense of the work, for several reasons: the many and mixed responsibilities and challenges confronting these leaders; the fact that superintendents spoke of their schools and districts as collective and shared enterprises involving many stakeholders with diverse viewpoints—but in reality often felt alone in the work; and most importantly, the fact that the voices of the superintendents in this study spoke about the challenges of making such connections happen.

Complexity Theory

Complexity theory, as it regards leadership, begins with the assumption that an organization is not a closed unit but rather part of a nested system of relationships that work in concert (Daly, 2010). In this type of system, "multiple elements interact and adapt to one another's behavior in self-organizing, nonlinear ways that suggest the system is 'learning'" (McQuillan, 2008, pp. 1773–1774). Each element, in this view, shapes and is shaped by the system. This perspective presents a challenge to leaders, as the nature of this self-organization is unpredictable.

Complexity theory is of importance to educators and scholars trying to make sense of an ever-changing educational terrain (Morrison, 2008). At its heart, complexity theory "is a theory of change, evolution, adaptation and development for survival" (Morrison, 2008, p. 16). Complexity theory views systems as dynamic, connected, and interacting with one another on many levels (Morrison, 2008). Snyder, Acker-Hocevar, and Snyder (2000) argue that "what is required for innovations to survive over time are strong connections and interdependencies that are continuously responsive to changing conditions" (p. 25). Such connectedness, however, "requires a *distributed knowledge* system, in which knowledge is not centrally located in a command and control centre. Rather, it is dispersed, shared and circulated throughout the system; communication and collaboration are key elements of complexity theory" (Morrison, 2008, p. 21). It is here that changing perspectives on district leadership must be developed. Strong connections and interdependencies may arise naturally, but it is the role of leaders to foster, develop, nourish, and build them. It is also here that the need to seek and grow connections acts in conflict with the kind of order and efficiency in ISLLC Standard 3, which some leaders may see as necessary to live up to.

If it is true, as Cilliers (1998) suggests, that connectedness requires a *distributed knowledge* system, then a priority of a district leader must be to see that knowledge is distributed. However, many superintendents feel overwhelmed with their workloads and the huge responsibilities placed upon them; the voices of small-district superintendents here suggest that they tend to take on the work themselves rather than share it. While this tendency may be due to an actual lack of other people to take on the work, it may also be attributable to tradition or habit. This tendency may be avoided with the assumption that distributing tasks in a sense creates more work for the district leader. Some research on distributed leadership supports this orientation. Gronn (2002) distinguishes between additive and holistic forms of distributed leadership. Additive forms are those in which multiple people are engaged in disconnected tasks without sense of what others are doing in the organization, whereas holistic forms involve conscious decisions and both rely upon and build strong relationships.

Perhaps more important than the idea of distributing *leadership* is the idea of distributing *knowledge*. As described above, distributed knowledge is a central facet of successful organizations, particularly organizations that thrive in complex situations. Distributing leadership in many ways serves to create the kinds of connections that are required for strong organizations, but distributing tasks, or the type of distributed leadership described above (Gronn, 2002), does not ensure that people within a system rely upon one another to share and build knowledge. Networked leadership can assist in this challenge. Related to complexity theory, networked leadership is also premised upon the assumptions that connections are key and that successful leadership builds upon and sustains them. The strongest organizations—and here, this idea is extended to districts—adapt and change as means of survival, not by just getting the work done but by developing and sharing knowledge. They embrace complexity rather than running from it, and they do so not by isolating themselves but by drawing upon the resources of people and communities inside and outside the system to sustain themselves (Morrison, 2008).

NETWORKED LEADERSHIP

While complexity theory provides a systems approach to understanding how schools survive and thrive within a nested system of relationships, networked leadership provides more of a theory of leadership and of how leaders in complex environments can best facilitate the kinds of connections required for working in such complexity. Networks are powerful and multifaceted. Earl and Katz (2007) suggest the following:

> The theory of action for networked learning communities presupposes that when groups work together they will *create new knowledge and spread it to others*. When adults interact in networked learning communities they engage with new ideas, new information and new skills. Systemic change depends on these individuals learning, and sharing their learning with each other. Once the knowledge is created and shared, the expectation is that it will influence practices—change what these teachers and headteachers do in their schools and classrooms and how they do it. Ultimately, the changes that teachers and schools make in their practices are intended to have an influence on pupils that will enhance their learning and their long-term success. (p. 6)

Chapman (2008) submits that a successful networking framework should facilitate meaningful conversations to generate and validate new knowledge and encourage participation that promotes trusting relationships between those involved and those who may potentially be involved in the network. This framework would also enhance the ability to support access to knowledge.

The current literature in the field about the use of networks in creating change demonstrates that networks can lessen the isolation of school leaders and promote shared learning and school improvement (Printy, Marks, and Bowers, 2009; Stone-Johnson and Kew, 2013). Even so, networks do not occur spontaneously; rather, they require much effort and maintenance. Further, leaders face challenges to entering into and staying in networks, including the amount of time involved, competing reform pressures, and a general lack of knowledge about how to actually engage in true networking activities

(Evans and Stone-Johnson, 2010). Networked leadership is also threatened by accountability and the pressure on schools to raise student achievement. This pressure oftentimes makes schools and districts turn inward, protecting human and fiscal resources in order to ensure that they are not seen as having left children behind (Stephenson and Bauer, 2010; Stone-Johnson and Kew, 2013), rather than seeking support from others. However, networks are understood to benefit not only students (Chapman and Fullan, 2007) but also teachers and leaders (Chapman, 2008; Harris and Muijs, 2005; Stone-Johnson and Kew, 2013) and the systems as well (Teddlie and Reynolds, 2000). Indeed, a key benefit of networking for schools is knowledge distribution; successful networks generate, validate, and create access to new knowledge (Chapman, 2008; Earl and Katz, 2007; Harris and Muijs, 2005).

While the research points to the positive impact of networking for schools, the challenges for superintendents, particularly small-district superintendents, to creating connections and relationships that serve to build and share knowledge are daunting. While people in small communities may all know one another, going beyond distributing tasks to distributing knowledge is at times highly challenging for superintendents in these districts.

Theory into Practice

To demonstrate the relationship between complexity theory, networked leadership, the work of small-district superintendents, and the realization of ISLLC Standard 3 in district and building leadership, let us again turn to the words of the superintendents in this study. Both networked leadership and complexity theory suggest that connectedness is a critical facet of successful organizations. However, superintendents describe the opposite of connectedness in many aspects of their work. Many researchers argue that the culture of schools and of education diminish leaders' opportunities for continued learning (Ackerman and Maslin-Ostrowski, 2002; Elmore, 2000; Fahey, 2011; Fullan, 2008; Stone-Johnson and Kew, 2013). The superintendents agreed with this finding. According to Superintendent 25, "The more buildings you have, the more layers, the farther removed your board and you tend to be from where it's impacting." Likewise, Superintendent 34 notes, "I think from a superintendent perspective it's when you get so distanced out three or four tiers away from the kids and it's tough to even offer advice without it coming to a screeching halt." Thus, at least for the leaders cited in this chapter, the work of district leadership appears to conflict with the kind of connectedness embraced by complexity theory and networked leadership. A question then arises: If connectedness helps strengthen systems, and superintendents rue their lack of genuine connectedness, how can meaningful and sustainable work occur?

Let us return to the description of complexity theory posited earlier: "Connectedness requires a *distributed knowledge* system, in which knowledge is not centrally located in a command and control centre. Rather, it is dispersed, shared and circulated throughout the system; communication and collaboration are key elements of complexity theory" (Morrison, 2008, p. 21). If this is the case, successful superintendents must not only utilize existing connections but also create new ones that serve to distribute knowledge. These connections may include intradistrict connections and interdistrict connections, both of which serve important functions for knowledge distribution.

Regarding the interdistrict level, here is some evidence that the superintendents with whom we spoke create connections and distribute knowledge through their work with other superintendents outside the district. One vital source of connection and new knowledge described by the small-district superintendents is peers. Superintendent 70 remarked,

> People I learned from are people like those sitting around this table that are involved in organizations like this one [the focus group took place at a conference] and [names a state association of school administrators]. Those people who are doing their job at home and they're willing to put in their time and serve on committees and lead organizations like we have here. They take time to be involved with what's happening today, rather than like so many people who are just concerned with dealing with what's in their districts. They do this stuff all the time. Those are the people that I've seen taking the next step. That I admire. That I can learn from.

Superintendent 72 also described the importance of peers, noting, "That's why I think when you go to quarter—regional meetings, state meetings, they're very collegial as superintendents because you're the only one in your district like you." Thus, even though it is challenging to find the time to connect with peers, doing so is an essential element of school, professional, and personal improvement and growth. Seeking connections may be one of the few ways to address the complexity of the work and ultimately to strengthen and sustain the organization—here, the district.

What is less present in the words of the superintendents is fostering the distribution of knowledge within their own districts. Several reasons discussed by the superintendents highlight why this aspect of leadership is so challenging. First, in small districts, there are few additional people in formal leadership positions upon whom a superintendent might call to take on some of these tasks, perhaps even only one other person. Second, regarding the type of leadership envisioned in ISLLC Standard 3, knowledge distribution is not viewed as a central task of maintaining a safe and efficient learning organization. Superintendents, as described throughout this chapter, focus so heavily on keeping the system afloat that at times it is difficult for them to see beyond maintenance. Related to this challenge, a third factor is the sense that there is only so much time in a superintendent's day. If he or she is indeed handling calls about bad biscuits and scooping buckets of water after a flood, the idea that he or she must also be out in the field making sure that everyone is talking and sharing feels overwhelming at best.

But creating these kinds of connections is important because not distributing knowledge keeps the organization from the learning needed for meaningful and sustainable change. Learning and connections that foster learning, as described, are the lifeblood of sustainable and strong organizations. It may well be the case that district leaders feel isolated from other leaders or people who may be of assistance. They may want to shield building leaders from noninstructional decisions at a time when pressures to raise student achievement and performance are greater than ever. Even so, both complexity theory and networked leadership urge that connectedness rather than isolation improves performance. Thus, district leaders and those who help them, including everyone from university professors to community members, must take on the challenge of building a web of leadership.

Conclusion

This chapter attempts to address a quandary in the work of small-district superintendents: What must be prioritized when the work is around the clock? Should leaders seek to minimize external pressures and view their role as that of gatekeeper, working to keep out problems and handle them themselves? Or, should leaders use pressures to bring people together and develop strong networks that engage multiple stakeholders in creating solutions and new knowledge? This quandary is juxtaposed with ISLLC Standard 3, which suggests that an education leader must promote the success of every student by ensuring management of the organization, operation, and resources for a safe, efficient, and effective learning environment. As described earlier, Standard 3 privileges efficiency over complexity. The question for leaders, then, is how best to live up to the standard while also embracing the kind of complexity that the standard seeks to minimize. This chapter conceptualizes this quandary from seemingly competing perspectives. Professionally and practically, school leaders are urged to manage organizations through minimizing pressures. In this view, leaders tackle problems as they occur. Theory and research, however, suggest that pressures should not be minimized but should, in a sense, be maximized. By this, I mean to say that pressures should be turned into opportunities for growth. The strongest organizations and leaders, according to this view, are the ones not who manage the existing problems but who have systems and networks in place to respond to the unpredictable problems. Organizations that use external pressures in this way live at the "edge of chaos" and thrive there.

As you begin to think about the skills you will need to be an effective district leader, it is important to think of the ways you can enrich your practice that go beyond the kinds of technical competencies you likely already possess. Undoubtedly, you are a skilled educator with deep knowledge about curriculum and instruction. You probably also have decent budgeting skills and are adept at drafting schedules, setting meeting agendas, and working with parents and communities. But how will you go beyond these duties to foster the kinds of connections required for strong and vital organizations? How will you reframe your thinking to see unpredictability as a positive? How can educational administration programs prepare future leaders to take on this perspective as well?

Each of the superintendents found that the role they took on as district leaders brought surprising levels of work that deeply challenged them. To help you think about how to address the quandary described in this chapter, as well as about how you might address some of the other quandaries presented in this volume in light of what is discussed here, consider the following questions:

1. What do you consider to be a successful, strong, and sustainable organization? What criteria do you use to support this belief? In what ways does your district meet these criteria? In what areas would you like to see improvement, and what plans do you have in the works to pursue these improvements?
2. Is your district, as ISLLC Standard 3 suggests, a safe, efficient, and effective learning organization? What aspects of your organization meet these criteria? What areas would you say still need to

be developed? In what ways might striving for "safe, efficient, and effective" hinder networking that would help you to learn continuously and adapt to the next challenge? In what ways might such striving facilitate networking?
3. In what ways can you, as district leader, strengthen connections between buildings and between yourself and other leaders in the district? What networks already exist? What networks might you seek to build going forward?
4. Whom do you turn to for support or advice in your work? Can you expand that network of support? What steps are required for this expansion?
5. What kinds of pressures does your district face? How are these pressures currently incorporated into your leadership? Is responding to these pressures part of what you consider your role as a leader? Why or why not?

Additional Reading

If you would like to read more about complexity theory, consider these works, which provide a strong theoretical framework for understanding the importance of connectedness and relationships:

Lewin, R. (1999). *Complexity: Life at the edge of chaos.* Chicago: University of Chicago Press.

Marion, R. (2002). *Leadership in education: Organizational theory for the practitioner.* Upper Saddle River, NJ: Prentice Hall.

McQuillan, P. J. (2008). Small-school reform through the lens of complexity theory: It's "good to think with." *Teachers College Record*, 110(9), 1772–1801.

Morrison, K. (2008). Educational philosophy and the challenge of complexity theory. *Educational Philosophy and Theory*, 40(1), 19–34.

Snyder, K. J., Acker-Hocevar, M., and Snyder, K. (2008). *Living on the edge of chaos: Leading schools into the global age* (2nd ed.). Milwaukee, WI: ASQ Quality Press.

The following works provide a strong theoretical framework for understanding networked leadership:

Chapman, C. (2008). Towards a framework for school-to-school networking in challenging circumstances. *Educational Research*, 50(4), 403–420.

Daly, A. J. (2010). Mapping the terrain: Social network theory and educational change. In A. J. Daly (Ed.), *Social network theory and educational change* (pp. 1–17). Cambridge, MA: Harvard Education Press.

Earl, L., and Katz, S. (2007). Leadership in networked learning communities: Defining the terrain. *School Leadership and Management*, 27(3), 239–258.

Evans, M. P., and Stone-Johnson, C. (2010). Internal leadership challenges of network participation. *International Journal of Leadership in Education*, 13(2), 203–220.

References

Ackerman, R., and Maslin-Ostrowski, P. (2002). *The wounded leader: How real leadership emerges in times of crisis*. San Francisco, CA: Jossey-Bass.

Bertalanffy, L. (1968). *General system theory: Foundations, development, applications*. New York: George Braziller.

Chapman, C. (2008). Towards a framework for school-to-school networking in challenging circumstances. *Educational Research*, 50(4), 403–420.

Chapman, C., and Fullan, M. (2007). Collaboration and partnership for equitable improvement: Towards a networked learning system? *School Leadership and Management*, 27(3), 207–211.

Cilliers, P. (1998). *Complexity and postmodernism*. London: Routledge.

Daly, A. J. (2010). Mapping the terrain: Social network theory and educational change. In A. J. Daly (Ed.), *Social network theory and educational change* (pp. 1–17). Cambridge, MA: Harvard Education Press.

Earl, L., and Katz, S. (2007). Leadership in networked learning communities: Defining the terrain. *School Leadership and Management*, 27(3), 239–258.

Elmore, R. F. (2000). *Building a new structure for school leadership*. Washington, DC: Albert Shanker Institute.

Evans, M. P., and Stone-Johnson, C. (2010). Internal leadership challenges of network participation. *International Journal of Leadership in Education*, 13(2), 203–220.

Fahey, K. M. (2011). Still learning about leading: A leadership critical friends group. *Journal of Research on Leadership in Education*, 6(1), 1–35.

Fullan, M. (2005). *Leadership and sustainability*. Thousand Oaks, CA: Corwin.

Fullan, M. (2008). *The six secrets of change: What the best leaders do to help their organizations survive and thrive*. San Francisco, CA: Jossey-Bass.

Glass, T. E., and Franceschini, L. A. (2007). *The state of the American school superintendency: A mid-decade study*. Blue Ridge Summit, PA: Rowman and Littlefield Education.

Gronn, P. (2002). Distributed leadership. In K. Leithwood and P. Hallinger (Eds.), *Second international handbook of educational leadership and administration* (pp. 653–696). Dordrecht, Netherlands: Kluwer Academic.

Harris, A., and Muijs, D. (2005). *Improving schools through teacher leadership*. Buckingham, UK: Open University Press.

Hatch, T., and Roegman, R. (2012). Out of isolation: Superintendents band together to improve instruction and equity in their districts. *Journal of Staff Development*, 33(6), 37–41.

Jazzar, M., and Kimball, D. P. (2004). Lonely at the top: The greatest challenge for some superintendents is the professional isolation they feel. *School Administrator*, 61(2), 10–14.

Lewin, R. (1999). *Complexity: Life at the edge of chaos.* Chicago: University of Chicago Press.
Marion, R. (2002). *Leadership in education: Organizational theory for the practitioner.* Upper Saddle River, NJ: Prentice Hall.
McQuillan, P. J. (2008). Small-school reform through the lens of complexity theory: It's "good to think with." *Teachers College Record,* 110(9), 1772–1801.
Morrison, K. (2008). Educational philosophy and the challenge of complexity theory. *Educational Philosophy and Theory,* 40(1), 19–34.
Orr, M. (2006). Learning the superintendency: Socialization, negotiation, and determination. *Teachers College Record,* 108(7), 1362–1403.
Printy, S. M., Marks, H. M., and Bowers, A. J. (2009, September). Integrated leadership: How principals and teachers share transformational and instructional influence. *Journal of School Leadership,* 19(5), 504–533.
Snyder, K. J., Acker-Hocevar, M., and Snyder, K. (2000). *Living on the edge of chaos: Leading schools into the global age.* Milwaukee, WI: ASQ Quality Press.
Spillane, J. P., Camburn, E., Lewis, G., and Pareja, A. S. (2007). Taking a distributed perspective on the school principal's workday. *Leadership and Policy in Schools,* 6(1), 103–125.
Spillane, J. P., Halverson, R., and Diamond, J. B. (2001). Investigating school leadership practice: A distributed perspective. *Educational Researcher,* 30(3), 23–38.
Stephenson, L. E., and Bauer, S. C. (2010). The role of isolation in predicting new principals' burnout. *International Journal of Education Policy and Leadership,* 5(9), 1–17.
Stone-Johnson, C., and Kew, K. (2013). Systemic educational change: Applying social network theory to lateral learning among principals. In R. Flessner, G. Miller, K. Patrizio, and J. Horwitz (Eds.), *Agency in teacher education: Reflection, communities and learning* (pp. 153–163). Lanham, MD: Rowman and Littlefield.
Teddlie, C., and Reynolds, D. (Eds.). (2000). *The international handbook of school effectiveness research.* London: Falmer.
Zellermayer, M., and Margolin, I. (2005). Teacher educators' professional learning described through the lens of complexity theory. *Teachers College Record,* 107(6), 1275–1304.

CHAPTER 7

GENERATIONAL DIVERSITY AND FEMINIST EPISTEMOLOGY FOR BUILDING INCLUSIVE, DEMOCRATIC, COLLABORATIVE COMMUNITY

Debra Touchton and Michele Acker-Hocevar

As is evident in the superintendent transcripts, building community today is different from in past decades. There are many underrepresented individuals in our school districts who either do not know how to make their voice heard or feel that when they use their voice, no one listens. We are charged as leaders to open spaces for those who have been marginalized. As we explore ISLLC Standard 4, we turn to generational theory and feminist epistemology for assistance in understanding what collaborating with faculty and community members means in terms of how leaders frame what they hear; how they respond to diverse community interests; how they interrogate *different ways of knowing*; how they balance their preferred ways of knowing with those of others; and how they might employ their ways of knowing to influence communicative structures and processes in their school districts to build more inclusive, democratic, collaborative communities.

It is important that we first define what we mean by epistemology. We will use the terms "different ways of knowing" and "epistemologies" interchangeably. Epistemology is a branch of philosophy that investigates the nature of knowledge. "To explore the nature of knowledge, is to raise questions about the limits of knowledge, the sources of knowledge, the validity of knowledge, the cognitive processes, and how we know. There are several 'ways of knowing'" (Webb, Metha, and Jordan, 2013, p. 55). Each way of knowing informs and limits how we listen; what we hear; what we know; how we evaluate what we hear; how we engage or disengage in reciprocal communicative structures and processes; and how our actions might foster or hinder collaborating with other faculty and community members.

By examining ways of knowing that are different from our own, we begin to identify potential spaces that can be created by involving others in building a more inclusive, democratic, collaborative community (Furman and Starratt, 2002). We may also begin to identify limitations and advantages within various communicative structures and processes and how to expand them to include and involve more diverse publics, thus, giving voice to those who have not previously been heard.

THE PROBLEM

The term "public" is not uniformly understood. For example, Superintendent 32 shared how he commonly heard such things from his stakeholders as, "It is how I think because this is how I was raised and we've always done it this way and by gosh, we shouldn't change the way we are doing things because it worked 30 years ago." The superintendent continued, "You have to give people a voice and let them know they are heard." The problem, he stated, "is balancing what you know to be in the best interest of students with what people tell you to do." He continued, "That is probably the biggest issue I have out there right now is walking that line about how things were done in the 40s and why we are not still doing them that way." Clearly, there are generational perspectives and different ways of knowing.

THE PERSPECTIVES

To explore such different perspectives and notions of how things should be done versus how they were done, we employ two perspectives to provide you with a historical backdrop for understanding different worldviews. First, we draw upon the concept of generational theory (Strauss and Howe, 1991), because it lends itself well to examining differences in generational thinking. It helps leaders understand what they might do to adopt communicative structures and processes that appeal to the various publics that represent their stakeholders. Second, we highlight feminist epistemology. We chronicle three waves of feminism to depict how feminist epistemology, much like the idea of "public," is not uniform. We will discuss feminist epistemology as women's ways of knowing. In fact, as women struggled to gain access and opportunity, the three waves represented three different struggles. Generational thinking and feminist epistemology, taken separately or together, can help you as a leader to interrogate communicative structures and processes in fresh and more inclusive ways. The questions, however, are different.

No Easy Answers

We are not suggesting an easy answer for how to design the most effective communicative structures and processes. What we are suggesting, however, is that understanding generational thinking and being conversant with feminist epistemology helps you to ask questions about appropriate media and the quality of your interpersonal skills (e.g., listening and hearing voices shaped by generational perspectives and feminist alternative ways of knowing). Yes, you can assess your readiness to reach out and adjust to multigenerational and diverse groups of people. Yes, you can begin to identify corresponding pathways needed for effective communicative structures and processes to take form. Yes, you can begin to engage all the publics in a process to access information more fully. No, you should not see this as the answer; it is not meant to be prescriptive. No, these are not the only ways you can wrestle with how to involve more diverse publics.

Generations and Waves

We situate superintendents' stories using generational theory and feminist epistemology in order to explore the complexity of creating inclusive, democratic, and collaborative community. Given the complex world we live in today, it is no wonder that a superintendent faces a growing number of issues involving others in building such inclusive, democratic, and collaborative communities.

Strauss and Howe (1991, 1994) define a generation as people born over a span of roughly 20 years, or about the length of one phase of life. Generations are identified by cohort groups that share three criteria. First, members of a generation share key historical events and social trends during the same phase of life. Second, they share certain common perspectives, beliefs, and behaviors. Third, they share a common perceived membership in that generation.

Just as the generations share common historical experiences, the three waves of feminism share historical epochs that convey their common struggles for equality, equity, and choice. The first wave, at the turn of the twentieth century, was about the right of women to own property and vote. The second wave of feminism concerned equal access of women to professions previously closed to women who insisted upon commensurate and equal pay. The third wave is about choice regarding a wide array of roles to which women may aspire. Waves, like the generational perspectives, share common characteristics. They serve to punctuate common understandings of historical events. It is important to note, nonetheless, that there are no agreed-upon exact dates for when a generation begins and ends and that such factors as socioeconomic status, race and ethnicity, and education may have moderating effects on the generations. Generational perspectives describe the historical and educational backdrops of these various generations. Often, these generations express points of view contrary to those of other generational groups based on their myriad experiences growing up in a particular era that shaped their values, their beliefs, and how they see the world today. These experiences, often referred to as defining moments, color and influence how generational groups experience similar events and might be collectively bound together around a common hinge of history— an epochal event that leads to similar points of view on issues. This is also true for the three waves of feminism. A second-wave feminist may see the world quite differently from a third-wave feminist. As a result, a person from each generation and wave possesses her or his own set of values, beliefs, life experiences, attitudes, and expectations, referred to as "generational personalities" (Lancaster and Stillman, 2002) and "wavers." Individual generational personalities and wavers often reveal their preferences for communicative structures and processes.

Exploring Diversity

For the purposes of this chapter, we define diversity as the differences between gendered perspectives of reality that constitute feminine and masculine perspectives (Alvesson and Billing, 1997) and—in this latter case known as "generational diversity"—among the four generations (Lancaster and Stillman, 2002): veterans, baby boomers, Generation X, and Generation Y/millennials. This chapter provides opportunities for the readers to explore and examine their values and beliefs in relation to how their generational perspectives of inquiry for fighting for inclusion and voice align with feminist epistemology and complement their understanding of how to build inclusive, democratic, collaborative community. In particular, the three waves reveal how the evolution of human consciousness underpins different leadership actions one might associate with the superintendents' narratives and worldviews related to self and community. Basic principles of the feminist epistemology grew out of the waves, and two key assumptions for educational leaders are that they must (1) recognize the invisibility of underrepresented populations seeking legal rights (e.g., people in poverty, people of color, people with disabilities, people of diverse sexual orientations, people with English as a second language) and (2) seek to give voice to the oppressed and invisible to right social and educational injustices. Addressing how to raise individual and collective consciousness for leadership action should foster a dialogue to address injustices and ensure representation of all groups. This is not easy. The leader's new role may well be to find unity among diversity through engaging others in listening, inquiry, and respect for difference (Sidorkin, 1999). This would occur while simultaneously acknowledging numerous ways of knowing. Finding unity among difference and diversity means it is important that leaders ensure that structures of civility are firmly in place, and tailored communicative structures and processes must recognize differences discussed within the generational theories and feminist epistemology perspectives.

Zemke, Raines, and Filipczak (2000) state, "It is diversity management at its most challenging. The obvious markers of race and sex have less clear impact on the differences and signal less in the way of differential treatment than do generational differences" (p. 25). This is not to say that one's gender, ethnic background, family makeup, socioeconomic circumstances, religion, or hometown is not important; it is just that for this chapter, we focus on the generational differences and corresponding feminist epistemologies within these three different waves of feminism to explore self and other. We inquire how leadership beliefs, values, and behaviors may affect personal communicative styles and exclude diverse voices by comparing personal preferences to feminist epistemologies. The idea is to use the different lenses to assess how to foster more inclusive, democratic, and collaborative community.

We briefly discuss the four generations, generational leadership for stakeholders, and implications for leadership approaches. We conclude with a discussion of feminist waves and epistemology. We encourage you to think about where you identify your generational personality and how you relate to the feminist waves and epistemology.

Four Generations

As mentioned, there are four generations presently interacting in the workplace: veterans, baby boomers, Generation Xers, and millennials.

The veteran generation, born between 1920 and 1943, has been described as loyal and patriotic. Members of this generation, also known as the traditionalists (Lancaster and Stillman, 2002), the World War II generation, and the radio babies (Gravett and Throckman, 2007), were born during the Great Depression and World War II. This generation built most of the nation's infrastructure, believed in duty before pleasure, embraced family values, and spent conservatively (Lancaster and Stillman, 2002; Lovely and Buffman, 2007; Raines, 2003). The defining events that shaped this generation's personality were the Great Depression, the New Deal, Pearl Harbor, the golden era of radio, the silver screen, and Superman. Leaders were FDR, Patton, and Eisenhower. Hence, their patriotism and view of the leader are based on these heroic archetypes.

Members of the baby boomer generation, born between 1944 and 1960, are known as optimistic and competitive. Unlike the veterans, the boomers grew up in an optimistic economic environment, and they have often been labeled the "me generation" because they were privileged to focus on themselves and where they were going (Lancaster and Stillman, 2002). Hence, this group may pursue their own gratification, perhaps sometimes at a price to both themselves and their families (Lovely and Buffman, 2007). Baby boomers are driven to succeed, and status and power, as well as making a difference, are important to them. It has been said that boomers live to work and will never retire. Defining events for boomers were the Vietnam War; the assassinations of three key leaders: John F. Kennedy, Martin Luther King Jr., and Robert Kennedy; the civil rights movement; women's liberation; the space race; television; the Beatles; and *Captain Kangaroo*.

Members of Generation X, also known as Xers, were born between 1960 and 1980; are sometimes described as detached, unmotivated, and skeptical; and were the first to be called latchkey kids. Xers grew up in an era of high divorce rates, struggling economies, and fallen heroes. They are self-reliant and skeptical of authority, and they seek a sense of family through a network of friends and work relationships (Lovely and Buffman, 2007). While previous generations were loyal to their employers for most of their careers, Xers do not have such a mind-set, and changing jobs is not an issue for them. While boomers may be described by the saying "live to work," Xers on the other hand may be viewed as those who "work to live." Lancaster and Stillman (2002) state that this is likely the most misunderstood generation in the workforce today, as they have carved out their own identity separate from the veterans and the boomers. Generation Xers' defining events were VCRs, Watergate and Nixon's resignation, the

Challenger disaster, the fall of the Berlin Wall, microwaves, computer games, MTV, AIDS, extreme sports, and *The Simpsons*.

Members of Generation Y, also known as millennials and nexters (Zemke, Raines, and Filipczak, 2000), were born between 1980 and 2000 and are described as pragmatic and realistic. They glean multiple perspectives from the previous generations—with loyalty and faith in institutions (characteristics from the veteran generation), optimism about their ability to make things happen (a characteristic from the boomers), and just enough skepticism to be cautious (a characteristic from the Xers) (Lancaster and Stillman, 2002). Millennials feel wanted and indulged by their parents, live busy lives, embrace core values—such as civic duty and confidence—similar to those of the veteran generation, are well mannered and polite, use technology in unforeseen ways (Lovely and Buffman, 2007), and have new ideas about gender stereotyping and racial and sexual categorizing (Zemke, Raines, and Filipczak, 2000). Defining moments for this present generation were 9/11, Columbine, the Oklahoma City bombing, *It Takes a Village*, the Internet, X Games, and reality TV.

As we stated earlier, aspects of one's "generational personality" affect how one perceives leadership—one's own style as well as those of others—and how one determines the communicative structures and processes intended to build inclusive, democratic, collaborative community. Individuals' perceptions have been influenced by a historical time period that colors their beliefs and values. Balancing the different perspectives of others with our own leadership preferences involves private versus public acknowledgments of who we are and what differentiates us from others. Let's take a brief look at what the four generations expect from themselves as stakeholders and leaders.

Generational Leadership Implications for Stakeholders

As stakeholders, veterans expect the leader to lead and the follower to follow (Lancaster and Stillman, 2002). They believe that an individual moves in the organization/career through perseverance and hard work, one rung of the career ladder at a time. They are driven by rules and order, strive to uphold culture and traditions, can leave work at work, and find technology intimidating. When it comes to working in teams, they are in agreement with the power of collective action as long as there is a central leader in charge (Zemke, Raines, and Filipczak, 2000). They want to know where they stand and what is expected of them, and they are eager to conform to group roles as long as they know what the roles are for them to adhere to. Boomers, on the other hand, have a strong need to prove themselves to others, may manipulate rules to meet their own needs, are deferential to authority, work long hours, and may become political if turf is threatened (Zemke, Raines, and Filipczak, 2000). When working in teams, they will go the extra mile. They are good at building rapport and solving problems, embrace equity and equality, and want credit and respect for accomplishments. Gen Xers strive for balance, freedom, and flexibility; expect to have fun at work; prefer independence and minimal supervision; and are good at multitasking. They like to work in teams with informal roles and desire the freedom to complete tasks their own way. They work best with teammates of their choosing, struggle to build rapport with other group members, and do not like being taken advantage of at any time (Zemke, Raines, and Filipczak, 2000). Last but not least, millennials want to fit in and are respectful of authority, but they are not afraid to approach the leader with concerns (Lancaster and Stillman, 2002). They value continual learning, are exceptional at multitasking, and, similar to the veterans, are drawn to organizations with career ladders and benefits (Zemke, Raines, and Filipczak, 2000).

Generational Leadership Approaches

Now that we know a bit more about the generations as stakeholders, let's examine generational leadership approaches. As one might expect, the veterans' leadership style is one that values dedication and loyalty from workers as well as themselves (Lancaster and Stillman, 2002). They equate age with status/power, believe in and impose top-down structures, are autocratic decision makers, keep work and home separate, and view change as disruptive and undesirable (Zemke, Raines, and Filipczak, 2000). Given what we know so far about boomers, it may not surprise you that they tend to lead through consensus. They do not like conflict, generally apply a participatory approach to leadership and decision making, and are less flexible with change (Zemke, Raines, and Filipczak, 2000). So what about Xers, you ask? They are drawn to leadership for altruistic reasons—not for power, status, and prestige as the boomers are. Gen Xers have a laid-back style of leadership. They work to create a functional and efficient environment; create and support alternative workplace structures, unlike the two previous generations; are willing to challenge those in higher positions; and adapt easily to change (Zemke, Raines, and Filipczak, 2000). Millennials, being the combination of the previous three generations, are resilient and open to new ideas (Zemke, Raines, and Filipczak, 2000; Lancaster and Stillman, 2002). They work well with varying employee styles and needs, prefer flattened hierarchy, display more decorum and professionalism than Xers, and often lack experience handling conflict and difficult people.

Feminist Waves and Epistemology

We draw on feminist waves and epistemology to explore the battles women fought to win a voice and inclusion in society at large. Considering the main goal of the first wave of feminism (addressing legal inequalities), we explore equity, especially in practice (Rowe-Finkbeiner, 2004; Sommers, 1994). We note that the first wavers "helped change the perception of women from voiceless and dependent with the dominant male culture to become independent thinkers for shaping policy and decision making for their inclusion through basic rights ensured through law" (Rowe-Finkbeiner, 2004, p. 23). This is important for educators to consider, because giving voice to the voiceless may involve a number of developmental steps that lead to creating the space and the legitimacy that ensure that certain members of the community have access to pathways to more fully express their views. While the first wave of feminist concerns focused explicitly on rights such as voting, owning property, and attaining an education, second wavers (1960s to early 1980s) focused primarily on women's independence from and equality with men (Rowe-Finkbeiner, 2004; Sommers, 1994). They based their efforts on a variety of issues: sexuality, the workplace, reproductive rights, and domestic violence. Third wavers (late 1980s to present), women and men born in the mid-1960s to the 1980s, identified a new way of thinking about women, a cultural change—"no one size fits all." The focus was on issues that may limit or oppress women and other traditionally marginalized groups. In other words, the third wave provided women and men with the freedom to pursue a variety of life options and more opportunities for inclusion in a more democratic community. The third wavers challenged the second wavers' definitions of femininity and focused on a more poststructural interpretation of what gender and sexuality paradigms mean to each individual in relation to what is and what is not good for women. In *Manifesta: Young Women, Feminism, and the Future*, Baumgardner and Richards (2000) suggest that feminism can change with every generation and individual:

> The fact that feminism is no longer limited to arenas where we expect to see it—NOW, *Ms.*, women's studies, and red suited congresswomen—perhaps means that young women today have really reaped what

feminism has sown. Raised after Title IX and *William Wants a Doll* [*sic*], young women emerged from college or high school or two years of marriage or their first job and began challenging some of the received wisdom of the past ten or twenty years of feminism. We're not doing feminism the same way that the seventies feminists did it; being liberated doesn't mean copying what came before but finding one's own way—a way that is genuine to one's own generation. (p. x)

The roots of feminist epistemology lie in the feminist waves that challenged the taken-for-granted ways of thinking and knowing within a male-dominated worldview. Alternative ways of knowing, or feminist epistemology, correspond to the three waves. Equity ways of knowing assume that sameness should be the standard. Ecofeminism, representative of the third wave of feminism and more encompassing, "recognizes the multiple contexts in which we live" (Enomoto and Kramer, 2007, p. 69). Lessons from each of the three feminist waves can teach us to increase inclusion of diverse groups; to see how we might cast a wider net to incorporate multiple communicative structures and processes through various strategies; to explore different ways of knowing; to tailor the message and the media to different groups; to recognize that "one size" does not fit all; and to acknowledge that our leadership preferences may fail to reflect various aspects of feminist epistemology. Making the personal public through discourse and linking the self with the community call for feminist epistemology together with an ethic of care for others (Gilligan, 1982) and Laible's (2003) loving epistemology. Each of these approaches asks us to walk in another's shoes. Creating safe spaces for others *to be* means that in addition to adopting an ethic of care, we learn to be comfortable with contradiction, work through these contradictions with others, appreciate dissent, and develop critical awareness of how we serve others, especially children (Grogan, 2003). Ferguson (1984) employs feminist epistemology to critique bureaucratic control that stifles women and results in we (men) against them (women) discourse. Feminist epistemology is not for women only. It opens the floodgates that allow us to relate self to other selves without reproducing binaries of self versus other.

Feminist Epistemology Implications for Stakeholders

Johnson (2005) states, "Every struggle to change the world needs a way to make sense of where we are, how we got here, and where to go—and the women's movement is no exception. It has developed feminism as a diverse and evolving framework for understanding gender inequality and interpreting women's experience in relation to men, other women, and patriarchy" (p. 99). Out of this struggle emerged women's exploration of how men and women are "fundamentally different in their development, life experiences, and perspectives. Gilligan's research concluded that women act with an 'ethic of care' and engage in 'connected knowing,' whereas men act with a focus on individual rights and justice" (Ginsberg, 2008, p. 19). What does this mean to you as a leader in developing more inclusive, democratic, collaborative communities?

If in understanding feminist epistemology the private is public and the personal is political, then every person in a community has a unique history and background that make the public domain inherently political. Some groups, historically marginalized and excluded, have not had their ways of knowing validated in the larger social and political systems. What are the implications for leadership approaches that feminist epistemologies provide as a mechanism for inviting others to engage in the dialogue? Feminist epistemologies challenge the status quo and the patriarchal system of power, privilege, and (in)difference. This means that stakeholders with varying perspectives do not hold uniform opinions. Conflict and controversy are part of growth and development.

Feminist Epistemology Leadership Approaches

We cannot talk about feminist epistemology or ways of knowing without acknowledging the limitations of broad and universal assumptions about men and women that ignore other differences. These differences include such things as race, class, ethnicity, religion, and sexuality. The question for leaders to ask is, "What unites us?" Just as all women are not alike, not all people from the different generational personalities are alike. Employing different lenses gives us different insights. As leaders, we must seek similarities. So where does that leave us? If our goal is to expand communicative structures and processes to be more open and inclusive to promote more inclusive, democratic, and collaborative communities, then it is important to have different interpretations of how to adequately attend to a fuller range of what represents reality through different ways of knowing. The dominant discourse of leaders operating in isolation, as if the school board were the only public, is exclusionary of other publics. An ethic of care (Gilligan, 1982) presupposes that for leaders to care, they must exhibit what Noddings (1984) points to as an empathetic and responsive relationship that is interactive. Gatekeeping devices that privilege one way of knowing over others is in opposition to building a more inclusive, democratic, and collaborative community. Leaders can seek to walk in another's shoes and understand their perspectives, and as Laible (2003) pointed out, we must be willing to travel and in so doing leave a part of ourselves behind (Young and Skrla, 2003). "This means, then, more of a mutual engagement and more of a mutual struggle for understanding, mutual benefit, and mutual responsibility are required than the term 'traveling' encompasses" (Young and Skrla, 2003, p. 208).

Superintendents' Stories

We read many different stories from the Voices 3 focus-group transcripts and selected stories we felt would provide the reader with enough information to deconstruct real events, using the dual lens of generational personalities and feminist epistemology that moderates between the private and public issues and concerns. Our selection of stories raises questions about how to assist leaders with moving toward more inclusive, democratic, and collaborative communities through the critique of existing communicative structures and processes.

Creswell (2013) explains that narrative allows us to re-story what our interviewees share with us. We encourage you to think about and write your own stories about how you might tell the stories differently, using the re-storying method that conveys your own story based on your generational values and beliefs and feminist epistemology, not those of the superintendents. Following each of the stories, the "things to consider" sections will assist you in thinking about the different viewpoints of balancing the self with others' perspectives.

The first story is told by a male superintendent who shares a story of what happens when you try to do "what's best for students."

> We extended the school day by adding 15 minutes in the morning and 15 minutes at the end of the day. Not—initially, it was because we lost time for a hurricane. But, what we wanted to do was lengthen the school day for more instructional time, which there was a good bit of debate about. But, the school board voted to support that recommendation 100%. We had an outspoken critic in the community who tried to sue the superintendent for violating state law. Now, the intent was to give more time in the day for instruction. Even 30 minutes, when you add it up over a week, you've got 2 and 1/2 hours. But, there I was in court trying to defend the fact that I was adding to the instructional day to help children. I was being sued. Luckily the judge took one look

at the case and told the parent never to show up in his court again. But, here you are being sued for doing the right thing. And, you don't walk into a court of law without being prepared. So, there were days and hours spent putting my defense together with the lawyer—all that time could have been better spent working on curriculum and instruction with principals and teachers, but here, I had to go defend myself because I was being attacked. And, that happens again and again.

Things to Consider

Let's look at the story through the dual lenses and the communicative structures that were in place. If from the veteran generation, would an individual agree with the superintendent, as this generation believes that the leader is the one in charge, and support the action because it was the superintendent's initiative and the board approved it? What about a baby boomer? Would he or she see what the superintendent did as "the right thing" and as making a difference in the educational lives of the students, or would he or she agree with the "outspoken critic," thinking that it was "the right thing to do" to bring the case to the attention of the courts? As an Xer representative, might the individual be skeptical of authority and choose to move on to something else more worthy of his or her time? Then there is the millennial, being a combination of all three—would the person tend to work with the three representative generations to find the balance between doing what is right for the teaching and learning process and the legal aspects of lengthening the school day? What about the different perspectives from the three waves of feminism? How might policy implications and the court battle align with the first wave? How might the third-wave feminists look at multiple ways to address this issue? What does feminist epistemology suggest about a bureaucratic solution?

The superintendent stated that he was trying to do the best thing for students, while the other players in the story most likely thought they were also. Why could a conflict arise between what different generations think about "what's best for students?" Where would you place this superintendent's perspective? How would you reconcile your personal preferences in order to think about communicative structures and processes that might create more democratic, inclusive community and build more support to address this issue and resolve the differences of opinion? How might feminist epistemology help us to understand that the first approach to increasing instructional time meant changes in policy while not addressing practice? How does this approach sidestep listening? What would a loving feminist epistemology suggest as follow-up action? Why is doing what is best for children a source of contention? What does it mean to see choices as a menu of possibilities? How did the superintendent's position leave little room for negotiation and space for seeing alternatives? What happens when we begin to personalize a situation and think in binaries of *us* against *them*? The superintendent said, "I had to go defend myself because I was being attacked. And, that happens again and again." What does this reveal about his thinking? What if he had balanced the two different perspectives? How might his self-analysis have been different? Why is it important to recognize that when the courts get involved, the issue may not be what it appears? How might resources have been better utilized in this situation? When leaders experience situations like this, what do you think happens to them when they are faced with opposition in the future? Is there anything that can be learned from this?

Another Story

A female superintendent tells the story of "feeling burned" as a result of putting structures in place to build a democratic, collaborative community in her district.

> When we were doing things a few years ago financially, when the state was withholding money and our school enrollments were declining and—the nice thing about that was because we were being paid for the 2 preceding years, we knew it was coming. When we were having to make decisions about having significantly less money—you know a hundred fifty thousand dollars—we set up structures to get people's voices heard. We did things where we worked with staff members about: "If you had more money, where would you put it?" and "If you had less money, where would you put it?" We did things in terms of any community groups we could wrestle together. We did parents together and parent groups in the high school and actually asked people some of the hard questions about, you know, you can only do so much per tab, what [should we not be doing]? Those are hard decisions for anybody. We tried that business in getting everybody's voice and we kind of really came up with a plan about what we could do in terms of when people plan to retire, etc. Our plan, what we hear, was that extra-curricular was important—not only the problem there, but what it ought to look like. We had lots of good information and the board agreed to do a community meeting. Very nicely, I mean all 7 people, basically they trusted me because I said, you know, "Are you willing to do this? We have some people requesting that we do a community meeting." The people who came to the community meeting, three-fourths of them

were our employees, and they just blasted the board, absolutely blasted the board—they jumped in up there with things we had not even considered or talked about. They didn't even talk to the principal about it. They didn't talk to anybody about it and that existing board, there's no way in the world I can ask them to do that.... Maybe it didn't backfire in terms of—we still had to make the cuts, but still half of it backfired in terms of the relationships. Like I said, they [the board] trusted me that it was a good idea. I don't know if it was or not, but I always believed the idea was to be open and direct.

Things to Consider

For this story, let's look at the generations from both the leader's and the stakeholders' views. In this case, the superintendent was blindsided at the community meeting. The superintendent couldn't understand why the employees (most likely teachers and staff) "blasted" the board. Was this attributable to her lack of understanding of the different generational thinking of teachers? She said, "They jumped in up there with things we had not even considered or talked about. They didn't even talk to the principal about it." She discusses that, in terms of relationships, the structures put in place backfired. What tension does this suggest between the superintendent's personal and private views about how to address differences of opinion and conflict? In what ways can generational thinking and feminist epistemology help us understand and interpret the superintendent's views and the views of those who did not do as she had anticipated? If the superintendent had possessed more of a generational and/or feminist epistemological understanding, how might the outcome have been different?

Democracy is messy, and if voices are going to be heard, how can you facilitate a positive outcome that balances personal desires with public concerns? Or can you? Why did the teachers use this meeting to voice frustration in a most public venue? Had they been heard before? We know from school personnel demographic data that most teachers are women. Using the feminist lens, how many times have these stakeholders (teachers are predominantly women) been asked what they think? What level of frustration might be a result of not being heard? According to feminist epistemology, the personal is political. Why is it important to ask the participants who seemed angry and spoke up and appeared to attack the board what was behind the outburst? In many respects, the board represents authority that might have been used in other ways to silence these educators. What would feminist epistemology suggest regarding what might be an appropriate response from the superintendent? How would different generations view the board's authority? How might a feminist critique of the superintendent's interpretation of the event reveal her way of knowing that may not have been similar to those of others at the meeting?

Another Story

This story is from a superintendent who, in his first year in the position, had a school building destroyed by fire.

> We had to make some plans to house our students for the coming year. And to reconstruct the building or close the system were the options. We established several groups to advise us. We listened to the business community of what their wishes were. We listened to the local government groups. We listened to the teachers; we listened to the parent groups and ended up relocating to classrooms. We had volunteers come in those groups because it was their decision; they were a part of that decision-making process. They helped us establish that by volunteering. We had some people come forth to make some monetary contributions to help us that we did not expect because they were involved in the decision-making process of rebuilding the school. In building the school, we reviewed the plans with the people who occupied [the school] asking them to make a "wish list" of what you would like included in the math area, the science area, the language arts area, the home economics area, vocational areas; and each one of them came back with a lot of things that they would like to have, which exceeded our ability to build. Then we had them prioritize those things; if you had to give up something and take on one, two, or three, which is of most importance? And we tried to incorporate that into the architect[ure] of the building process. One of the items I reminded was teachers don't have any storage and teachers were adamant about having some place to store their materials. That was probably one of the most successful projects because there was very little finger pointing, or complaining or frowning after. I think that was a success story. A lot of people came together and formed a consensus and we implemented many of the recommendations.

Things to Consider

What made this a positive experience for this superintendent, and what role does generational/feminist understanding play in this story? How did this superintendent include diverse groups of stakeholders who represented the differing learning perspectives, values, and beliefs of the individuals? What generational perspective and feminist epistemology did this superintendent exhibit? How did the personal perspectives of the superintendent mesh with the successful outcomes for the greater public? What did the superintendent believe to be important when seeking members to determine what was best for the district? How did the superintendent manifest personal beliefs and values along with the public or community perspectives? How did managing the process remove the superintendent from engaging in conflict? The superintendent spoke about listening to different groups. How does this leadership approach align with the generational personalities and feminist epistemology? How is this story different from the two previous stories? How were different ways of knowing honored in leadership action? How was space created for multiple perspectives to be heard? How did asking people to prioritize what was most important to them result in the overall project success? What are the benefits and drawbacks of taking this much time?

So What?

Superintendents were aware that past communicative structures had not been successful but were unclear about what to do differently, and they rarely raised questions about whether to address "one size fits all" perspectives. When building communicative structures, leaders should consider choice of media and the varied pathways the generations use to access information today, how to employ strong interpersonal skills of listening, hearing through alternative ways of knowing, and reaching out and adjusting for multigenerational stakeholders. The challenge for leaders is to recognize these differences and consider their own generational personality and ensuing epistemology as they strive to develop communicative structures that build inclusive, democratic, collaborative community. One must focus on how best to promote self and others in consciousness-raising leadership actions that move beyond where things are stuck. The negotiation between building individual and communal views, between private and public spheres of influence, and between personal and community notions of inclusion might well challenge our thinking about how we interpret events (Acker-Hocevar, Ballenger, Place, and Ivory, 2012). One more thing to consider: regardless of what communicative structures a leader puts in place or what lens she or he uses to build inclusive, democratic, collaborative community, if there is no leader commitment to include all voices, then the structures do not matter. What does this mean for you in terms of creating access for others to more fully participate in an inclusive, democratic, and collaborative community?

Additional Reading

Ashcraft, K., and Mumby, D. K. (2004). *Reworking gender: A feminist communicology of organization.* Thousand Oaks, CA: Sage.

Ashcraft and Mumby situate gender in critical organization studies. They base their communicology of organization on six premises. Their goal is to propose a feminist communicology that develops the potential of feminism as a guide to recenter gender. In doing so, they hope to expose a discursive process that underlies organizational arrangements.

Baumgardner, J., and Richards, A. (2000). *Manifesta: Young women, feminism, and the future.* New York: Farrar, Straus and Giroux.

Baumgardner and Richards argue that feminism is at a crossroads, yet it is not dead! Setting up an intelligent argument for this, the authors address political issues as personal and discuss the media influence against feminism and the need for activism for equality.

Coates, J. (2007). *Generational learning styles.* River Falls, WI: LERN Books.

Coates examines the four generations from the perspective of learning—that is, how the generations differ in their learning styles. She discusses learning theory and the brain and how to manage diverse generations in the workplace, and she provides guidance in meeting the challenges.

Gravett, L., and Throckman, R. (2007). *Bridging the generation gap: How to get radio babies, boomers, Gen Xers, and Gen Yers to work together and achieve more.* Franklin Lakes, NJ: Career Press.

The authors provide the reader with hands-on experiences, real-life cases, strategies, and solutions for how to manage the generations in the workplace and build bridges between them. Gravett and Throckman use an unusual "point-counterpoint" style of writing, as the two of them are from different generations, baby boomer and Generation X.

Johnson, A. G. (2005). *The gender knot: Unraveling our patriarchal legacy.* Philadelphia: Temple University Press.

Johnson explores patriarchy in a way that provides us with personal ways to empower ourselves to grapple with its systemic effects. He encourages us to raise questions about gendered constructions of reality that hold binaries of femininity and masculinity in place. He faces the myths of feminism head on.

Lancaster, L. C., and Stillman, D. (2002). *When generations collide.* New York: HarperCollins.

In this book, Lancaster and Stillman discuss the four generations—traditionalists (veterans), baby boomers, Generation Xers, and millennials—in the workplace. They discuss who the generations are, why they clash in the workplace, and how to solve the "generational puzzle" at work.

Lovely, S., and Buffman, A. G. (2007). *Generations at school: Building an age-friendly learning community.* Thousand Oaks, CA: Corwin.

In this book, Lovely and Buffman (educators) discuss the school as a multi-generational workplace (teachers and school leaders) facing a new generation of parents. The purpose of the book is to introduce school leaders to the four generations working in schools, with ideas and strategies with which teachers and leaders can understand and manage the mix of generations.

Noddings, N. (1984). *Caring: A feminine approach to ethics and moral education.* Berkeley, CA: University of California Press.

Noddings challenges the reader to accept her definition of caring as a means to approach ethics and moral education differently. It is about treating others according to this ethic of care. Noddings moves beyond the traditional trappings of philosophical logic to explore caring as a means to accomplish what is good.

Raines, C. (2003). *Connecting generations: The sourcebook for a new workplace.* Berkeley, CA: Axzo Press.

Raines writes a "must read" for all who manage or lead organizations and are working to bridge the generation gap in the workplace. This is a how-to book with practical advice and training ideas for dealing with the stress, conflict, and frustrations that come with the multigenerational workplace. He writes, "The generation we belong to is one of the many differences we may have with our coworkers" (p. 1).

Strauss, W., and Howe, N. (1994). *The fourth turning: An American prophecy.* New York: Broadway Books.

Experts on generational theory, Strauss and Howe explain generations, generational archetypes, and the four turnings in the history of generations. They discuss how the cycles of history can tell us what is coming.

Zemke, R., Raines, C., and Filipczak, B. (2000). *Generations at work: Managing the clash of veterans, boomers, xers and nexters in your workplace.* New York: American Management Association.

Zemke, Raines, and Filipczak, cross generational experts, have written a book that describes the four generations and the defining moments of each generation; uses case studies of four companies that struggled with managing a workplace made up of the four generations; and identifies the challenges and successes of integrating and mixing the generations in the workplace.

References

Acker-Hocevar, M., Ballenger, J. N., Place, A. W., and Ivory, G. (Eds.). (2012). *Snapshots of school leadership in the 21st century: Perils and promises of leading for social justice, school improvement, and democratic community.* Charlotte, NC: Information Age.

Alvesson, M., and Billing, Y. D. (1997). *Understanding gender and organizations*. Thousand Oaks, CA: Sage.
Baumgardner, J., and Richards, A. (2000). *Manifesta: Young women, feminism, and the future*. New York: Farrar, Straus and Giroux.
Creswell, J. (2013). *Qualitative inquiry and research design* (3rd ed.). Thousand Oaks, CA: Sage.
Enomoto, E. K., and Kramer, B. H. (2007). *Leading through the quagmire: Ethical foundations, critical methods, and practical applications for school leadership*. Lanham, MD: Rowman and Littlefield.
Ferguson, K. (1984). *The feminist case against bureaucracy*. Philadelphia: Temple University Press.
Furman, G. C., and Starratt, R. J. (2002). Leadership for democratic community in schools. In J. Murphy (Ed.), *The educational leadership challenge: Redefining leadership for the 21st century* (pp. 105–133). Chicago: University of Chicago Press.
Gilligan, C. (1982). *In a different voice: Psychological theory and women's development*. Cambridge, MA: Harvard University Press.
Ginsberg, A. E. (Ed.). (2008). *The evolution of American women's studies: Reflections on triumphs, controversies, and change*. New York: Palgrave Macmillan.
Gravett, L., and Throckman, R. (2007). *Bridging the generation gap: How to get radio babies, boomers, Gen Xers, and Gen Yers to work together and achieve more*. Franklin Lakes, NJ: Career Press.
Grogan, M. (2003). Laying the groundwork for a reconception of the superintendency from feminist postmodern perspectives. In M. Young and L. Skrla (Eds.), *Reconsidering feminist research in educational leadership* (pp. 9–34). Albany: State University of New York Press.
Johnson, A. G. (2005). *The gender knot: Unraveling our patriarchal legacy*. Philadelphia: Temple University Press.
Laible, J. (2003). A loving epistemology: What I hold critical in my life, faith, and profession. In M. Young and L. Skrla (Eds.), *Reconsidering feminist research in educational leadership* (pp. 179–191). Albany: State University of New York Press.
Lancaster, L. C., and Stillman, D. (2002). *When generations collide*. New York: HarperCollins.
Lovely, S., and Buffman, A. G. (2007). *Generations at school: Building an age-friendly learning community*. Thousand Oaks, CA: Corwin.
Noddings, N. (1984). *Caring: A feminine approach to ethics and moral education*. Berkeley, CA: University of California Press.
Raines, C. (2003). *Connecting generations: The sourcebook for a new workplace*. Berkeley, CA: Axzo Press.
Rowe-Finkbeiner, K. (2004). *The F word: Feminism in jeopardy: Women, politics and the future*. Emeryville, CA: Avalon Publishing Group.
Sidorkin, A. (1999). *Beyond discourse: Education, the self, and dialogue*. Albany: State University of New York Press.

Sommers, P. (1994). *Who stole feminism? How women have betrayed women.* New York: Simon and Schuster.

Strauss, W., and Howe, N. (1991). *Generations: The history of America's future, 1584 to 2069.* New York: William Morrow and Company.

Strauss, W., and Howe, N. (1994). *The fourth turning: An American prophecy: What the cycles of history tell us about America's next rendezvous with destiny.* New York: Broadway Books.

Webb, L. D., Metha, A., and Jordan, K. F. (2013). *Foundations of American education* (7th ed.). Upper Saddle River, NJ: Pearson.

Young, M., and Skrla, L. (2003). Research on women and administration: A response to Julie Laible's loving epistemology. In M. Young and L. Skrla (Eds.), *Reconsidering feminist research in educational leadership* (pp. 201–210). Albany: State University of New York Press.

Zemke, R., Raines, C., and Filipczak, B. (2000). *Generations at work: Managing the clash of veterans, boomers, Xers, and nexters in your workplace.* New York: American Management Association.

CHAPTER 8

Promoting the Success of Every Student with Integrity, with Fairness, and in an Ethical Manner: What If the Way Is Not Clear?

Gary Ivory, Cristóbal Rodríguez, and Rhonda McClellan

We are pleased with the opportunity to write about ISLLC Standard 5, which serves as the main title to this chapter. Nearly every word of this standard resonates with us. We are excited to envision a system of schooling in which all students can succeed. Furthermore, as the three of us together have decades of experience as educators, we have certainly come to recognize the satisfaction of working with leaders of integrity, rather than those who are at best self-serving and at worst duplicitous. Fairness is a virtue we value highly. Doing things in an ethical manner is similarly appealing. So, we looked forward to writing a chapter that would help readers pursue these ideals.

But because of our experiences in education, both as leaders and as followers, we emphasize our subtitle as well. Sometimes the way is not clear, even to the wisest and best-intentioned leader. In education, you, the leader, are pursuing the goals of ISLLC Standard 5 simultaneously with the goals of the other five standards. Sometimes these goals may compete with one another for your attention. The needs and wants of all those in your organization and community (students, faculty, staff, parents, and other community members) will differ. Sometimes these constituents will have views that differ from yours on how (or even if) you should work to live up to these ideals. As Leithwood, Begley, and Cousins wrote more than 20 years ago, "Schools operate in a dynamic environment which exerts constant, often contradictory pressures for change: future schools are likely to experience even greater pressures of this sort" (1992, p. 8). You regularly will lack time, money, or other resources to pursue all your goals with equal dedication. Sometimes random events will throw you totally off course. We hope this chapter leads you to examine ways to retain your commitment to and effective pursuit of these ideals even when the way is not clear.

Organization of This Chapter

We begin with an anecdote about a colleague who is a superintendent. He is Native American, and his school district at the time was in a remote, low-income, and culturally and linguistically diverse community. To lead off our discussion of pursuing lofty visions when the way is not clear, we relate to you an account he gave one of us about an incident in his district.

From there, we present two perspectives on thinking about the work of human beings, namely, the normative and the empirical. These two perspectives have been prominent since the time of Plato and Aristotle. They are often in competition with each other, but we believe that your problem solving can be enhanced if you appreciate the merits, and understand the limits, of each. We make the case that two modern perspectives, critical theory and recognition of satisficing, extend the 2,500-year conversation we have been having about normative and empirical perspectives.

Then, we present some passages from our focus groups with superintendents where they talk about their experiences. We will ask you to consider how normative and empirical approaches in general and critical theory and the concept of satisficing in particular can inform our understanding of the challenges these superintendents recounted, and of how one might persist in pursuit of the ISLLC Standard 5 ideals in the face of such challenges. We offer questions for reflection and/or discussion that we hope will lead you to think deeply about important issues related to the pursuit of ideals.

Finally, we send you back to work again on your leadership platform. Is the current version of your platform adequate for your emerging understanding of the quandaries you met and considered in this chapter? Do you need to change it? To change any emphases in it? To enhance any explanations you have in it?

A Story

Now back to our superintendent colleague. He seems totally committed to the ideals stated in ISLLC Standard 5. But perhaps he sometimes finds the way unclear as well. He called a couple years ago with this announcement: "Gary, I just ordered 29 Port-A-Potties!" He went on to explain that his community (not just his school system) had suddenly lost its water supply. The plumbing was so old that some of the pipes were wooden, and the maintenance staff did not know where to begin to look for the failure. They stood around looking to the superintendent for guidance.

He had sent the children home on Friday; he was calling on Monday. He could not keep the children out of school indefinitely—missed school days equate to lost state funding and lost learning time—and so he had ordered the Port-A-Potties and cases of bottled water, preparatory to resuming school. Then, a staff member had reminded him about the evaporative coolers. In dry regions of the country, buildings can be cooled through evaporation. Water is poured over fibrous pads around a large blower. As the water evaporates, the air is cooled and blown through the building. It is much cheaper than refrigerant-based air conditioning. But you need running water for it to work. The district now lacked running water. "So," he said to me, "we'll get lots of fans."

He went on, "I'm calling all the school board members to let them know about my decision to bring the kids back to school tomorrow. But they don't know [what to do]—they've never faced anything like this!" In one of the few times he has ever been anything but upbeat, he said ruefully, "I'm going to be criticized for this, whatever I do." He did not feel he could keep the children out of school any longer—"We only have so many 'snow' days." On the other hand, the teachers would be upset about coming back to work with no running water in the school and community. He mimicked their complaint: "I haven't had a shower in three days!"

This story is relevant to our chapter because it highlights a leader wanting to do the right thing but not knowing exactly how to proceed in a very complex situation. Do you see how events were piling up and might have distracted him from pursuing the ideals of Standard 5? Maintenance people and board members lacked the knowledge or experience to solve a problem and looked to the superintendent for solutions. The superintendent sounded unsure about the best way to proceed and had forgotten the effect of the plumbing failure on the air conditioning. Finally, it seemed that whatever he decided would have some negative outcomes. We maintain that in organizations, this happens frequently. Leaders are often unsure about what to do next. They regularly forget that decisions will have unforeseen consequences and that one event can cause a chain of problems down the line. They regularly cannot put their fingers on the "best" decision. In fact, we have plenty of evidence that not being sure of what to do next is a common experience for leaders.

Normative and Empirical Approaches

Let us move now to philosophical perspectives. We can characterize efforts to consider the human condition under two broad approaches: the normative and the empirical. These two approaches might be represented most simply by a choice: Do we want to focus on ideas, or do we want to focus on facts that can be verified by experience? Another way to describe this is to ask if we believe that there are ideas in our minds that are more fundamental than any lessons we learn from experience. Or do we tend to agree with those who believe that experience is the best teacher? Normative approaches emphasize ideas; empirical approaches focus on experiences and on research, data, and facts. We have selected these two perspectives because they have characterized Western culture's conversation for 2,500 years. For example, the philosopher Plato built his philosophy around ideas. Plato's star pupil, Aristotle, built his philosophy on what he could learn from experience. Drawing on insights from both traditions can help you improve your understanding of decision making in education today (Johnson, 1996a, 1996b).

Notice that ISLLC Standard 5 mentions virtues: integrity, fairness, and promoting student success in an ethical manner. Standard 5 is concerned with morality, with what education leaders *ought* to do. In other words, it is about values. Many writers have maintained that we cannot derive values from facts, data, or experiences; that values cannot come from empirical approaches; and that they are best derived by looking inward, by examining ideas.

Normative approaches, which are concerned with looking inward to our ideas, attempt to assess leadership practices according to standards of morality. They focus on approaches "to leadership that would be exhortatory, morally uplifting, or even critical" (Johnson, 1996a,

p. 14). Adherents of normative approaches see no point in leading if you are not leading toward a value. They also tend to see values as points on which most or all right-thinking people will agree most or all of the time. They see a primary goal of leadership preparation to be helping students to identify what Plato referred to in *The Republic* as "the good" and to commit themselves to it (Johnson, 1996a, 1996b). They fear that obsession with facts might blind people "to the hopeful possibilities, that is, the promises of their work" (Lindle, 2004, p. 169; see also Foster, 1986).

Empirical approaches, by contrast, emphasize that "leadership is an empirical phenomenon conducive to study from a descriptive, social scientific and value-free standpoint" (Johnson, 1996a, p. 13). These approaches emphasize how much we can learn about leadership by making disciplined and value-free examinations of our experience. They see a primary goal of leadership preparation to be helping students become disciplined thinkers, well grounded in the lessons of experience. In the twentieth and twenty-first centuries, some philosophers have been unconvinced of the clear distinctions between values and facts, between the normative and the empirical, but for the purpose of considering quandaries and how to be a better quandary negotiator, let us focus on the differences between these two approaches.

Normative approaches are more idealistic; empirical approaches are more practical. Both approaches to studying leadership have their merits. It is important to attend to both values and evidence. Ignoring either one leaves us with too narrow a view. As Fullan wrote, "It is possible to be crystal clear about what one wants and be totally inept at achieving it. Or to be skilled at managing change but empty-headed about what changes are most needed" (2001, p. 8). So, let us work to enhance our understanding by using both approaches.

A Normative Perspective: Critical Theory

Critical theory is a perspective that emphasizes the importance of working for social justice. In education, critical theorists ask, "Who benefits from our educational policies and practices and who loses out?" (Grogan, 2004, p. 223). Its adherents set out to promote justice by investigating and pointing out ways in which society falls short of being just. In fact, critical theorists call attention to forces in society that systematically, and perhaps deliberately, work against social justice or the common good. Critical theorists are not surprised when school systems do not promote the success of every student or when people and organizations do not act with integrity and fairness or in ethical ways. They assume that *not* being fair occurs systematically all the time and that it is part of how the world generally works unless individuals take deliberate steps to counter it. Critical theorists see their most important work to be identifying injustice and urging people to work against it (Barbour, 2006; Foster, 1986). Critical theorists also emphasize how those with power, wealth, and certain "privileged" identities promote the notion that the society in which they are on top is in fact the most natural, the most commonsense, and even the inevitable way for things to be. Critical theorists point out examples of how those on top tell their story so that the rest of the people accept it. Through lobbying, control of the news and entertainment media, support of literature and the arts, and even through public education and religion, those with wealth and power influence members of their society to see things their way—to their benefit. Those in charge win consent for their ways of valuing and thinking about things. Critical theorists' term for this process is *hegemony* (Gramsci, 2006). Because of their concern about hegemony, critical theorists are cautious about accepting mainstream or "commonsense" explanations of things. They work to point out problems in those explanations (we often see them describing their own efforts with the verb, "problematize"), and they offer what they call "counter-narratives" (Grogan, 2004, p. 223), which provide alternatives to commonsense explanations.

We claimed above that normative views, like critical theory, can be contrasted with empirical views. We also said that empiricists focus on facts. Do critical theorists disparage facts? No. Critical theorists do see the value of empirical approaches (Bohman, 2012). But they problematize them. As the philosopher Richard Rorty (1989) pointed out, "About two hundred years ago, the idea that truth was *made* rather than *found* began to take hold of the imagination of Europe" (p. 3, emphasis ours). In light of Rorty's claim, we think that critical theorists would explain "facts" this way: Facts are expressed in sentences; the sentences we make depend upon our language. Our language develops within our culture. And our culture is heavily and constantly influenced by hegemony. So, we must be wary of claims that anything is a fact. Similarly, we must be skeptical of claims of neutrality and objectivity. Claims about facts, neutrality, and objectivity are claims we should problematize (because they come from a culture influenced by those protecting their own power and privilege). For this reason as well, critical theorists would probably be skeptical of many claims from the normative tradition, e.g., that there are objective and universally valid moral standards, as Plato affirmed (Johnson, 1996a, 1996b). But we see critical theorists as standing among the normative thinkers because they emphasize values and moral choices (Bohman, 2012).

An Empirical Perspective: The Concept of Satisficing

Empiricists are wary of ideas that cannot be grounded in lessons from experience. Grand ideas are fine, empiricists say, but grand ideas have been held by the naive, the deluded, and the psychotic, even by those who are downright evil. We can best protect ourselves from naiveté, delusion, and psychosis by checking our ideas against experience. Empiricists are not opposed to moral virtues but are wary of ideologies and their tendency to inhibit one's ability to think clearly. Empiricists are impatient with any claim that cannot be anchored in experience. So, they set out to describe organizations, education, and educational leadership in terms of facts related to our experience. They look at all organizations, including education organizations, in terms of our experiences of them.

One scholar in this tradition was Nobel Prize–winning economist Herbert Simon. He described leadership in terms of *satisficing*. The key insight of his concept of satisficing is this: faced with solving problems amid overwhelming complexity and conflict, and faced also with the limits of their own cognitive processing, leaders make decisions that are *good enough*—not the best, not perfect, but good enough.

Empiricists do not see satisficing as "settling" or as embracing the status quo. They do not see satisficing as lazy or slovenly. They see it as necessary, as an approach validated by experience. Rainey (2001) contrasted traditional economic theory with insights that Herbert Simon took from psychology:

> Economic theory usually assumed that human beings engage in rational decision processes in which they systematically and consistently maximize utility. . . . One can describe Simon as taking the position that human beings cannot really do that, especially when facing complex decisions. . . . We may not have enough information in some ways or we may have too much in other ways, and we often do not have enough time, resources, and cognitive capacity to make a systematically rational, maximizing decision. Especially when faced with complex decisions, human beings do not "maximize," they "satisfice." They find ways to reach a decision that is good enough rather than assuredly maximal or the best. (p. 494)

In Simon's words, "Maximizing utility bears no resemblance whatsoever to what we human beings actually do" (1993, p. 396). Facing complex problems, leaders (including education leaders) make a good enough decision, rather than the best—or even the "right"—decision. To do otherwise may in fact be counterproductive because to delay long enough to get more information or better understanding may also be to lose time confronting and working on a problem that may further deteriorate and cause other problems (Feuer, 2006). Our friend's quandary with the plumbing problem illustrates some of the complexity. It illustrates why satisficing seems such a useful concept with which to approach leader decision making.

Before we consider the data from Voices 3 superintendents, let us put on our philosopher hats and consider these questions:

1. How do we live up to ISLLC Standard 5: promoting the success of every student with integrity, with fairness, and in an ethical manner? How much of our time and effort should we spend critiquing the status quo? How do we maintain our energy, commitment, and hope in the face of critical theory's claims about hegemonic control of society in general and education in particular? How do we maintain those qualities in the face of evidence that we will spend much of our careers making good enough decisions rather than best decisions?
2. To what extent can critiques of the status quo enhance our decision making, even though we may only, much of the time, be able to satisfice?
3. How do you lead with integrity, with fairness, and in an ethical manner when your student population has many needs, you have lost the water supply, and if you keep the students out of school longer, you will lose resources to help them meet those needs?

Notice that ISLLC Standard 4 reads, "An education leader promotes the success of every student by collaborating with faculty and community members, responding to diverse community interests and needs, and mobilizing community resources" (CCSSO, 2008). Should you mobilize community resources to confront the fact that some communities have regular supplies of clean water and others do not? Or should you accept such differences as natural and inevitable? Do you believe a superintendent should lobby the "powers that be" for better community services, or would his or her time and energy be better spent working to improve instruction in the district? How much do you believe good instruction depends on the fulfillment of basic human needs?

How might an understanding of the concept of satisficing help you make a decision to deal with the lack of water and the consequences for the district's effectiveness? Given that your time and energy are finite (and that your understanding of the complexities of any problem will be limited), how will you "promote the success of every student"? What will it mean to lead "with integrity, with fairness, and in an ethical manner," as Standard 5 calls you to do? Might a thorough understanding of both critical theory and satisficing lead you to enhance or modify your leadership platform?

After you have thought about these broad questions, continue reading this chapter. We provide two examples of superintendents dealing with complex situations, and we will ask you to consider the situations and the superintendents' perspectives in terms of satisficing and concepts from critical theory.

SUPERINTENDENTS' VOICES

First, some background information. Superintendents, with their wealth of preparation and experience in school leadership, generally answer to elected boards made up of people with far less of that preparation and experience. Principals generally answer to the superintendents. But board members sometimes working to represent their own communities might approach their local school principals for advice on district policy. So, we have a circularity problem: superintendents take direction from the board members, who take direction from the principals, who take direction from the superintendent. Who's really in charge here? Is this a wonderful way to give voice to the community? Is it a recipe for organizational chaos? Is there a way to manage this quandary? What insights can we get from critical theory? What insights can we get from the concept of satisficing? Can the two perspectives together help us make sense of the quandary or arrive at a way to proceed that promotes "the success of every student with integrity, with fairness, and in an ethical manner," as the ISLLC standard calls for?

Democratic School Leadership

Now, here is a quandary to consider from the Voices 3 transcripts. Superintendent 63 is commenting on the issue of how democratic a school leader should be. Just a heads-up: critical theorists tend to push for leadership that is democratic because they believe that democracy allows more voices to be heard and reduces the odds that a few people with wealth, power, and privilege will dominate the conversation. Empirically oriented people will focus on the lessons of experience and on how being democratic plays out in practice. In particular, empiricists who agree with the concept of satisficing will say that leaders are never going to have a formula to allow them consistently to make the perfect decision about how much voice to give others. Let us read from the transcript.

Superintendent 63: Can I just bring up quickly. . . . It's the issue of the role of principals in regards to the school board. I think it's . . . unique to [this region], but really in many schools—and it differs from school to school, but really in some of these schools, I'm kind of along for the ride. I mean [board members] respect me. If I said something and I raised a big concern, I think I would get my way. So it's not that. It's not trying to rip away power or anything. But it really is those boards look to that principal as their advisor, and I think sometimes that can be okay because it's close to the ground, but boy, there are times when they can get crossways on that stuff. But it's a function of our governance.

And I think particularly it's small schools, where everybody knows everybody. This is a rural phenomenon I think, because everyone knows everyone; they know their kids; they know the kids that are having challenges; and it's just small.

Superintendent 65: Yes, at one of my schools we have almost as many board members as staff members. It's way too close.

Superintendent 66: And this was true at the other district I worked in— the superintendent is responsible for everything, no matter what. And that means that the superintendent is the one who is going to work directly with the boards in any place where I work. And I worked that out with the principals ahead of time. We work as an administrative team. If it's going to the board, we have agreement on it, and I believe that you could go to any principal that works with me and they would tell you, to use [Superintendent 63's] analogy, I'm the best corner man they've ever had. They don't mind going into the ring to fight, but they want to—at the school level, they want to know that they've got a good corner person. In the board setting, I never let principals take abuse. That—I stop it, period. I absorb it. Whatever way it takes, the principals are—they're not—that's not their role. It's mine.

And conversely, they don't go out on their own at the board meeting, and they know it, and they understand it and we're in total agreement about it. If you're not there, you don't get hired in this system, because it confuses the board and the public, when the administrative team doesn't speak with one voice. And the way for it to speak with one voice is to have done the work ahead of time. It's not on the agenda, unless we're ready for it to be on the agenda. If something comes up, it's a surprise, they know—I'm taking the lead, and I'm taking the fall. So that's the way it is.

Questions on Dealing with the School Board

Respond to the following questions as you consider the exchange among the superintendents above. Develop your responses in light of your understanding of normative and empirical perspectives, particularly critical theory and satisficing.

1. How do you promote the success of every student with integrity, with fairness, and in an ethical manner when you need the approval of school board members that may have perspectives that differ from yours and from those of other board members? How do you accomplish this when the school board members' perspectives are being influenced by people other than you?
2. To what extent does it make sense to you that people with money, power, and privilege actively promote ideas that enable them to hold on to those things rather than to pursue the common good? How likely does it seem to you that school board members will be influenced by messages from those people? How likely is it that superintendents will be?
3. What is your reaction to the superintendent emphasizing to principals that the administrative team should speak with one voice? Is that a necessary step to get board approval for measures to promote the success of every student? Is it a form of hegemony? How much dissent is good in an organization? How much unanimity is needed?
4. To what extent does it make sense to you that leaders generally do not act to maximize utility but only make decisions that are "good enough"? How much democratic input is good enough to promote the success of every student with integrity, with fairness, and in an ethical manner? How much unanimity is good enough?
5. How might a critical theorist analyze the conversation of the superintendents above? How might a person who accepts the concept of satisficing?
6. On a personal level, how will you deal with claims that you are not being democratic enough in your decision making? Or that you are being too democratic? How will you maintain the energy to pursue your ideals in light of the claim that you might well only ever be able to satisfice?
7. Review your leadership platform. Do you need to revise it in any way in light of ideas you have encountered so far in this chapter?

Student Behavior Problems

Now, here's a second quandary, involving a painful decision that any administrator might face: whether to expel a student for misbehavior. On the one hand, ensuring that schools run peacefully, safely, and in an orderly fashion is a genuine good and is perhaps necessary for promoting the success of every student. Some students might so disrupt that peace, safety, and order that, if they remained in school, they would hinder the learning of everyone. On the other hand, keeping students in school has clear benefits both for the individual students and for society.

Consider these points: A leader might well have learned from painful experience (either personal experience or someone else's) that he or she cannot allow too much disruption in an organization. Otherwise, there would be *dis*-organization. But we also know from experience that students from certain groups tend to receive more severe punishments (U.S. Department of Education, 2012). Critical theorists suggest that schools may be treating certain groups and classes of students differently because they cannot function within the traditional rules and norms of the school community (Giroux, 2010). From the concept of satisficing we learn that in each individual situation, we must make decisions that get at the immediate inappropriate behavior; thus, within the demands of the work, school leaders cannot take the time to focus on the complexity of underlying systemic or covert social biases. They are responsible for what they can control and for what occurs on their campuses and cannot ameliorate all the social ills present.

Read the following account of a conversation among superintendents and then analyze it in terms of the two perspectives we have presented. Consider for yourself how a critical theorist would describe the events. Then consider how an empiricist interested in the concept of satisficing would describe them. Finally, think about how the two perspectives in combination might enhance our understanding of the events and expand our vision of how to proceed.

> *Superintendent 1*: Let me tell you a little story here. We've had two students show up this year with a knife in their cars. They didn't bring it in the school but—they [had knives] in their cars. Student #1 was recommended for suspension long-term, the rest of the semester, plus all the next one. Student #2—same thing was recommended, however—and that's within policy—and by the way, within policy we can change if we want to and provide services or not provide services to either one of these kids. The parent . . . of the first student didn't care enough, really, to really pursue the whole thing,

so that student was gone for the entire suspension period. He still is gone. Parent #2 was in our office today. . . . Here's the situation and it calls for common sense: Here's a parent who came with her son today, pleading on behalf of him. . . ., And he did a good job in a hearing, explaining why he wanted to go to school. Now, he's still unmotivated. He's still lazy, but the parent—we're talking about the difference in parents here; that's what the question was—this parent said, "I need to do whatever I can to help, to get him through school. I know he's not doing well. What can I do, as a parent, to help get this job done?" And, as a result of that, plus with a conversation, we decided to give him an opportunity—now the suspension, still, on paper, is for the rest of the semester, plus all the next, but he has an opening now—to come up, after he goes to Vo-Tech, and stop by. He'll finish a project or a class off campus this semester and if he does it, and does it well, it shows us that he's interested in doing this. Then he's gonna be allowed to come back. That's where you stay away from black and white. If I was to treat them as black and white to make it easier on me, neither one of them would be in school now. But, because we have a parent who would have enough interest to say, "I need help," we're gonna do what we can to help and that's our responsibility.

Superintendent 2: That's where you get back to doing what's right for the kid.

Superintendent 1: Using common sense. I mean we've talked about a lot of different things, in terms of—what would happen if our valedictorian showed up, on campus, and had a knife in her car? Accidently. Common sense dictates that we deal with that issue differently than we've done with the other ones. We can still follow the letter of the law; recommendations still remain the same, because he was concerned about—well, what would it look like if he just recommended a three- or four-day suspension? But it was my advice that he go ahead and stay with the whole thing and then come back at a theory level and give this kid something to work for and show that he's innocent. And because a parent is there to support [him].

Questions on Dealing with Student Behavior Problems

As you did previously, consider the quandary described by the superintendents above in light of different perspectives, including your developing leadership platform.

1. Consider these possibly contradictory claims. We are grateful to Pitner and Ogawa (1981) for pointing them out: (1) superintendents, and other school leaders, have incredibly full days and are never able to get everything done they would like; and (2) they

still make decisions regularly that show their priorities. As you lead an educational system in which the plumbing sometimes fails, students sometimes bring weapons to school, accountability systems can impugn your effectiveness, and principals disagree about what superintendents should be doing, what will be the priorities that will be reflected in your daily decision making?

2. In the discussion of the students who brought knives to school, what do you think of the superintendent's reasoning for the different treatment of students? What did his descriptions reveal about his value system? Would you have arrived at the same conclusions? Are there values you would want to hold onto over all others? What are they? Why are they important to you?
3. Could one argue that the superintendents in the discussion ended up favoring one type of student over another? In so doing, are they perhaps protecting wealth, power, and privilege?
4. Defend the perspectives of critical theory. What insight(s) from satisficing do you, as a critical theorist, find informative? How might this impact your leadership and decision making?
5. Defend the role of a hard-nosed empiricist who relies on facts and who is convinced of the validity of satisficing. Now, what insight(s) from critical theory do you find informative? How might this impact your leadership and decision making?
6. Can you be an empiricist who is committed to integrity, fairness, and ethics, to making every effort to ensure that everyone is treated well under your leadership? Will your view of the "facts" of satisficing make you believe you can never achieve your goal? Then, what will be the implications for your leadership efforts? For your efforts at professional growth?
7. Can you imagine a situation in which you would critique conditions that others around you think are natural, commonsense, and even inevitable? Can you live with being the critic day after day in your normal work life? What might you gain by such a stance? What price might you have to pay? How might you need to grow personally and professionally to critique effectively?
8. Can you imagine a situation in which you would believe that others around you were not attentive enough to facts and experience? In which they were too unforgiving of the failures of organizations and their leaders' limitations? How might you work to get people to focus more on logic and evidence? How might you need to grow personally and professionally to do this effectively?
9. If you followed the instructions in Chapter 1, you have generated a leadership platform. How will you base your actions on that

platform if you will never get everything accomplished that you would like to? If an observer followed you around for a year, how would that person describe your leadership? Would that person be able to see your platform being carried out?

Conclusion

Great thinkers have struggled with the duality highlighted in this chapter. It is our nature to aspire to the highest ideals. Many people see working for the benefit of others to be one of the surest ways to attain fulfillment as humans. Certainly many educators and education leaders see life this way. Furthermore, part of working for the benefit of others may well involve pointing out when systems and situations work counter to the benefit of others. Critique can be a means of working for the general welfare.

At the same time, we regularly encounter situations where we seem not to be up to the task. We lose our enthusiasm, fatigue sets in, and we become inclined to pursue our own welfare rather than the welfare of students and communities. Or, as illustrated in this chapter, conditions become so complex that we lack the cognitive ability to consider and weigh all the variables and possible outcomes. When we face such quandaries, the words of the critic or the idealist seem to offer little assistance or support.

We three chapter authors maintain that no matter how much we grow as leaders, we will never be able to break free from the tension between our ideals and our capabilities. The challenge is to realize that while we can never reach the ideals (we will regularly "satisfice" rather than optimize), the ideals give our work meaning. We must learn to accept the reality of our own limitations and continue pursuing the ideals despite those limitations. Simultaneously, we must develop the capacity to accept ourselves as imperfect. We must both learn to hear the voices of the critics as pointing to better ways to lead and learn to take with a grain of salt their constant reminders that education institutions and those who lead them are flawed. The flaws will persist, and there is no particular reason to think the critics would lead education better than those now in the leadership roles.

Finally, we urge superintendents and aspiring superintendents to take from this chapter one final lesson: just as we regularly encounter struggles between our ideals and the realization that we fall short, all other people in the education enterprise find themselves in the same struggle. We pursue ideals, we critique, and we fall short. But we must proceed with the understanding that we are all in the same boat. We all have aspirations, we all fall short, and we all can benefit from critique. We must all sometimes be the critic, and we must all, at other times, resist the inclination to let the critic dampen our spirit in the pursuit of the noble ideals of education leadership.

Additional Reading

We have set out in this chapter to give you simple introductions to two complex perspectives: critical theory and the concept of satisficing. We are proud of the job we have done in simplifying these two notions. At the same time, we have risked oversimplifying, and we want to avoid that as well. We invite you to dig further to deepen your understanding of work that has been done with these two approaches. To that end, we suggest here some works that can support your efforts to better understand the ideas we have presented and their relevance to education leadership.

Educational Administration Quarterly (2004). Special issue: The legacy of William P. Foster: Promises for leadership and schooling.

After William Foster's death, a number of scholars extended the conversation he had started about critical theory and education leadership.

Feuer, M. J. (2006). *Moderating the debate: Rationality and the promise of American education.* Cambridge, MA: Harvard University Press.

This little book applies the principles of satisficing to school reform issues. Feuer laments the tendency in school reform to settle for nothing less than the best and makes a strong case that satisficing might well be the smartest and most effective tack we can take.

Foster, W. P. (1986). *Paradigms and promises: New approaches to educational administration.* Amherst, NY: Prometheus Books.

William Foster was probably the first scholar of education administration to draw on critical theory. This is a very readable introduction to his ideas.

Lehrer, J. (2009). *How we decide.* Boston: Mariner Books.

Lehrer is a journalist writing about cognition. *How we decide* was a *New York Times* bestseller and is a fun read. Satisficing gets little explicit attention in this book, but Lehrer illustrates well the complexity of making decisions in tough situations and explains how the brain can work to enhance or to interfere with good decision making.

Mumford, M. D., Zaccaro, S. J., Harding, F. D., Jacobs, T. W., and Fleishman, E. A. (2000). Leadership skills for a changing world: Solving complex social problems. *Leadership Quarterly,* 11(1), 11–35.

These authors argue that leaders' effectiveness depends upon their problem-solving abilities and explore how to develop leaders' skills in creative problem solving. Baughman and Mumford noted that "ill-defined problems cannot be solved simply through the routine applications of extant knowledge" (as quoted by Mumford et al., 2000, p. 17). The problem-solving models presented in this article call upon the skill to use previous experience, creativity, social perceptiveness, knowledge about the organization, and particular personality characteristics (e.g., openness, tolerance for ambiguity, and curiosity) to identify approaches and solutions. The eleventh volume of *Leadership Quarterly* may offer insights into grappling with complex problems.

Simon, H. A. (1993). Decision making: Rational, nonrational, and irrational. *Educational Administration Quarterly*, 29(3), 392–411.

In this article for the premier journal in education leadership, the founder of the concept of satisficing applies his ideas to our field.

References

Barbour, J. D. (2006). Critical theory. In F. W. English (Ed.), *Encyclopedia of educational leadership and administration* (pp. 237–240). Thousand Oaks, CA: Sage.

Bohman, J. (2012). Critical theory. In E. N. Zalta (Ed.), *The Stanford encyclopedia of philosophy* (Spring 2012 ed.). Retrieved from http://plato.stanford.edu/archives/spr2012/entries/critical-theory/.

Council of Chief State School Officers. (2008). *Educational leadership policy standards: ISLLC 2008*. Retrieved from http://www.ccsso.org/documents/2008/educational_leadership_policy_standards_2008.pdf.

Feuer, M. J. (2006). *Moderating the debate: Rationality and the promise of American education*. Cambridge, MA: Harvard University Press.

Foster, W. P. (1986). *Paradigms and promises: New approaches to educational administration*. Amherst, NY: Prometheus Books.

Fullan, M. (2001). *The new meaning of educational change* (3rd ed.). New York: Teachers College Press.

Giroux, H. A. (2010). Memories of hope in the age of disposability. Retrieved from http://archive.truthout.org/memories-hope-age-disposability63631.

Gramsci, A. (2006). Hegemony, intellectuals and the state. In J. Storey (Ed.), *Cultural theory and popular culture: A reader* (3rd ed.; pp. 85–91). San Francisco, CA: Pearson.

Grogan, M. (2004). Keeping a critical, postmodern eye on educational leadership in the United States: In appreciation of Bill Foster. *Educational Administration Quarterly*, 40(2), 222–239.

Johnson, P. F. (1996a). Antipodes: Plato, Nietzsche, and the moral dimensions of leadership. In P. S. Temes (Ed.), *Teaching leadership: Essays in theory and practice* (pp. 13–44). New York: Peter Lang.

Johnson, P. F. (1996b). Plato's *Republic* as a leadership text. In P. S. Temes (Ed.), *Teaching leadership: Essays in theory and practice* (pp. 83–103). New York: Peter Lang.

Leithwood, K., Begley, P. T., and Cousins, J. B. (1992). *Developing expert leadership for future schools*. Washington, DC: Falmer.

Lindle, J. C. (2004). William P. Foster's promises for educational leadership: Critical idealism in an applied field. *Educational Administration Quarterly*, 40(2), 167–175.

Pitner, N. J., and Ogawa, R. T. (1981). Organizational leadership: The case of the school superintendent. *Educational Administration Quarterly*, 17(2), 45–65.

Rainey, H. G. (2001). A reflection on Herbert Simon: A satisficing search for significance. *Administration and Society*, 33, 491–507.

Rorty, R. (1989). *Contingency, irony, and solidarity*. New York: Cambridge University Press.

Simon, H. A. (1993). Decision making: Rational, nonrational, and irrational. *Educational Administration Quarterly*, 29(3), 392–411.

U.S. Department of Education. (2012). *New data from U.S. Department of Education highlights educational inequities around teacher experience, discipline and high school rigor*. Retrieved from http://www.ed.gov/news/press-releases/new-data-us-department-education-highlights-educational-inequities-around-teache.

CHAPTER 9

POLITICAL PERSPECTIVES ON RESOURCE ALLOCATION IN RURAL SCHOOL DISTRICTS

Chad R. Lochmiller

As described by ISLLC Standard 6, "An educational leader promotes the success of every student by understanding, responding to, and influencing the political, social, economic, legal, and cultural context" surrounding his or her school or school district. Superintendents working in rural school districts face many of these contextual factors, directly owing both to the small size of their school districts and to the close connections between the school district and the community. A central challenge for their work, then, is to bring competing stakeholders together to advance the goals of the school district. Quite often, superintendents must accomplish this task with limited or declining resources. Further, in the process of bringing these forces together, superintendents are to act as instructional leaders and public stewards. As instructional leaders, superintendents are responsible for the quality of the education provided to a community's children. They are responsible for ensuring that each child is provided with a rigorous education that prepares him or her to attend college or pursue a career. Superintendents also act as public officials, responsible for the prudent management of the school district's resources while being subject to the (perhaps changing) priorities of their school board and the demands of the surrounding community.

The choices facing these leaders, particularly when budgets are tight, are fraught with political considerations. Even the most seasoned administrator can quickly find himself or herself embroiled in conflict as a result of unexpected political conditions. These conditions weigh heavily on superintendents, acting to eliminate some choices, advance others, and make some seem unrealistic. These forces are both internal and external to the district, and they require the superintendent to become astute at identifying the political conditions around them and adjusting his or her leadership accordingly. Although superintendents are pressed to provide *more* resources in response to competing demands, the fiscal reality of many school districts suggests that it is rarely as simple as "throwing money at the problem." Poor economic conditions have reduced state revenues and have thus made it difficult for states to increase education spending. Today, superintendents are expected to lead with less. Given the limited resources available to them, it is essential that superintendents develop both the skills needed to think critically about these political forces and the ability to adapt their leadership to respond productively to these forces. As such, their work is very much about identifying, managing, and responding to the political forces surrounding their leadership.

This chapter provides you, the reader, with a theoretical lens and reflective questions with which you can consider the impact of politics on a prototypical decision. Drawing upon data from the Voices 3 project, the chapter presents a case study of a rural superintendent facing the politics inherent in a declining resource environment. The purpose of this case study is to provide you with an opportunity to use a theoretical perspective to think critically about the decisions that a superintendent might make given the challenges he or she is facing. Before presenting the case study, I briefly discuss the current fiscal status of school districts throughout the United States. I focus specifically on the recent declines in resources available to school districts, as these recent experiences will likely inform your thinking about the decisions facing the superintendent. Next, I present an overview of David Easton's (1965) *A Framework for Political Analysis*, which explains the interaction between stakeholders, the policy-making environment, and policy decisions. I also discuss Wirt and Kirst's (1997) adaptation of Easton's framework that focuses on K–12 schools. I encourage you to use these frameworks to think about the political forces, choices, and various options available to the superintendent. Then, I present the case of Samantha Cohen (pseudonym), a superintendent who leads the small, rural school district described in the case. Finally, I conclude the chapter by considering reflective questions centered on the decisions and tensions facing the superintendent as well as the implications that these decisions and tensions have for your practice as a superintendent or educational leader.

Identifying Assumptions about Resources

Although the Voices 3 data collection occurred before the Great Recession (2008–2010), the impact of the most recent recession likely shapes your thinking about the fiscal challenges that will be discussed in this case. The current challenges facing school districts are of a magnitude not seen previously and will likely influence how you think the superintendent in the case presented should approach the resource-related challenges facing her. Prior to discussing the case, then, it is important to acknowledge the current fiscal reality surrounding public school districts, as this likely influences your assumptions about resource allocation.

A recent report suggests that schools and districts throughout the United States have weathered significant fiscal crises in the past five years; yet, many schools and districts are still grappling with the remaining effects of the worst recession since the Great Depression. A report commissioned by the American Association of School Administrators, for example, indicated that as recently as February 2012 schools across the nation were continuing to endure significant financial distress while also experiencing significant reductions in the number of teaching positions available and the elimination of academic programs (Ellerson, 2010a). Nearly three-quarters of school districts across the nation indicated that they were "inadequately funded" at that time and that funding levels had not returned to prerecession levels. As Guthrie and Peng (2011) noted, "A unique set of constitutional, structural, financial, and political arrangements has, up to now, ensured that school systems and professional educators are buffered from revenue losses when the economy declines" (p. 20). These protections have allowed many school districts and the superintendents who lead them to avoid making dramatic cuts to existing education programs. The dramatic contraction in state revenues that forced significant cuts in schools and districts was effectively a "fiscal tsunami" that wiped out decades of stable and increasing public investments in public schools (Guthrie and Peng, 2011, p. 20).

Conditions have improved since the recession, affording some schools and school leaders the opportunity to invest in new programs and initiatives. Yet, this is not the case in many districts, as they continue to face flat or reduced funding levels. As reported by the Center on Budget and Policy Priorities, "Schools in around a third of states are entering the new year with less funding than they had last year" (Leachman and Mai, 2013, p. 1). Fifteen states are providing less funding per pupil to school districts than they provided a year ago (Leachman and Mai, 2013). Compounding matters, school districts have also experienced reduced funding from the federal government because of automatic cuts required by sequestration (Ellerson, 2013). According to a report issued by the American Association of School Administrators, sequestration has resulted in the reduction of professional development opportunities, academic programs, and personnel, and it has increased class sizes in many districts throughout the nation (Ellerson, 2010b). Thus, difficult choices remain for many school districts across the United States.

At the time the Voices 3 data were collected, superintendents had not yet encountered many of these fiscal challenges and thus were not familiar with the draconian cuts that they have dealt with more recently. Thus, the case presented here is positioned before the Great Recession and is intended to shed light on the more common situation of superintendents managing slight reductions in funding from one year to the next. Previous research indicates that stability in education resources often prompts educational leaders to make minor changes in the allocation of resources from one year to the next (Chambers, Shambaugh, Levin, Muraki, and Poland, 2008; Monk, 1994; Miles, 1995; Odden and Picus, 2008). Research on district and school resource allocations suggests that previous budgets often predict how resources will be allocated in the current year, with modest adjustments (Erlichson and Goertz, 2002; Hartman, 1999; Odden and Archibald, 2000). Thus, for many of the superintendents interviewed during the Voices 3 project, their leadership had not yet required them to consider dramatic resource allocations, nor were they required to consider how the investments they were making at the time supported their district's learning improvement goals. Not surprisingly, though, the comments that the superintendents in the Voices 3 data offered highlighted the growing interest of parents, principals, and teachers in the allocation of resources, as well as the increasing pressure on superintendents to make strategic use of scarce resources. More generally, each of these factors shapes how superintendents engage in fiscal leadership and what they are able to do given the political conditions surrounding them.

Political Perspectives on Fiscal Leadership

Resource allocation decisions are political decisions. Superintendents must develop the capacity to think critically about the various factors that might influence how these decisions present themselves. According to Bird, Wang, and Murray (2009), "The superintendent is the only person who has the positional authority to access the power domains of the Board of Education, central staff, principals, teacher associations, parental groups, community groups, and local/state governmental structures" (p. 141). This authority gives them the opportunity to influence the political conditions surrounding their school district. Moreover, it means that these conditions influence their ability to exercise fiscal leadership.

Within the context of school district budgeting and resource allocation, superintendents act as policy makers, public stewards, and advocates. They exercise fiscal leadership by making decisions that maintain the district's fiscal integrity while also addressing the learning needs of students. Thus, they make decisions that "either explicitly, or implicitly . . . presume that the resources they allocate purchase learning opportunities, offer incentives, and otherwise underwrite activities that—over time—develop the capabilities of teachers" and thereby improve the learning opportunities for students (Plecki, Alejano, Knapp, and Lochmiller, 2006, p. 2). At their core, resource allocation decisions made by superintendents "must reflect an understanding of the imperative to close the achievement gap" by providing students from less advantaged social positions with access to the resources, programs, staffing expertise, and support needed to ameliorate inequities that lie beyond the school system (Plecki et al., 2006, p. 2). This perspective pressures superintendents to improve student learning and promote equitable achievement outcomes using resources that are finite. The complexity and volatility of resource allocation decisions, therefore, require that superintendents move beyond their technical capacity to monitor resource levels (i.e., their ability to understand budgets) toward a broader understanding of the values and interests of those who vie for resources and the ways in which resources can be used to support them. As Plecki (2000) stated,

> The exercise of fiscal leadership in schools occurs in a highly political environment. Issues related to the allocation of scarce resources, by definition, become political, as interests compete with one another for attention and support. Embedded in the political perspective is the notion of the exercise of power and authority relationships

by contending parties and the need for leaders to broker competing interests. (p. 548)

Plecki's assertion is that resource allocation decisions reflect political dynamics associated with individual stakeholders, their individual agendas, and the specific interests they have that are distinct to the organization (the school or district) as a whole.

Resource Allocation as a Political Endeavor

Resource allocation decisions should be viewed through the lens of politics. This perspective situates the superintendent's leadership in a broader policy arena (Mazzoni, 1991) while acknowledging that a superintendent's primary responsibilities include identifying stakeholders within the arena, managing information given to stakeholders, and constructing a policy agenda that enables them to meet the teaching and learning needs of the students they serve. Bird, Wang, and Murray (2009) noted that superintendents live in "highly charged political arenas" (p. 141), with these arenas engaging multiple constituencies and demanding that superintendents become skilled at "orchestrating the interchange of educational providers and consumers" and "mediating the competing values of constituencies as they hover over scarce resources" (pp. 141–142). The task in this chapter is not to describe the strategies that superintendents use to orchestrate these constituencies. Rather, the tasks are to provide reflective opportunities for you to use political theory to understand the work that superintendents engage in and to prompt you to consider how political theory might inform your practice as an educational leader.

A Political Systems Perspective

Theoretical perspectives from the field of political science serve as useful tools for superintendents seeking to make sense of the influence, roles, and agendas of competing stakeholders. David Easton's (1965) framework, described in *A Systems Analysis of Political Life*, provides one possible description of the intersection between the broader political environment, the demands of and support from individual stakeholders, the political process, and the decisions or actions that result. As Easton (1965) noted, a systems analysis model rests on three assumptions. First, his model assumes that political systems can be identified for the purpose of analyzing the broader social and environmental context that surrounds them. Second, he assumes that political systems have discernible units, which he suggests consist of specific interests, actions, and stakeholders. Finally, the system has some form of boundary and therefore can be defined in a way that allows it to remain distinct from the broader context that surrounds a given political activity.

Adapting Easton's Model to School Districts

Wirt and Kirst (1997) adapted Easton's model for use in public schools. They noted, "Schools are as much political systems as are Congress or the presidency, the state legislature or executive. School systems perform [politically] in a society in which other institutions—economic, religious, family, and so on—themselves seek certain valued resources from schools" (p. 57). They suggested that school district resource allocation decisions may be "material," referring mostly to the physical resources of the school system (e.g., where a building will be constructed or where a teacher will be assigned). In contrast, resource allocation decisions may be "symbolic," referring to the ideals, beliefs, and positions of the school system. These symbolic actions could include investing in a particular math curriculum or deciding upon a school mascot. More simply, "schools allocate *resources*—revenues, programs, professionals—and they also allocate values—teaching Americanism or the importance of learning for intrinsic or occupational purposes" (Wirt and Kirst, 1997, p. 57).

Much like Easton's (1965) original model, Wirt and Kirst (1997) asserted that resource allocation decisions are fundamentally political in nature and are made in response to a combination of demands and supports. Demands are "pressures on the government for justice or help" (p. 60), with this reference to government applying also to a school district. School districts and their superintendents face numerous demands from their communities, particularly in relation to resources. For example, a parent seeks assistance for his or her son or daughter with special education needs. A news story in the local paper expresses concerns over the district's math curriculum. The teachers union threatens to strike over increases in their health care premiums. A citizen's comments at the local school board meeting stir up controversy and angst over one school board member's decision to support a district initiative. Supports, on the other hand, refer to the community's "willingness to accept the decisions of the [school district]" (p. 60). Unlike demands, which place added pressure on the school superintendent, support offers the superintendent leverage to address the demands using the resources available. Examples of support include a local levy that passes, a community forum that is well attended, or a school board member who is reelected.

The political system identifies, interprets, and responds to the demands and supports from the community and district stakeholders. Superintendents exercise fiscal leadership within this system by creating conditions to solicit opinions and views from stakeholders, gathering and disseminating information about the district's priorities, and assessing the district's capacity to serve specific needs given the resources available. Within this system, the superintendent adopts a specific orientation and role. According to Wirt and Kirst (1997), a role refers to "expectations of one's behavior by significant others within the social structure" (p. 164). Superintendents respond to the demands and pressures placed on them by constructing a process to engage stakeholders and by orienting their leadership style in ways that allow them to respond to the stakeholders. Wirt and Kirst characterized the superintendent's style using a three-by-three matrix to describe the ways that superintendents (within the context of the broader political system) orient their leadership.

Wirt and Kirst (1997) assumed that superintendents orient their leadership style within the political system in response to the degree of conflict in the community. In communities with less conflict, the superintendent avoids the conflict by delegating decisions to subordinates, mediates the conflict by facilitating dialogue among the community's stakeholders, or fights the conflict by focusing the school district on administrative routines and practices that effectively reduce the potential for conflict to begin. In communities with more conflict, the superintendent might avoid conflict by deferring to others or by simply not taking stands on issues. The superintendent might also mediate the conflict by engaging stakeholders in a process that facilitates compromise. Finally, the superintendent might choose to be more assertive and engage with stakeholders in order to influence their perceptions or advance a preferred policy alternative. In a community with less conflict, the superintendent may adopt a professional style, focusing on the efficient and orderly operation of the school district.

Wirt and Kirst's (1997) adaptation of the political systems framework enables practitioners to understand the broader political environment that surrounds the exercise of fiscal leadership as well as the specific leadership styles that a superintendent might adopt given the potential conflict in the political environment.

In the next section, I present a case study developed from the Voices 3 data. This case illustrates the political context surrounding a superintendent's leadership as well as the style of leadership adopted.

Herbert Valley School District: An Illustrative Case

Samantha Cohen (pseudonym) became the superintendent of Herbert Valley School District (pseudonym) five years ago. Before that, she was an elementary school principal, assistant principal, and classroom teacher in a neighboring district. As a veteran superintendent, she has guided the small rural school district through a significant period of both instructional transformation and declining resources. Under her leadership, the district has adopted new curricula and enhanced the amount of professional development provided to classroom teachers and school principals. Many of the changes in the district have been achieved through collaboration with the district's six-member school board, the broader community, and the parents of children in each of the district's five schools. Community members describe Cohen's style as collaborative and consensus oriented. She has received high marks from the community and has a positive relationship with the current school board, although she acknowledges that they are wary of additional reforms because of the costs.

Herbert Valley is a small, rural school district located 180 miles south of a major city. The district is surrounded by large agricultural facilities and smaller family farms. In the past five years, the district has experienced declining student enrollment and reduced state support for basic educational services. Today, the district enrolls approximately 4,750 students compared to nearly 6,800 five years ago. Approximately one-third of the district's students are Latino, and nearly 90 percent of the Latino students are English language learners. Half of the students in the district are now eligible for free or reduced-price lunch, which reflects the region's declining economy. The district operates five schools—three elementary schools, one middle school, and one high school. In the past five years, a combination of declining enrollment and changes in program requirements has reduced the district's general fund budget by nearly $1.8 million. The district also has had difficulty passing a levy that would provide funds for replacing two of the district's aging school buildings and upgrading the district's bus fleet. Thus, the superintendent and her administrative team face constant challenges related to declining revenue.

The district's school board is composed of six members in addition to the superintendent, who serves as secretary to the board but does not vote. Three members own farms in the community and have strong connections with the schools, the district, and the town. Their commitment to the schools, however, is not strong, and they balk at raising taxes to pay for new district facilities or raising fees to cover additional district programs. They operate from the perception that the district has enough resources but is "top-heavy" or "wasteful." The next two members are local business owners who support the district's mission yet are hesitant to embrace increased taxes and fees, fearing the impact on their businesses. These members tend to be more moderate than the first three and to vote in support of the district's initiatives, but they have pressed the superintendent to pursue greater efficiency and to focus only on those subjects that are tested. The final member is a retired classroom teacher from the school district, a former union president, and an activist. She is a "wild card," as described by the superintendent, as she is able to garner support for district initiatives among the other board members. She has been handily reelected with support from the local teachers union. The board's membership has been stable during the past three years.

The teachers union serves as an additional stakeholder. The union has developed a somewhat acrimonious relationship with the superintendent and her administration. Early in her tenure, Cohen worked aggressively to improve teaching and learning in classrooms across the district and specifically focused on improving reading achievement in the district's elementary grades. The superintendent focused much of her leadership on improving instruction in reading and sought to bring additional supports to students who struggled. This required her to reallocate resources from other programs that were not focused on literacy, especially since the district lacked substantial new revenues. These efforts upset the teachers union, as they felt the reforms were "top-down" and aligned with the requirements of No Child Left Behind rather than the wishes of the union's members. They perceived that these reforms were adopted without the superintendent fully considering the impact on union members or taking into account the members' views. Reflecting on her early leadership challenges, the superintendent recalls that "one of the biggest roadblocks in doing what's best for kids has been our union. The roadblocks get thrown in your face all the time because we can't do this and we can't do that because of our contracts." Both she and the board supported a Reading Recovery model, with after-school support provided to struggling students, many of whom came from low-income families or from families for whom English was not their first language. The union felt the proposed model would not be as beneficial as additional time for collaboration or non-instructional days for professional development. They perceived that the issue was that teachers lacked an understanding of the new curriculum, not that the students required additional support. Superintendent Cohen noted that the union resisted these reforms and ultimately tried using provisions in the teacher contract to scuttle them, particularly a provision requiring increased compensation for classroom teachers who would be expected to work after school with struggling students.

Despite her early focus on teaching and learning, the superintendent has realized that teaching and learning issues quickly become challenges related to resources. People, money, time, and programs are among the most common concerns that she deals with in her day-to-day work. As she reflects on her rise to office, she notes that she was "unprepared" for the challenges related to allocating resources, particularly the political challenges associated with resource decisions. While her preparation experience covered "budgets," the challenges that would confront her as a superintendent had inherently political dimensions for which she was largely unprepared. As she sees it, "Superintendents have to understand what the children need, over politics and over individuals' self-serving needs," and "we have to understand how to handle different perspectives."

Given declining enrollment and reduced state support for general education, Cohen feels as though she lives in a "perpetual budget cycle"—always making decisions about resources for the coming year while protecting those in the current year. Inevitably, the resources she must work with for the upcoming year will be equal to or less than those from the previous year. This is the case for the current year, as the district faces a shortfall of approximately $750,000, which is the largest one-year decline she has faced. Whenever she considers making major changes, she has to remind herself and those she leads that "the district's finances are not plentiful." She and her administrative team must make resource allocation decisions to maintain a sense of equilibrium—both fiscal and political. In terms of resources, she frequently considers whether programmatic choices can be sustained from year to year. She asks her administrative team to make clear decisions with "the best interests" of students in mind; yet, these decisions often face resistance from the teachers union.

REACTING TO RESOURCE DECISIONS AND GAUGING COMMUNITY SUPPORT AND DEMANDS

As she considers her original decision to redirect resources from a small intervention program toward the district's reading initiatives, Cohen recalls how principals and classroom teachers reacted. Her teachers and principals were aghast that she asked what proportion of the program's resources could be reallocated. Teachers and principals reacted fiercely, claiming that their hard work could not be sustained with a penny less. In responding to the principals and teachers, Cohen recalls explaining to them that she had to make difficult choices in relation to the district program and that her decision may run counter to their views. She recalls telling them,

> We can't say, "Oh you can't put a price on that," because our jobs require us to do that. We have to make those decisions. We can't just give blank checks to everyone, you know unless—you do that for a while, and then pretty soon your financial position is in the dumpster, and you're looking for another job and so . . .

In her mind, preserving the district's financial position is key, but an equally important responsibility relates to the preservation of the district's programs and services for students who, as she describes, "need them most." This approach defines her attempt to maintain a sense of fiscal equilibrium given declining resources.

The superintendent has worked to maintain a positive relationship with stakeholders in the community. She does so by engaging them in the resource allocation process and by asking them about their preferences and needs. This, she claims, is how she maintains a sense of political equilibrium. This endeavor, she says, "requires a significant amount of effort and energy and is easily the biggest responsibility a superintendent has." Her challenge is primarily to find productive ways to engage the community in order to identify stakeholder demands and current levels of support. From her vantage point, it is not enough to simply keep the community informed and infrequently ask them for their preferences. Rather, the challenge is to identify what the community wants and will accept given the resources available. This work is ongoing. Based on the information she has gathered, she perceives that the community (including her school board) is supportive of her efforts to improve reading achievement. The community's support has allowed her to focus resources on reading. As she states, "A few people want everything, some people want some things, a couple people want nothing, and trying to get everybody to be wise about resource allocation is pretty significant, especially with the budgetary issues that we face all the time."

In the past year, she has faced the community's demand for an updated elementary school to be built in a neighborhood with declining enrollment. The teacher's association has asked, at the same time, for a modest salary increase and increases in professional development funds. Parents have expressed concerns about the district's aging bus fleet, demanding that new buses be purchased soon. Principals have argued for more control over their building allocations at the expense of resources allocated for district-wide initiatives. And teachers have made specific requests for software, technology, and other tools to help reach an increasingly diverse student population. The superintendent has grown increasingly aware that she cannot serve all of these needs if she intends (which she does) to maintain the district's investments in reading. She finds that her role is less about communicating decisions she makes than about weighing the competing (sometimes conflicting) perspectives of those she leads and seeking to find a workable compromise with those around her, while still adhering to her commitment to provide reading support to students.

Despite her commitment to these investments, the superintendent points to the local teachers association as being the most difficult stakeholder to keep at bay. She notes that the association was furious when the district was unable to fund increased teacher salaries, despite receiving a significant infusion of resources from the state and continuing to invest in its reading initiatives. The situation worsened when the local paper published the school district's budget and noted that the state had provided an increase in appropriations for schools in the coming school year. This was not something the superintendent factored in during the budget process. As the superintendent recounted,

> What's going to happen to me when the town puts the budget in the [newspaper] because the state is giving us additional money—it's going to [look] to the average person that we're getting all of this extra money and so we should be in good shape. They don't even realize, unless we come out screaming, that we are getting leveled-funding locally, and by the time we pay the increase in retirement, the state retirement that we're all required to belong to—a small school division—for someone like us—it's going to cost us something like $284,000 more . . . For us, that's a lot of money. And, that's without the pay raise! And the state is giving us $500,000, so that's a big chunk of it right there. And, throw in oil and gas prices. So, by the time I pay all of that, there's nothing for

teacher salary increases. And, that's the part that's confusing because in a small area, people see that chunk of money and say, "Oh, they've got tons of money. They don't need any more money!" And, they don't understand administration either. They think you've got three people in your office and that's three too many! That we're top heavy!

Internal demands and support matter as well, though the superintendent has not experienced significant resistance from the district's administrators and classroom teachers. However, the superintendent sees that the principals and teachers are increasingly attempting to shape the district's agenda by demanding more support at the building level. This conflicts with the mandates being pushed by the state, which require greater alignment in teaching practices so that students are able to meet performance expectations. These demands often shape the goals of the larger district at the expense of the goals at the building level, creating conflict. As the superintendent notes, "I think sometimes teachers and principals—principals get very building minded—which is good, they're out to support their building, . . . and teachers are out to protect their classroom, to get what they need for their kids." Continuing, she adds, "I think that sometimes they [teachers and principals] lose sight of why decisions are made for the good of the whole and for the good of all kids, not just this one group of kids, or not just this one building." As superintendent, her task is to reconcile the demands of individual schools with the larger needs of the school district. According to the superintendent, she does this through her approach to decision making and gathering input from the staff in the district. In the past two years, conflict between the district and schools has emerged as a result of the district's reading initiative. The superintendent has required that each school withhold a portion of its Title I allocation to support reading efforts. This reduces the amount of discretionary resources available at the school level. These reduced resources have upset principals who feel as though the district is attempting to tie their hands.

PRODUCTIVELY ENGAGING STAKEHOLDERS IN THE POLITICAL PROCESS

As she considers how to proceed with the district's reading programs this year, Cohen faces the complicated task of structuring a process whereby stakeholders are engaged, interests are stated or made public, and differences between the interests are resolved. This process broadly forms the "political system" that she uses to bring divergent stakeholders to consensus regarding the resources available to the school district and the priorities that these resources will be used to address. As the superintendent reflects on the past year, she recalls her approach to this important work:

> When we were having to make decisions about having significantly less money—you know a $150,000—we set up structures to get people's voices heard. We did things where we worked with staff members asking "If you had more money, where would you put it?" and "If you had less money, where would you put it?" We did things in terms of any community groups we could wrestle together. We did parents together and parent groups in the high school and actually asked people some of the hard questions about, "You know you can only do so much. What is it that we should not be doing?" Those are hard decisions for anybody. We tried that business in getting everybody's voice and we kind of really came up with a plan about what we could do.

The superintendent has sought to cultivate support among the various stakeholders and ensure that all demands are known and addressed, but she has found that these efforts often prove less successful than she hoped. She acknowledges that these efforts are often hindered by the political interests of those who participate.

For example, at one of the forums she initiated last year, teachers and staff showed up at the meeting and used the forum to express their frustration that the budget for the coming year did not include increased salaries. The superintendent views this as a political "show of force" by the teachers union aimed at making the board uncomfortable and trying to disconnect them from their commitment to the district as a whole. The superintendent described the meeting as one in which employees "blasted the board" and raised a fuss about issues that conflicted with the expressed requests or commitments that they made previously. According to the superintendent,

> They jumped up there with things we had not even considered or talked about. They didn't even talk to the principal about it. They didn't talk to anybody about it. And that existing Board, there's no way in the world I could ask them to do that.

The fallout from this exchange has been significant. The superintendent acknowledges that the board's willingness to support previous commitments has now been weakened. As Cohen notes,

> The board's changed. . . . I had a board that was willing to trust. I was willing to involve people in the community and it backfired. Maybe it

didn't backfire in terms of—we still had to make the cuts, but still half of it backfired in terms of the relationships. Like I said, they trusted me that it was a good idea. I don't know if it was or not, but I always believed the idea was to be open and direct.

Adjusting Leadership in Response to the Stakeholders

Looking at the budget process for the coming year, Cohen acknowledges that she must often adjust her approach to respond to the stakeholders' concerns, objections, and support. This has been particularly true of her exchanges with the teachers union, which she describes as more "hostile" and "combative" than in years past. While the superintendent sees the community, her board, and the district's staff as supportive, the teachers union has been resistant and is attempting to influence the board's decisions. Their resistance to continued investments in the Reading Recovery program, for example, makes her feel as though she is required to "fight for what's best for kids," and she recognizes that each of these exchanges "costs her politically" as the union becomes increasingly defensive toward her position. Last year, the union opposed the district's investment in the Reading Recovery program with increases in time for teacher professional development not provided and compensation for the after-school component of the program not offered. This year, they promise to continue their objections.

Given current contract provisions, the superintendent has been required to pay classroom teachers $15 to $20 per hour for the additional time they devote to the program. Her inability to pay all teachers to work in the program has created tense relationships at some of her district's schools, making principals skeptical about continuing the program. As the superintendent states,

> One of the big issues we deal with is just intrinsic and extrinsic rewards for the staff. What we have created is a situation now with a lot of burnout. We really don't have the money to pay people for their time but we are asking a lot of them to comply with new mandates.

In previous years, the superintendent and her administrative team limited the number of teachers working in the program and instead relied on a combination of teachers and paraprofessionals. It was an affordable solution given the pressures on the district. However, the union objected as they felt that teachers should be leading the program and were entitled to compensation given that they were required to work beyond their contract period. As Cohen notes,

You try to offer them $15 to $20 dollars an hour. They will come right back and say, "You know, I just can't do it." So you have to start putting money on these extra hours to get over the old, "You pay me more or I'm not doing it." So now we have people who are really sticking around [for free] and volunteering after school for some of them and have somebody else that is getting paid for it. It's created a little problem that way for us.

While increasing compensation for teachers enables her to engage the district's staff in the program, it also limits the resources available to her to support other initiatives. Given union resistance, growing skepticism among her district's administrators, and increasing pressure to improve reading achievement scores, the superintendent faces a challenging year.

Reflecting on the Case Using Easton's Framework

Given the superintendent's recollections, it is now possible to reflect on the context surrounding the superintendent and consider how her experiences can be understood from the political perspective characterized by Easton's (1965) framework. More importantly, we can begin asking questions about what the superintendent can do given the political context surrounding her decisions. If we follow Wirt and Kirst's (1997) adaptation of Easton's framework, the first questions we must ask relate to the environment surrounding the school district, which shapes the superintendent's work. These questions consider, for example, the composition of the community, the various interests represented by the board, and the nature of the school district's relationship with the citizens. The following questions might help us begin to consider the environment surrounding the superintendent and her school district:

- How does the environment surrounding the school district shape the political activities that ultimately influence the superintendent's decisions about the allocation and use of resources?
- How does the environment promote or prevent certain resource decisions from being made, and what effect does this have on students, schools, and the community?
- What are the "boundaries" of the political system—that is, how might we know whom to include, whom to exclude, which interests to consider, and which interests to ignore?

- What previous decisions or actions might influence the environment? In what ways might these decisions or actions shape the current opportunities and restrictions?
- How does the superintendent's leadership agenda (e.g., her strategic priorities, values, or goals) influence her response to the political pressures in the school district?

Next, we can begin to consider how various inputs are influencing or are beginning to influence the superintendent's decisions. At this stage, inputs might be considered "signals" that are informing or are beginning to inform the superintendent's decisions. We can distinguish these signals—consistent with Easton's (1965) framework—as *demands*, which are expressed as needs or interests that the school district may or may not be able to meet, and as *support* that may embody the community's willingness to accept current and future decisions. We might ask the following questions:

- What inputs are currently actively influencing the superintendent's work and/or the decisions that the superintendent may be preparing to make?
- What demands have the community, stakeholders within the community, and interest groups made on the superintendent and her school district?
- What support has the community historically or recently given to the school district?
- What will threaten the support given to the school district if existing decisions are implemented as planned?

Up to this point, the questions primarily aim to identify the conditions surrounding the school district and superintendent that may (or may not) influence their resource allocation decisions. These questions help us identify the context in which political decisions may be made and the stakeholders who might impede or support these decisions, and they help us to begin to identify the stakeholders whom the superintendent must have "at the table" to begin making decisions.

The next questions relate less to the environment and more to the actual political process, which might be described as the way in which the superintendent navigates interests so as to reach a resource allocation decision. These questions relate to the political strategy that the superintendent might adopt as well as to her approach to fiscal leadership. Possible questions include the following:

- What process will the superintendent establish to solicit input from stakeholders who are making demands and expressing support for resource allocation decisions?
- How will the information be evaluated and prioritized given the scarce resources available?
- What information must be relayed to the community to inform them about the process and sensitize them to the resources available?
- How will interests be prioritized given the resources available and the rationale presented by the stakeholders?

An additional set of questions relates to the superintendent's decision as well as to the potential impact the decision may have on the stakeholders who sought to influence the decision-making process and consequently the broader environment surrounding the school district. These questions include the following:

- How might resource allocation decisions impact the stakeholders?
- How might information about decisions be relayed to the stakeholders?
- Which stakeholders will receive this information, and how might they react?
- How might the impact influence, shape, or alter their current support for and demands on the school district?
- What might the long-term impacts be on the political environment surrounding the school district and the potential to advance other initiatives?

Politically, we must also consider how the superintendent orients her leadership to the political environment given the pressures and demands presented to her, as well as the limitations on resources and room to act. Although this case does not make explicit reference to the superintendent's leadership style, we can use the leadership styles framework advocated by Wirt and Kirst (1997) to explain which style the superintendent might adopt given the political conditions at hand. While it may be tempting to assume that the superintendent's leadership style is static and unchanging, it seems feasible that the superintendent may adapt her style in response to the changing demands and support as well as in recognition of the roles that the stakeholders assume. The questions presented below invite you to consider how a superintendent's style evolves given both higher levels of conflict in the community and pressures placed on her by the stakeholders.

- What style of leadership does the superintendent adopt at various stages of the decision-making process?
- What prompts or causes the superintendent to adopt this style?
- What behaviors, statements, or concerns from stakeholders influence the style she adopts?
- How might the style help her to address the stakeholders' behaviors, statements, or concerns?
- When should the superintendent consider adopting a different stance or style?

Conclusion

The purpose of this chapter is not to provide clear-cut solutions. Rather, much like the other chapters in this volume, this chapter presents a case and asks you to think critically about the political conditions surrounding the superintendent and to determine whether there are opportunities that she could consider given the resource constraints imposed on her. In this regard, Easton's (1965) and Wirth and Kirst's (1997) work serves as a lens through which you can think about the leadership challenges presented in the case and consider how this superintendent, similar to other superintendents, might respond.

References

Bird, J. J., Wang, C., and Murray, L. M. (2009). Building budgets and trust through superintendent leadership. *Journal of Education Finance*, 35(2), 140–156.

Chambers, J. G., Shambaugh, L., Levin, J., Muraki, M., and Poland, L. (2008). *A tale of two districts: A comparative study of student-based funding and decentralized decision making in San Francisco and Oakland Unified School Districts.* Washington, DC: American Institutes for Research.

Easton, D. (1965). *A systems analysis of political life.* Chicago: University of Chicago Press.

Ellerson, N. M. (2010a, December). *Surviving a thousand cuts: America's public schools and the recession.* Arlington, VA: American Association of School Administrators. Retrieved from http://www.aasa.org/research.aspx.

Ellerson, N. M. (2010b, June). *Projection of national education job cuts for the 2010–11 school year.* Arlington, VA: American Association of School Administrators. Retrieved from http://www.aasa.org/research.aspx.

Ellerson, N. M. (2013). *Surviving sequester, round one: Schools detail impact of sequester cuts.* Arlington, VA: American Association of School Administrators. Retrieved from http://www.aasa.org/research.aspx.

Erlichson, B., and Goertz, M. (2002). Whole school reform and school-based budgeting in New Jersey: Three years of implementation. In C. Roellke and J. Rice (Eds.), *Fiscal policy in urban education: A volume in research in education fiscal policy and practice* (pp. 37–64). Greenwich, CT: Information Age.

Guthrie, J. W., and Peng, A. (2011). A warning for all who would listen: America's public schools face a forthcoming fiscal tsunami. In F. M. Hess and E. Osberg (Eds.), *Stretching the school dollar: How schools can save money while serving students best* (pp. 19–44). Cambridge, MA: Harvard Education Press.

Hartman, W. (1999). *School district budgeting*. Reston, VA: Association of School Business Officials International.

Leachman, M. L., and Mai, C. (2013, September). *Most states funding schools less than before recession*. Washington, DC: Center on Budget and Policy Priorities. Retrieved from http://www.cbpp.org.

Mazzoni, T. L. (1991). Analyzing state policymaking: An arena model. *Educational Evaluation and Policy Analysis*, 13(2), 115–138.

Miles, K. (1995). Freeing resources for improving schools: A case study of teacher allocation in Boston public schools. *Educational Evaluation and Policy Analysis*, 17(4), 476–493.

Monk, D. H. (1994). Resource allocation in schools and school systems. In T. Husen and T. N. Postlethwait (Eds.), *The international encyclopedia of education* (pp. 5061–5066). Oxford: Pergamon Press.

Odden, A. R., and Archibald, S. (2000). Reallocating resources to support higher student achievement: An empirical look at five sites. *Journal of Education Finance*, 25, 545–564.

Odden, A. R., and Picus, L. (2008). *School finance: A policy perspective* (4th ed.). New York: McGraw-Hill.

Plecki, M. L. (2000). Money isn't everything: Teaching school finance in a leadership development program. *Journal of School Leadership*, 30(6), 542–560.

Plecki, M. L., Alejano, C. R., Knapp, M. S., and Lochmiller, C. R. (2006). *Allocating resources and creating incentives to improve teaching and learning*. Seattle: Center for the Study of Teaching and Policy, University of Washington.

Wirt, F. M., and Kirst, M. W. (1997). *The political dynamics of American education*. Berkeley, CA: McCutchan Publishing Corporation.

Chapter 10

Choosing a Superintendent: A Decision Framework

Susan Printy

Hiring the right personnel has been shown to be among the best forms of quality control for organizations (Collins, 2001). Hiring a superintendent can be a quandary for selection committees, since it is impossible to know how things will work out in the future when decisions are based on each candidate's past history and the district's current status. Who will adequately lead the district into the projected future? What are the critical considerations? How do you make decisions? This chapter introduces the quandary of hiring a new superintendent for a small, rural, but rapidly changing school district. In this case, a decision needs to be made about which of two finalists should be offered the superintendency.

While other chapters in this text focus on superintendents' beliefs, dispositions, and actions, this chapter considers candidates for the superintendency. Each candidate in this particular case has experience in the role, but careful consideration must be given to matching the skill set of each candidate to the expectations and context of the job as described in the case. The decision framework presented here can be applied to describe any problem situation, so it is a useful tool for any educational leader to add to his or her tool kit. Additionally, it could be used by current superintendents to gauge personal fit to an open position before beginning the application process. Working through the case provides you, an educational leader, with a basic understanding of the utility of the decision framework.

Each candidate is a composite drawn from the transcripts of multiple superintendents who participated in focus groups for Voices 3; the community session transcripts are developed around the superintendents, using their issues and their own words. While both fictional candidates are highly qualified for the open position, each has definite opinions about a preferred direction for the district's schools. Importantly, however, both have needed expertise that they can bring to this growing community and the challenges it faces.

In Chapter 1, the editors of this book argue for the benefits of a thorough analysis of possible alternatives before adopting strategies for problem solving. Complex problems can overwhelm leaders as they strive to make the right decision. As a result, leaders can settle quickly on simplistic solutions or become paralyzed and fail to act (Cameron, Quinn, DeGraff, and Thakor, 2006). This chapter offers leaders and decision makers a framework to support development of their cognitive complexity, that is, the ability to understand the complexity of a phenomenon in terms simple enough to enable one to take action (Cameron et al., 2006). Such a condition seems analogous to "epistemic sophistication" discussed in Chapter 1 (Day, Harrison, and Halpin, 2009). The Competing Values Framework (CVF) assists leaders to describe thoroughly the quandary of hiring a superintendent before making a decision. In doing so, leaders illuminate the source of competing cultural values, recognize that the resulting tensions are endemic to organizational life, and sustain inquiry until the best choice becomes apparent.

The case centers on hiring a new superintendent for a small, rural, but rapidly changing school district. In this case, you will have the opportunity to take the perspective of a school board member or of a principal, teacher, or community stakeholder who serves on a hiring advisory committee. The chapter provides data about the district and transcripts of each candidate's comments to a community forum in response to a set of prepared questions. After describing the case using the provided data and the CVF, you will venture an opinion about which of two finalists should be offered the superintendency.

A development such as that described in the case can come on suddenly. The CVF will help you, in the role of a stakeholder, consider many ramifications of the case. In addition to the primary driver of the case—hiring a new superintendent—the case involves a multitude of school culture orientations and challenges. As you consider the case, you will draw on your own experience, certainly, but you also are pushed to develop cognitive complexity, that is, to take into account and benefit from multiple perspectives. Key values that motivated the

Voices 3 investigation—school improvement, democratic community, and social justice—are embodied in the cultural tensions identified by the CVF. As suggested earlier, the CVF is a tool that is useful for describing any problematic situation.

The Competing Values Framework

The Competing Values Framework (CVF) incorporates four dominant culture types that have been recorded in the organizational literature (Cameron and Quinn, 2011). The CVF offers leaders a coherent yet simple framework for organizational decision making based on an understanding of organizational culture, which results from a "complex, interrelated, comprehensive, and ambiguous set of factors" (Cameron and Quinn, 2011, p. 29).

The CVF was developed through a series of studies that examined indicators of organizational effectiveness (Quinn and Rohrbaugh, 1983). Statistical analyses described two major dimensions that organized the indicators into four main clusters (Cameron and Quinn, 2011). One dimension differentiates effectiveness criteria that emphasize flexibility, discretion, and dynamism from criteria that emphasize stability and order. That is, some organizations are viewed as effective if they are changing and adaptable (e.g., online schools), and other organizations are viewed as effective if they are stable and consistent (e.g., universities). The second dimension differentiates effectiveness criteria that emphasize an internal orientation, coherence, and control (e.g., religious schools) from criteria that emphasize an external orientation, differentiation, and competition (e.g., charter schools).

Together, these two dimensions form four quadrants, each representing a set of organizational effectiveness indicators. **Figure 10.1** illustrates the relationship of these two dimensions to each other (the shaded cross in the center) and to associated effectiveness indicators. These indicators of effectiveness represent what people value about the organization's culture and approach to work. They characterize what people hold as good and right and appropriate for the organization. "The four clusters of criteria define the core values on which judgments about organizations are made" (Cameron and Quinn, 2011, p. 31).

The **Hierarchy Culture** represents the earliest approach to organizing in the modern era, based on the work of Weber (1947). This cultural type prioritizes **control**, with indicators of effectiveness related to efficient, consistent processes for utilizing resources. The focus is internal, on stable work technologies and routines. The leader

	Flexibility and Discretion		
Collaborate	**Clan Culture** Leader Type: - Facilitator - Mentor - Team builder Value Drivers: - Commitment - Communication - Development Result: Human development and high commitment produce effectiveness	**Adhocracy Culture** Leader Type: - Innovator - Entrepreneur - Visionary Value Drivers: - Innovative outputs - Transformation - Agility Result: Innovation, vision, and constant change produce effectiveness	**Create**
Control	**Hierarchy Culture** Leader Type: - Coordinator - Monitor - Organizer Value Drivers: - Managing resources - Timelines - Consistency and uniformity Result: Control and efficiency with capable processes produce effectiveness	**Market Culture** Leader Type: - Hard-driver - Competitor - Producer Value Drivers: - Market share - Goal achievement - Profitability Result: Competition and accountability to customers produce effectiveness	**Compete**

Internal Focus and Integration — *External Focus and Differentiation*

Stability and Control

Figure 10.1 Competing values for organizational effectiveness
Source: Adapted from Cameron and Quinn, 2011, p. 53, used with permission.

emphasizes timelines and uniform work through organization, coordination, and monitoring.

Moving clockwise, the next quadrant introduces the **Clan Culture,** which is similar to a family-type organization. Attention to concerns of individuals was identified by theorists such as McGregor (1960), but connections between a people orientation and business success were not made until researchers studied Japanese firms in the late 1960s. An organization with a Clan Culture seeks to increase internal human capacities and flexibility and emphasizes the ability to **collaborate**. Effectiveness results from developing employees and increasing their commitment to the organization. Leaders work as mentors, team builders, and facilitators. Frequent processes relate to professional development, communication, shared decision making, and creating buy-in for new projects.

A third cultural type depicts the **Adhocracy Culture**, which was most recently described as the world shifted from an industrial orientation to an information orientation. The root of this label is "ad hoc"—meaning temporary or specialized. Such an organization values the ability to **create**. There is continual scanning of the environment and creation of dynamic and quick response; the organization must respond to the environment in order to survive. Effectiveness is determined by innovation, vision, and constant change. Innovative, visionary, and entrepreneurial leaders seek new ideas and products, agile employees, and organizational transformation. Senge's (1990) work on the learning organization reflects this perspective on organizations.

Finally, the **Market Culture** is based on the work of theorists such as Peters and Waterman (1982). An organization that represents market values emphasizes the ability to **compete**. The organizational focus remains external, but it is accompanied by interest in stability. Accountability to agents or customers and aggressive competition determine effectiveness. Hard-driving, competitive leaders achieve goals and demonstrate productivity, thus carving market share and maintaining profitability.

Those who have studied organization theory will recognize the above approaches to thinking about organizations and their actors. In fact, the CVF integrates four traditional approaches. As an analytic tool, it clearly reflects the editors' comments about theory in Chapter 1: theory describes "(1) which elements of a situation are most worth paying attention to and (2) how these elements relate to one another"(p. 8).

Designers of the CVF claim that effective organizations need to pay attention to *all* of the organizational issues encompassed in the framework, though it is clear that (1) some organizational members and leaders will have preferences for certain orientations and values and (2) organizations will need to prioritize certain quadrants at various points in time. An organization operating in chaos, for instance, needs to introduce stable operational routines, while an organization with few customers might focus on developing new products or securing new clients.

After reading the case that follows, you, the reader, will assume a role on the Selection Advisory Committee for the school district. To help you make a decision about your preferred candidate, you will complete three tasks using the CVF.

The Summerland Community

Summerland Township spans 652 square miles across terrain marked by rolling hills and cornfields in the southern region of a midwestern state (the community context, while based in fact, is fictional). Three green energy facilities have announced firm plans to begin operation within the district taxation and attendance area in the near future, spurred by the support of both the previous and the current governor, by the state's generous tax exemptions, and by collaborative development efforts by the state's three major universities. With the recent shifts in the auto industry, green technology start-ups can capitalize on the state's skilled workforce and on cheap, available industrial facilities and land. The start-ups near Summerland will be lean, but there are already plans for rapid expansion in the next decade. Commercial developers are moving full speed ahead with plans for building necessary housing stock and retail/commercial infrastructure.

The Green Technology Companies

- Last year, **CBY Technologies of China** announced a partnership with wealthy investor Winchell Barclay to open a **battery** plant on the eastern boundary of the school district. Already, CBY has cornered the market on batteries for cell phones, iPods and iPads, and low-cost computers through its current Silicon Valley plant. The company plans to exploit its Midwest location to build batteries for electric cars and, within a few years, to open a factory for electric cars. A recent case study by the Harvard Business School indicates that CBY is one of the top four manufacturers worldwide—and the largest Chinese manufacturer—for each of the dominant rechargeable battery technologies (Li-Ion, NiCad, and NiMH).
- During the summer, the **State Biofuel Conglomerate** announced a new sweet corn hybrid being grown throughout the Midwest. With a higher sugar content than even sugar cane, the corn is economical for use as a **biofuel** because it does not require the starch-to-sugar conversion of other corn products. A processing plant for the new corn is under construction on the southern edge of the district, near the corn belt that crosses into adjacent states to the south.
- A local man has a new **wind turbine** design for residential and small industrial use and is ready to begin production in an old automotive power drive plant just west of the town of Summerland. J. D. Swayle and two other collaborators will have one production line ready for operation by Christmas. All graduates of the

engineering and entrepreneurship programs at the nearby land-grant university, the partners are committed to investing in the state and helping to turn around the stressed economy.

The Summerland School District

Advertising itself as a school district that blends the old with the new, Summerland Community Schools are headed for big changes. More classrooms will be needed in a hurry! The current superintendent, Ralph Jansen, a longtime stalwart of the community, realizes that retirement is the next phase of his career. He has laid the groundwork for change and growth, but he has remained insistent on stability and efficiency as core values that should guide all decisions. He has provided all stakeholders with information about the schools, and established decision-making processes are in place. As superintendent, Jansen has emphasized open communication with his stakeholders. As an example, board agendas, minutes, budgets, and other documents are available on the school website. He blogs on the superintendent's page several times a month, and he invites constituents to email him directly, promising a response within 24 hours. The following excerpts from the most recent Summerland School District annual report (see **Figure 10.2**) offer evidence of a good school district that has not yet faced the rapid economic and demographic shifts that the new industries portend.

Summerland Community Schools Annual Report	
District Profile	**Community Profile**

Mission Statement   April 2013
The mission of Summerland Community Schools is to engage the community in providing a quality educational environment that promotes successful lifelong learning for our students, staff, and community. In the accomplishment of this mission, our actions will reflect these values:
   Integrity,
   Responsibility,
   Tradition,
   Respect,
   Dedication,
   Pride.
	The Summerland Community School District encompasses parts of seven townships (Coolidge, Glover, Franklin, Rogers, Rome, Comstock, Hilldale) and the town of Summerland, including seven post office districts. Situated in the midst of rolling farmland and scenic lakes and streams, the school district typifies a community working to blend the old with the new. Summerland Community School District provides employment for many local residents as well as quality educational and enrichment opportunities. Residential construction has been a major source of

(continued)

(continued)

revenue and community growth. Family and tradition remain strong in our community as we continue to develop and grow.

Belief Statements April 2013

We believe that . . .

- Well-kept facilities provide appropriate environments for productive learning.
- Communication is the key to effectiveness, in classrooms, schools, and across the district.
- Appreciation of cultural diversity strengthens our schools.
- Caring, competent, and informed staff support the learning of all students.
- The school must provide all students with a technologically proficient staff.
- Students learn best when they feel good about themselves and their accomplishments.
- Personal investment and discipline contribute to a quality education.

Summerland Teaching Staff

The Summerland professional staff consists of 99 teachers and four counselors. Master's degrees are held by 74 percent of the faculty, and 100 percent of our teachers have a bachelor's degree and teaching certificate and are teaching in their endorsement area. All staff members continually strive for improvement by attending seminars, workshops, and conferences. A committee of representatives from each building organizes professional development to meet district-wide school improvement goals and to help our district provide the best educational opportunities for our children.

Continuous Improvement Goals, 2013–2015

Picking up the PACE

People

- Recruit, hire, induct, support, and retain high-performing staff
- Ensure all employees are highly qualified and skilled for their positions
- Develop and nurture a district professional culture of leadership, integrity, and creativity

Achievement

- Accelerate learning and raise expectations for every student
- Increase student achievement and teacher development through focused, individualized professional learning aligned with achievement goals
- Adopt models and structures based on practices that are research based and demonstrated to be effective

Community

- Strengthen collaboration with parents to enhance learning for their own children and all children
- Expand and strengthen community involvement and partnerships to foster ownership of and shared responsibility for our school

Environment

- Provide environments that optimize learning and teaching and that are safe, secure, and well maintained
- Support a high-performance learning culture based on trust and mutual respect

School Profiles*
Summerland Elementary School

The elementary school hosts 735 students, kindergarten through fifth grade. We offer full-day kindergarten as well as a kindergarten prep program. We also run an after-school latchkey program for those working parents who need some after-school child care.

Points of Pride:

- Northwest Evaluation Association formative testing in all grades for instructional planning
- DIBELS and MLPP formative assessments
- Building-wide Response to Intervention
- Students score at/above state averages in MEAP tests
- Differentiated instruction and inclusion
- Class and individual goal setting
- Students of the Month in all classes
- School and community service partnerships and celebrations
- Parent-teacher organization
- School and community literacy activities, such as book fairs and author visits
- Family dances, picnics, and holiday festivities

Ed Now! School Report Card*

Summerland Elementary teachers and staff are very proud of the status we earned for the 2012–2013 school year.

English/Language Arts	B
Mathematics	A
Indicators of School Performance	A
Adequate Yearly Progress (AYP)	Met AYP

Composite Grade A
Percent Proficient
Midwest Educational Assessment Program

Year	ELA	Math
2013	85%	76%
2012	87%	80%

Summerland Middle School

Our school is a place where we believe that student safety and achievement are priorities. We believe that all students can learn, and we provide a supportive learning environment as students navigate their way through this time of adolescence. We have a very dedicated staff that is committed to delivering a great education for our 425 students.

Points of Pride:

- MS students scored at or above the state averages in all MEAP testing areas
- Opportunity to earn high school credit in Algebra I, Spanish I, and Earth Science
- Coteaching with Special Ed and General Ed teacher in seven different classes
- STAR tutoring program
- Grade-level teaming for teachers
- Student Assistance Team to help struggling students
- Positive Behavior Support system
- Incentive day each trimester for students who turn in all work and have good behavior

Ed Now! School Report Card*

Summerland Middle School received the following grades for the 2012–2013 school year.

English/Language Arts	C
Mathematics	A
Science	A

(continued)

(*continued*)

Social Studies   C
Indicators of School Performance   A
Adequate Yearly Progress (AYP) Did not meet AYP

Composite Grade   B
Percent Proficient
Midwest Educational Assessment Program

Year	ELA	Math	Science	Soc. St.
2013	82%	78%	84%	85%
2012	76%	73%	78%	82%

Summerland High School

Our high school offers a wide variety of subject areas appealing to our 584 students. It is our desire to prepare students for the many aspects of living. Some will be pursuing further education in such institutions as colleges, universities, and technical schools. Others will want to immediately enter the job market, and we will do everything possible to see that each individual will be prepared to succeed in the area best suited to his or her needs. We appreciate the dedicated interest of the school staff and members of the community, as they all contribute to the overall educational process.

Points of Pride:

- 33 students completed Advanced Placement classes in Calculus, Chemistry II, Art History, Psychology, English Language and Composition, U.S. History, American Government, Statistics, and Microeconomics
- Fine Arts and Performing Arts classes
- Mentoring program
- Tutoring
- Responsible Thinking Program

- 50 percent of students participate in 50 Cougar teams in 18 sports
- Full schedule of extracurricular activities, including:
  - Debate
  - Drama
  - Environmental Club
  - Math Club
  - International Club
  - Key Club
  - National Honor Society
  - Student Council
  - Youth in Government
  - Yearbook
  - Writer's Club

Ed Now! School Report Card*

Summerland High School received the following grades for the 2012–2013 school year.

English/Language Arts   B
Mathematics   C
Science   A
Social Studies   B
Indicators of School Performance   A
Adequate Yearly Progress (AYP)   Met AYP

Composite Grade   B
Percent Proficient
Midwest Merit Assessment

Year	ELA	Math	Science	Soc. St.
2013	53%	49%	65%	84%
2012	42%	42%	49%	81%

Retention Rate

2011–2012	96.4%
2010–2011	95.1%
2009–2010	96.6%
2008–2009	98.4%

Graduation Rate

2011–2012	86.15%
2010–2011	85.42%
2009–2010	83.34%

Choosing a Superintendent: A Decision Framework

Dual Enrollment Data		
Juniors and Seniors in College Classes	2010–2011	96% completion (N = 26)
	2009–2010	100% completion (N = 32)
2011–2012 100% completion (N = 25)	2008–2009	100% completion (N = 12)

Figure 10.2   Excerpts from the 2013 Summerland School District Annual Report

*Note: All of Summerland's schools have subgroups with fewer than 30 students, and there are no students in the Limited English Proficiency category. Ed Now! is the state accountability system based on student achievement and schools' self-assessment. Indicators of School Performance are self-reported by each school and provide an indication of the school's culture, educational program, and allocation of resources. Students in grades 3–9 participate in the MEAP—Midwest Educational Assessment Program. The MMA—Midwest Merit Assessment—assesses students in grade 11 and eligible students in grade 12 on state-mandated high school core content expectations.

Meet the Candidates

The Summerland school board worked with a regional superintendent search agency to find candidates for Jansen's replacement, and the board has narrowed the applicants down to two preferred candidates: Mr. Edward Hill and Dr. Jayne Broward. In separate community forums, each candidate responded to the same set of questions. The audio files were then posted on the district website. As a Selection Advisory Committee member, you were present at the original interview sessions; you subsequently read both transcripts carefully. Each transcript consists of a brief biography of the candidate and his or her responses to the same set of questions.

Mr. Edward Hill

Mr. Hill is an experienced superintendent, having turned around two chronically underperforming school districts that also experienced financial difficulties. Originally from Kentucky, Mr. Hill most recently lived and worked in Indiana.

1. **Warm-up question: Can you tell us something about being a school leader that has been important to you?**
"To me, as a superintendent, it is not one event, but what has been most purposeful for me has been that it's not one person, but it really has required building leadership capacity. And I think that my role as a superintendent—that was the biggest 'aha'—yes, as superintendent you oversee and you're responsible for all the principals and others.

Really it has been about building that leadership capacity and particularly the role of the administrative leadership team. It doesn't just happen, but it really requires nurturing and then setting goals with them and holding people accountable, not accountable as individuals but as the whole team. And I think our greatest accomplishments have been as a result of building leadership capacity with the administrators, but also recognizing teacher leaders and recognizing what their roles can be in influencing and improving student learning in the respective schools."

2. What does it mean when you say, "What's best for kids?"
"For me, it is about student achievement, bottom line. When I first got to the district office, we were just coming out of an under-performing label. And so, through a school improvement plan, we had to focus to drive back to what we were really after, which was student performance and opportunity and succeeding for all kids. Within a year we were able to get out of that status. What we did was set up strategies through professional learning communities. What that did was give us an umbrella under which to focus everything and then work down towards that improvement. We asked those critical questions, 'What do students know? How do they know it?' and 'If they are not learning it, what do we do about it?' That kind of drives everything.

"As a leader, the tiers of administration kind of get in the way. The higher up you go, if you want to say it that way, the further you can get away from students and what they need. It's probably been my professional liability over the years, but I do everything I can to stay back at the level of the students. As a principal and now as a superintendent, I attend every banquet, every awards assembly. I go to athletic events. When I'm having the worst possible day, it's sort of like a principal with kindergartners, but I do it with high school. I go over to the school and luckily my office is pretty darn close to one of them. Or I go to an activity and I see the things that these kids are doing that don't always get in the paper and I think, 'This is why we're doing what we're doing.'

"Our focus this year will be whatever it takes for those who aren't still at that level. And I encourage teachers too. They live in a real sheltered world sometimes and a home visit is probably one of the best things they can do. I'll give you an example. A teacher can go through college, get a job in the educational community and that is who they are, surrounded with every day, and they think everybody lives in their world. Administrators are guilty of the same thing. For many, many students, school is the best part of their day. Teachers sometimes lose sight of what those kids go home to at night. For a lot of them, it is not a very wonderful experience. I try to provide activities and things where they can see the bigger picture of what the student's world is like."

3. What particular ability are you proud of?

"Having come from a primarily business background as well as education, I brought two skills to the table, if you will. Being a finance person and sitting in every chair in every educational spectrum, when I became a superintendent eight years ago, I had the good fortune of getting my first job in a school district where the superintendent and the business administrator were removed. I had to reconstruct the finances as well as support the educational structure. And I guess that kind of set the stage for me for the rest of my career because my next move was five years in another school that had woeful financial problems. So I've never had the opportunity to go to a school district that was the, you know, the 'dream job.' I've always been—had the opportunity to go in and be a troubleshooter. And that wouldn't be the case here.

"The districts I've been recruited to go to were always districts that were in high need. I guess that's good that I've found my niche in the industry. And I've come to one conclusion, that money drives the whole system because if you know where the dollars are then you can do the education. I remember when I worked for my first superintendent who was an esteemed academic and I was his assistant. After working for him for over a year, I finally had the guts to say to him, 'You can have all the great dreams in the world but if I can't put the resources at your disposal, your dreams evaporate.' And I think that as superintendents we probably feel most that particular area, the finance side of our industry, because if you look at the news reports and research, it's usually finances that are the Achilles' heel of all quality educators in moving their districts. Money is something people relate to."

4. How do you motivate teachers?

"I'd say as a superintendent, I intentionally and regularly use every opportunity I can find to put a face on the work that we do. So often the work that we do—we talk about students but we don't really know the students. We don't always listen to them and so on. When I was in Kentucky, we had an enormous number of kids dropping out of school. We started to realize the assumptions that we made about why those kids dropped out or what those kids' needs were. In fact, our assumptions often were just the furthest thing from true.

We started to realize the fact that dropouts probably worked harder than kids that are in school, in order to make their lives work. I do an open-ended focus group with our at-risk kids, just saying, 'We're trying to understand what we should be saving, what we should be changing in the schools that you guys attended. You're the experts. We're trying to figure out what are the things we should be asking some hard questions about.' And then I let them go, talking to me. It takes about an hour.

"And I bring those results back to the elementary school teachers, and we talk about the school. I can do that because I'm superintendent, if you know what I mean. What it does is something that I think is really lacking in our system on a couple of dimensions. One is, I think, that elementary school people stop thinking about kids that they've had. They care deeply in the year when they personally have them as students, and for sure at the end, wherever they transition into the next school. Okay? And I think that we need to do a much better job about caring for all our kids.

"I did that once at a school board meeting. The board members still say that was the best board meeting they ever went to in their lives. Those kids were so great when they talked. They didn't talk to the board members; the board members were [eavesdroppers]. They talked about their lives, why they left school. All we did was just say, 'Why did you leave? Is there anything we could have done differently that would have kept you in school?' Those were the only two questions for a couple hours. The schools I am referring to were in some challenging areas. You might think you don't have these kinds of kids in your rural school. Your community will change, is changing. The Internet and the phone lines have broken down a lot of those barriers about distance. We might think we are really isolated. I think those days are over."

5. What is your attitude toward the latest school reform legislation?

"I would say that one of the things that has occurred and continues to occur is that educators have started to take responsibility, beginning with for No Child Left Behind. Early on, after a visit to Washington, DC, I realized that NCLB had everything to do with politics and nothing to do with kids. Eventually, educators made NCLB about kids, as they took on the accountability and recognized that, for all the 1100–1200 pages that are in the law, there were some parts that we could use to benefit our students. Do we generally complain about the reform legislation? Yes, because there is usually a lot to complain about.

"I also believe that behind the scenes there are more interventions being put in place for students that we didn't have in our classrooms before. There is more focused money and more focused curriculum on standards for improving teaching and learning than there ever has been in the history of education. I think that there are a lot of things that initially were bad for education. But I think what has happened is that educators have forgotten about the politics and have tried to apply policies to improve education. I don't think anybody is looking for credit for that, but I think that, in reality, we have tried to look beyond the politics. I listened to a man at a conference one time and he made the comment that those kids that we leave behind, many times it is because they are coming to our schools with an entirely different framework of education. Our expectation has always been that they and their families and their history will change to fit our education system. For us to make sure that students aren't left behind, we have to figure out a way that we change our framework to fit the needs of those kids. I think those are some of the things that have occurred because of the accountability piece."

6. What are your thoughts about shared decision making?
"The decisions we make are so important because they do impact the children. If we ever get to the point where we think that only our opinion covers all the needs of all those children out there, and the community and all, it would take a pretty good person to be able to do that. For me, the whole shared decision-making process has always been positive. I've had good results. For example, as a principal in hiring teachers, I never had people come in and sit and talk to me and I hired them. I've always involved—I hate to use the word 'committee,' but I would have the department chair, depending on what the job was, and a couple of teachers. They would create and ask the questions about learning and instruction and how it all fits. I would ask more general educational theory questions. When that decision was made, there was never the feedback of 'Oh he picked them.' It was 'We picked them' and there was real ownership in that. The more ownership you have in a decision, the fewer problems you will have in implementing the decision.

"It is sometimes hard to get the people to come forward and be part of it. All of us have found that you can invite them to come in and they don't always do it. I'm getting ready to start planning a third high school for our district, so I've sent out a letter inviting some people to come in. About 18–20 will be on this core committee. I won't make decisions single handedly about what that school will be like because there is too much history and tradition in the whole area. We'll do some programming of staff next week on what that might look like. I can think of very few things that haven't worked well as a result of using more of an inclusive, empowering approach as opposed to a single-handed dictatorial approach, in my career anyway."

Dr. Jayne Broward

Dr. Jayne Broward has held the position of superintendent of the North Huron School District, about one hundred miles north of Summerland, for six years. Before her appointment in North Huron, she was a superintendent in Ohio. She is originally from northern Indiana, where her children and grandchildren reside.

1. Warm-up question: Can you tell us something about being a school leader that has been important to you?

"I am always excited about working with principals to get them to become educational leaders. With many, it is just a matter of time. A lot of our principals were trained to be managers and they are very competent there. It took us quite a while—book study and discussion. Some veteran principals needed to be kicked out of the building and told to get professional development and be involved in the Leadership Academy and those kinds of things. You can tell a real difference whenever our principals have been involved in those learning experiences in terms of coming back and working with staff. Principals have made a turnaround in terms of recognizing that kids need to learn and that it's not just our job to teach but to teach all the kids who need to learn.

"The thing that's moving us now is to work with the staff as professional learning communities. We are really trying to work hard on our own, in terms of learning through book studies and collaboration."

2. What does it mean when you say, "What's best for kids?"
"Truly what is best for kids is to help them improve their academic achievement. Particularly in today's world, if kids don't have a core of academic skills, they can't go any place in the world. So, for me, it's what happens in the classroom that is most important. And I see my job as providing the resources, the training, the support, the vision, the passion, to get these things done. So, it's all about what happens in classrooms, and it's all about learning.

"In my schools, we value teachers, but we provide them guidance for what they teach. With reading, we don't give people a whole lot of choice. Our organization has evolved now as expectations have been set and met and we've involved people in setting new expectations. We have a K–12 math curriculum group that has now implemented a brand new math program, which is trying to get more to a conceptual based math. I think conceptual math is being more readily adopted, certainly at the elementary level and perhaps at the middle school. The high school seems to be a bastion of not wanting to change. We ended up having a teacher leader that we moved from the middle school to the high school and made a couple of changes in personnel and through that essentially had success on adopting conceptual math K–12. So it was a real celebration for us to watch the growth of our faculty and our teachers come together, research best practices of math, have discussions over a two-year period of time and culminate with a presentation to the board of education saying, 'This is what we want to do.' All of this in service to the kids, doing what's best for them.

"We do need to work hard to bring our high schools along, but we can't expect the high school to change in a vacuum. We won't be successful. I think it has to be a systemic change, all the way up from pre-K, actually all the way up through grade 16 or 20. And I think we have a disconnect there, too, that we need to look at. The focus is always on the high school and certainly there are some changes we would need to make there. But if we don't have the foundation before the kids get there, I'm not sure *just* changing the high school will make the difference. I think the American high school has to change. . . . I think that it has to, if only to be competitive. I think globally . . . that's the only way. It will continue to happen. We need to continue to figure out how we want to change 9–12 education for our kids."

3. What particular ability are you proud of?
"I was very fortunate to actually be involved as a teacher leader in a school district that was very progressive. In particular, the emphasis that they put on professional development for teachers really shaped a lot of my beliefs and a lot of things that I have carried with me as I moved into both the principalship and then subsequently into a superintendent position. We had so many marvelous individuals that were a part of that leadership group that actually went on to other positions. I'm not sure what the count is, at one time I did know, but it is easily 10–15 people eventually went somewhere else, primarily as superintendents. I think the ability to be able to transform an organization because of the professional development provided to both teachers and the leadership staff—that really made an impact on me

and shaped the kind of superintendent I strive to be. We now spend a lot of money on professional development and focus in on what it is that we want to try and accomplish. We bring quality training to our teachers. We'll send them wherever we have to, whatever it costs to get what they need so that they can be successful. And then everyone benefits through their professional community activities."

4. How do you motivate teachers?
"I believe it comes down to communicating. I would call it also building those relationships. It is your presence and the relationships you build. When it comes down to you making a decision on something, people know you and know your credibility and know you're there for kids, maybe because you've gone into classrooms or touched base with teachers.

"Another important thing I do as superintendent is to have that consistent message that we are about students, pre-K through 12. I want teachers having that sense that they aren't just teachers for a set time that the children are in their class or their elementary school, but that they want to continue to know kids as they move up through the high school. Similarly, I want the high school teachers having some sense of what happens in the lower grades. Connections between our elementary schools, middle schools and high schools are important.

"And then I guess just another piece for me is about talking with people continually about continuous improvement. And we do a pretty good job in that arena, but we aren't there. It's just that we can keep getting better. And so I think there are certain messages that are really important for us to be sharing—and again, with our staff, in the schools and in our central office."

5. What is your attitude toward the latest school reform legislation?
"Going back to the start of 'reform' as I have experienced it, I think No Child Left Behind helped us immensely. I think that dealing with accountability over the years, the reality is now, it has been worth it. We're much better than we were fifteen years ago and that's because we now know where our kids are in terms of their learning. We know that we need to be responsive to all our children. We know that these are the strategies that we need to employ to take us from point A to point B. I'm not sure, had we not had that push from NCLB, that we would have moved in that direction. I'll be the first one to say that there are pieces in much reform legislation that are absolutely abominable in my estimation, you know, the one-size-fits-all approach

to education is a real concern. But, in fairness to legislative efforts to push reform, I think public education is doing a better job today than it was even a decade ago, and I think a lot of that can be tied back, from my standpoint, right back to NCLB. The reform work around Common Core, though not legislative reform, has furthered our ability to help all kids reach high standards.

"I can tell you about my experience as an Ohio superintendent that goes to the heart of the discussion here. I went in to our elementary buildings and told teachers, 'You are the most important group here because you are the first ones that any kids see. If you don't get the groundwork laid, you know, it makes it doubly hard at the high school because the kids aren't prepared, and don't have the skills they need to build upon.' So I outlined the expectations I had: we will have every child reading above grade level as they leave second grade (actually what I said was 90 percent). I freaked them out; *90 percent* freaked them out. As a matter of fact, the funny thing about the story was that they sent an emissary back to negotiate the 90 percent figure with me in my office. Of course, this was more than ten years ago; teachers weren't even tracking kids' learning. They had no idea the first question to ask. How many kids were reading at or above grade level? They couldn't answer that. Which told me volumes about where they were with respect to knowing every child. The emissary tried to negotiate: 'How about 72 percent, or 78 percent, or 80 or something like that?' And I said, 'No, we aren't going to do that. We can do this.' And it's really about your beliefs and what you can accomplish and I held that line. It took us about five years to get there.

"Our schools steadily saw that progression of kids reaching that goal, all it did was to reinforce them to feel that, in fact, they can do it. A lot of this can just be daunting to our teachers who look at this and think, 'Every kid, every time, every day.' That can be hard, particularly when you are adding on more and more and when new students are entering your schools. The good thing, though, is that conversations are changing everywhere. . . . I hear teachers actually talking about instructional practices. I hear principals, when I go in the community, it's very exciting."

6. What are your thoughts about shared decision making?
"I always come back to simple things. I guess my current district, before I got there—I guess there was a run of superintendents and principals that were pretty autocratic. So, when I was hired as superintendent, I put committees together to hire my high school principal

and my elementary principal. And I remember my secretary saying to me, 'This is pretty good, [Dr. Broward.] Where'd you learn this?' And I thought, 'This is sort of a common sense thing.' But they thought it was really high-level stuff and I just thought that was odd. And it was the same thing with our curriculum adoption last year. Math was a big issue as far as what program to go with, and I called the teachers in and asked them for input and direction on where they wanted to go. They were very thankful and very supportive and we had great debates and discussions and when it was all over a group of them said, 'Well, thanks for letting us just be a part of this.'

"I thought that was incredibly odd that teachers weren't a part of making those kinds of decisions and, for me, it was a common sense thing. And it worked out really well. I mean, they complain less about it if they're a part of the decision. They can't complain about it if they were there to decide it. And they have a vested interest in being supportive of that. So it's one of those things, that it's a win/win situation. Sharing decisions, in my experience, has been very, very helpful."

Using the CVF for Decision Making

After attending the interviews and reading the transcripts closely, you have a good idea of each candidate's vision for schools and of each one's leadership style. As a member of the Selection Advisory Committee (pick one role: principal, teacher, or community member), you plan to do some reflective work before the SAC meets to decide the next steps. (Alternatively, this exercise could be carried out with a group.) The process described here helps you, as an educational decision maker, to delve deeply into both the current reality of the district and the impending changes within the broader community that will challenge the way the schools currently operate. The CVF is a tool that helps leaders stay engaged in "inquiry" for the time required to understand the situation thoroughly.

It is not uncommon for educational decision makers to be barraged with conflicting information, new mandates and requirements, and social problems or social innovations that reach into schools. Labels such as *opportunities* or *threats* are often applied to such developments. These labels, however, might limit the range of responses that are considered. School leaders often find uncertainty and ambiguity to be intolerable, and so they might take steps to quickly explain away the uncertainty. (That's what "organization" does—puts order to ambiguity.) To solve problems quickly, leaders often rely on intuition, incomplete information, saliency, concreteness, beliefs, or political interests in selecting both which issues to pay attention to and how to approach the issues. Unfortunately, in so doing, leaders can also limit their understanding of all the facets of the problems and make decisions that are less effective than they could be.

Task 1: Describing the Current Reality

Your first task as a member of the Selection Advisory Committee is to use CVF Worksheets A and B (**Figures 10.3** and **10.4**) to map out Summerland Community School District's current reality and culture. You will use any information found in the early pages of this chapter—that is, information about the Summerland community, the green technology companies, and Summerland School District. You should also draw on the Summerland School District annual report. **The worksheets should be copied from the text so that you can record your notes on the printed page. You will also need to make reference to Figure 10.1 to guide your inquiry.**

Begin by familiarizing yourself with the CVF Worksheet A (**Figure 10.3**) in relation to **Figure 10.1**. On the horizontal axis, write the word "internal" on the left end. This will remind you that issues located in both the Hierarchy and Clan quadrants deal with issues internal to the school district. On the right end of the horizontal axis, write the word "external" to remind yourself that issues located in both the Adhocracy and Market quadrants relate to the external environment. With the vertical axis, write "flexibility" at the top and "stability" at the bottom. The Clan and Adhocracy quadrants both deal with change, while the Hierarchy and Market quadrants value stability.

Using information in the case, you will describe Summerland Community School District—*as it currently operates*—according to the four culture profiles of the CVF. Do not, at this point, consider the kinds of changes that the new industries will necessitate for the district. Record key ideas in the appropriate quadrant on CVF Worksheet A. Start with the Hierarchy Culture. What evidence in the case suggests that Summerland Community School District has controlled and stable internal operations? Is there evidence of coordination, monitoring, and organization? Are resources well managed? Are school routines consistent? Make notes on CVF Worksheet A (see **Figure 10.3**) in the Hierarchy Culture quadrant.

Consider the Clan Culture and write notes in the corresponding quadrant. What evidence points to collaboration and professional

Clan Culture	Adhocracy Culture
Hierarchy Culture	Market Culture

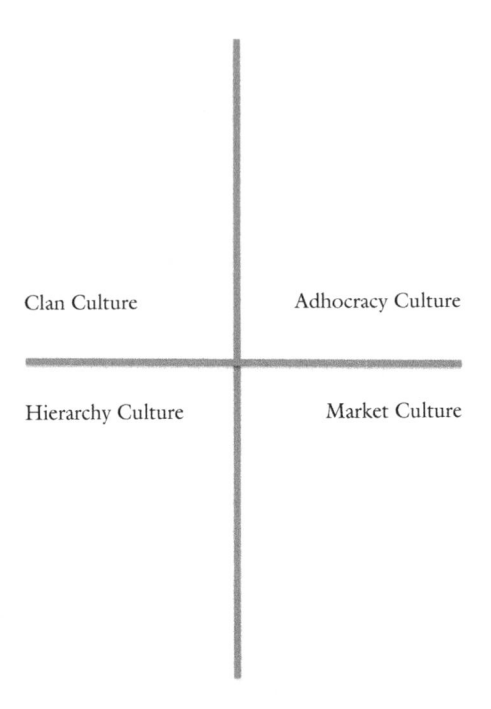

Figure 10.3 CVF Worksheet A

development? Are leaders facilitators and team builders? Do teachers demonstrate commitment? Are strong communication processes in place? Record your notes on the worksheet.

Continue around the framework in a clockwise direction. The Adhocracy Culture is defined by innovation and entrepreneurship. To what extent is the current superintendent, Mr. Jansen, a visionary? Has he readied the district for transformation? Is the district agile? Record your notes.

Finally, consider the current reality from the Market Culture perspective. Is the Summerland district focused on achieving high goals and maintaining a strong client base through competition? Is accountability to the community a prevalent value? Complete your notes on the current situation of the district. With evidence about the case gathered from all four perspectives, you have a thorough description of the Summerland district on CVF Worksheet A. You might also have some questions that are not answered by the information presented.

Task 2: Exploring the Tensions Introduced by the Green Industries

The CVF assists in exploring potential tensions resulting from a new "trigger" situation. The new green industries will bring new families to Summerland School District, resulting in a larger and more diverse student population. The impending changes result from developments "external" to the schools and will require that schools become more "flexible" in order to respond. Summerland schools will need to create varied responses and will benefit from an Adhocracy Culture in the near term. New resources will be available, but the district will also have new expenditures. CVF Worksheet B (see **Figure 10.4**) positions the green technologies in the Adhocracy Culture quadrant.

Think about specific ways in which the new industries will force the district to change its current operations. The pressure to change, which originates in the external environment, will introduce tensions that reach into all the other quadrants (indicated by the three arrows in **Figure 10.4**), demanding accommodation through other cultural perspectives. For instance, new students will require more class sections and probably new schools. The coordination of expansion and the management of resources will put pressure on the district's established processes and routines; thus, tension will be located between the Adhocracy and

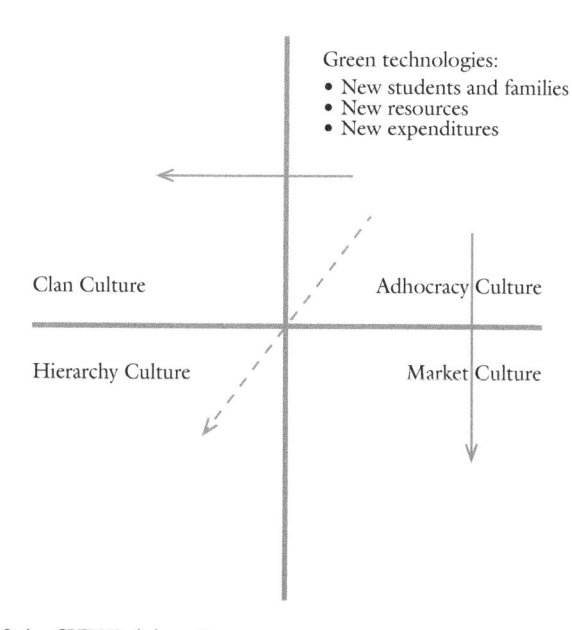

Figure 10.4 CVF Worksheet B

Hierarchy quadrants, represented by the dotted-line arrow in **Figure 10.4**. A more diverse student body will introduce new challenges for the professional staff and will require new training. Will the professional staff have a say in the new plans? These kinds of conditions introduce tensions as illustrated by the solid arrow going from the Adhocracy quadrant to the Clan quadrant. Finally, new members of the community are likely to have different expectations for the school district in terms of program offerings, achievement, and public perception or reputation. Tensions around these issues reach into the Market quadrant from the Adhocracy quadrant, also represented by a solid arrow.

Use CVF Worksheet B to imagine other sources of tension the district can expect as a result of the rapid changes brought about by the new technological investments, and record them on your worksheet. Tensions can be described between any two quadrants in the framework. As an example, teachers will need to retool many instructional practices in response to the more diverse student population. This is a tension between the Hierarchy quadrant (i.e., instructional processes) and the Clan quadrant (i.e., development of teachers' capabilities). Spend enough time in this inquiry to exhaust consideration of possible sources of tension.

Task 3: Select the Best Candidate for Superintendent

Having completed both Worksheet A and Worksheet B, you are ready to consider the skills and experience of each candidate for the superintendent's position. Given your description of the current situation and your analysis of tensions likely to be introduced by the green technology sector, take each candidate and consider which is best positioned to lead Summerland School District into a future where the schools are deemed "effective" from multiple perspectives. Working in groups can facilitate more complete consideration of issues, as different individuals will pay attention to different facts of the case.

Finally, review all of your analytic information. What is missing? What additional questions would you like to ask the candidates? Which candidate has strengths that will help address the complex situation of the school system? Your goal is to make a decision about which candidate has the best fit for Summerland's future.

Working through all possible developments—describing situations, identifying tensions, and aligning talents and values of individuals with the situation at hand—helps you, as a decision maker, to thoroughly explore possible solutions to problems. Looking at developments in this way allows you to be strategic, to take balanced perspectives, and to search for underlying difficulties before acting.

Reflection on Your Leadership

Everyone has different preferences based on what they value, how they interact with others, and the kinds of organizations they like to be involved with. Did you, in your analysis, put priority on "control," "compete," "collaborate," or "create"?

- Which of the four quadrants represents your preferences? Said another way, in which organizational culture would you be most comfortable? In which culture would you be most uncomfortable?
- Remember that effective organizations pay attention to all four quadrants. How does using the CVF push you as a leader to consider the benefits of incorporating other perspectives into your decision-making processes?

Conclusion

The Competing Values Framework (Cameron and Quinn, 2011; Cameron et al., 2006) assists in the development of future leaders because use of the framework encourages cognitive complexity. Developments such as those described in the case can come on suddenly. The CVF encourages those who hope to make strategic decisions about schools to explore a more thorough set of possibilities before acting. While the primary driver of this case is the need to hire a new superintendent, the district faces a multitude of value orientations and challenges. Those who consider the case draw on their own experience, certainly, but they also are pushed to develop cognitive complexity, that is, to take into account and benefit from multiple perspectives. Key values that motivated the Voices 3 investigation—school improvement, democratic community, and social justice—are embodied in the cultural tensions identified by the CVF. The approach to using the CVF for decision making described in this chapter can be applied successfully by aspiring or current educational leaders to reach better decisions by utilizing new leadership skills.

Additional Reading and Resources

Many books, chapters, and dissertations have used the Competing Values Framework as a theoretical basis for describing organizational leadership, culture, change, and effectiveness. Leaders with facility in using the CVF add value to their organizations by creating new leadership behaviors through the "interpenetration of the positive opposites" (Cameron et al., 2006, p.80). For an explanation of this leadership skill, see Cameron, et al., (2006).

The CVF can be effectively utilized for assessing—and then deliberately changing—organizational culture. See Cameron and Quinn (2011) for tools to use and processes to follow to create a preferred future culture. If your interest is more personal—that is, you seek understanding and development of individual leadership—Robert Quinn has written several books utilizing the CVF, including Quinn (1996) and Quinn (2004). Both build on the CVF to illuminate the source of difficulty in challenging situations and a path to personal transformation.

REFERENCES

Acker-Hocevar, M., Hyle, A. E., Ivory, G., and McClellan, R. (2014). Chapter 1. In G. Ivory, A. E. Hyle, M. Acker-Hocevar, and R. McClellan (Eds.), *Quandaries of the small-district superintendency* (pp. 1–19). New York, NY: Palgrave Macmillan.

Cameron, K. and Quinn, R. E. (2011). *Diagnosing and changing organizational culture: Based on the competing values framework*. San Francisco, CA: Jossey-Bass.

Cameron, K. S., Quinn, R. E., DeGraff, J., and Thakor, A. V. (2006). *Competing values leadership: Creating value in organizations*. Northampton, MA: Edward Elgar.

Collins, J. (2001). *Good to great: Why some companies make the leap . . . and others don't*. New York: HarperCollins.

Day, D., Harrison, M. M., and Halpin, S. M. (2009). *An integrative approach to leader development: Connecting adult development, identity, and expertise*. New York: Routledge.

McGregor, D. (1960). *The human side of enterprise*. New York: McGraw-Hill.

Peters, T., and Waterman, R. (1982). *In search of excellence*. New York: Harper and Row.

Quinn, R. E. (1996). *Deep change: Discovering the leader within*. San Francisco, CA: Jossey-Bass.

Quinn, R. E. (2004). *Building the bridge as you walk on it: A guide for leading change*. San Francisco, CA: Jossey-Bass.

Quinn, R. E., and Rohrbaugh, J. (1983). A spatial model of effectiveness criteria: Towards a competing values approach to organizational analysis. *Management Science*, 29, 353–377.

Senge, P. (1990). *The fifth discipline: The art and practice of the learning organization*. New York: Doubleday.

Weber, M. (1947). *The theory of social and economic organization*. A. M. Henderson and T. Parsons (translators). New York: Free Press.

Chapter 11

The Self and Leader Expertise

Rhonda McClellan, Gary Ivory, and Adrienne E. Hyle

If you are a superintendent of a small district, or if you aspire to be one, then you are setting out to be a quandary negotiator. It would do you no good to seek to be a quandary avoider; our examples in this book show that quandaries are inherent in the superintendency. Nor do we see superintendents as quandary solvers, for many quandaries never go away, or they go away only temporarily—rising again in new forms or with new parties concerned. But we do believe you can learn to negotiate quandaries: to make good decisions rather than ones that exacerbate quandaries, to make conditions as good as they can be for the greatest number of people, to face difficulties rather than letting them fester or passing them off to others, and to foster solutions that will be of long-term—rather than merely short-term—benefit and that will "support the higher level goals of [your] organization" (Bereiter and Scardamalia, 1993, p. 57). Part of being a great leader is quandary negotiation.

In part, negotiating quandaries requires your ability to draw upon a variety of resources (1) the formal skills you have learned in your preparation program; (2) others' experienced voices, theories, frames, and models that help capture patterns of human thought and behavior; and (3) what you have within you. Your ability to use these resources improves your ability to negotiate quandaries and advances your leadership expertise. Expertise should not be confused with knowing the answers to quandaries. Expertise is your ability to draw upon knowledge, experience, and yourself simultaneously—to arrive at more quality decisions (see **Figure 11.1**). The preparation you have received in your program and the encouragement in earlier chapters of this book to construct and rely upon a leadership platform, to enlist the wisdom of experienced superintendents' voices, and to play out decisions based upon the theories and models have provided a big step in your leadership development. We have yet, however, to take the time to talk about you, and who you are, and how you yourself influence your leadership. This is what we will do in this chapter. Let's talk about one of the most significant contributors to negotiating quandaries; let's talk about cultivating your leadership expertise. Let's talk about you.

Consider, if you will, the many superintendents that you have known. Did you find among them great range and diversity in their ability to work within the ambiguity of the job? For example, did you find that regardless of a superintendent's training and experience—many years or few—some of them did a better job of leading than

Problem/Quandary
"Experience" and "Context"

Leadership Platform
Beliefs and Values

The Self
Self-Efficacy
Goal Orientation
Self-Regulation

Skills and Theories
Formal Education/Experience

How well you recognize, reflect on, and respond to all of the above influences your level of expertise. With reflection and adaptation, you are **developing your leader expertise.**

Leader expertise fosters quality decision making.

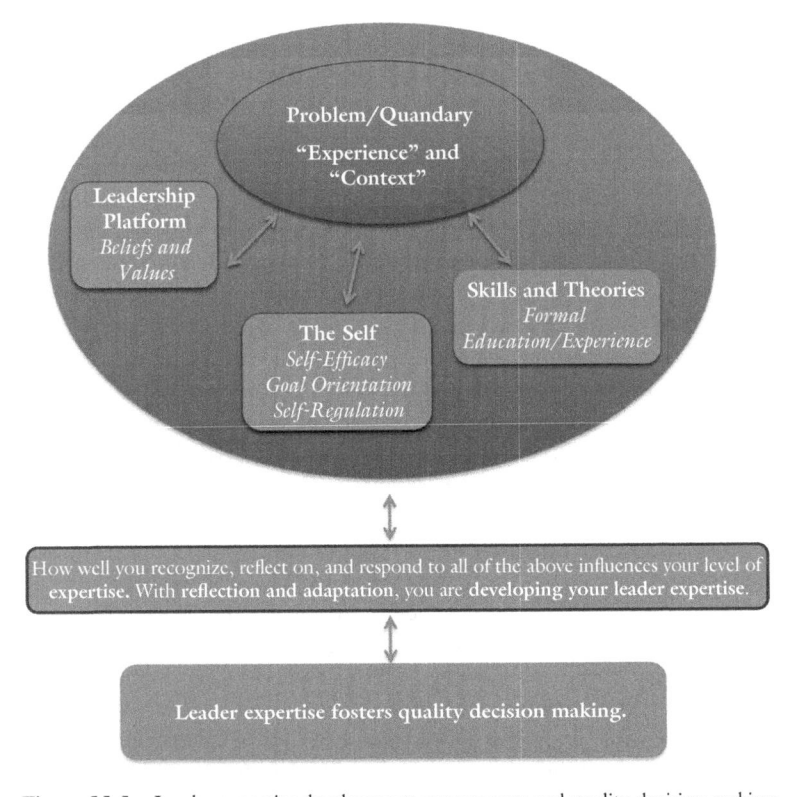

Figure 11.1 Leader expertise development components and quality decision making

others? Why do you think this is so? To put the example in the context of a classroom, have you considered why students if given the same set of information end up having varying degrees of knowledge and varying degrees of ability to use that knowledge? Although the students are given the same information, they comprehend and use it very differently. In time, we see some of these students deepening this knowledge—they test it, adapt it, and arrive at new conclusions based upon the initial information. Other students, however, do not.

So back to our point about superintendents: Is it possible for someone to have ample information and many years of experience and not have expertise? Do knowledge and experience result in expertise? Why is it that some superintendents are good and others aren't so good?

For the past few years, the three of us have entertained this question. We wondered (and we still wonder), How does a person cultivate expertise? We've read and thought a lot about what scholars have learned about experts (the chess master, the Olympic athlete, the concert pianist). How did they get that way? And how can those of us who will never be world-renowned experts use the lessons of expertise research to become something more than competent? Particularly, we've come to appreciate that negotiating quandaries requires developing expertise. We find great usefulness in Bereiter and Scardamalia's (1993) characterizing expertise in terms of one's career and their distinction between the expert and nonexpert career:

> *The career of the expert is one of progressively advancing on the problems constituting a field of work, whereas the career of the nonexpert is one of gradually constricting the field of work so that it more closely conforms to the routines the nonexpert is prepared to execute.* (p. 11, emphasis in the original)

Bereiter and Scardamalia tell us that experts recognize and embrace the need to negotiate quandaries—to make thoughtful decisions in a constant state of flux and ambiguity—whereas the nonexpert attempts simply to fix problems and maintain stability. Surely, we have all seen and worked with nonexperts. We have seen products of their work: a focus on daily procedures or policies that fix problems; a focus on maintaining things as they are—with little reflection on what might be done differently; and a focus on minimizing problems and squelching dissonance. We describe them as "being in a rut," "maintaining the status quo," "taking the easy way out," or "phoning it in." They are not exciting or inspiring to work with, and they may not seem particularly excited about their own work. They demonstrate little or no professional growth. You may be asking yourself, "Okay, I don't want to be like that. So, what can I do and how do I start to develop my leader expertise?"

Leader Expertise Development

We ask you to reflect upon the historical arguments shaping our understanding of leadership and of what it takes to develop leadership. One set of scholars argued that traits determine a person's ability to lead. You have probably heard the claim: leaders are born and not made. It's that simple. Just who you are coming out of the womb determines if you can or cannot be a leader: smart, tall, good-looking, male. This rigid, and frankly out-of-date, thinking was replaced by belief in skills-based and behavioral approaches. These researchers claim that for individuals to lead, they must learn the right stuff and act upon that information in the correct way. Knowing a multitude of skills, behaviors, contingencies—and yes, even theories—can make you a leader. Sounds familiar, doesn't it? So often in leadership programs, and even in leadership scholarship, a lot of energy is spent discussing and promoting these "competencies." To stop here, though, we believe is a bit shortsighted. Think about it this way: In our book about navigating quandaries, we may have tempted you to believe that with the right theory, framing just the right episode, you could arrive at a way to deal with the issue. This, we are afraid, is leading you down the wrong path. Quandaries are too ambiguous for clear-cut answers. Your target is the quality decision.

You may have with this book guidance and encouragement to think and act beyond the simple response—but we regret to inform you that this book has *not* made you an expert leader. Leader expertise development is not dependent solely on formal sets of knowledge—it comes from something more than the traits you were born with and a book about skills and procedures. Leader expertise is an amalgamation of who you are, what you know, and *factors hidden within you and your ability to draw upon and develop them all.*

So how do you influence your own leadership expertise development? As Bandura (1997) notes, you are a "partial contributor to what you become and do" (p. 6). "The greater your foresight, proficiency, and means of self-influence, all of which are acquirable skills, the more successful you are in achieving what you seek" (p. 8). He further explains that your "capacity for self-influence" allows you to be "architects of your own destiny" (p. 8). So, how do you influence—you?

We start with an easy one: self-awareness. Know yourself. One of the pivotal components of leadership, and one commonly overlooked in leadership programs, is self-awareness. Your leadership platform serves as a promising foundation to help you understand what you think and believe. You may need to reflect on *why* you believe what you do. Take the time to reflect upon influential experiences and encounters you have had, of the person you want to become, the passions you want to pursue, injustices that spur you to act, things that come easily for you, pet peeves that really get under your skin, and reactions that you later are proud of or regret. You are your key to becoming a leader. Everything that happens is viewed through your lens.

To complicate matters, contemporary leaders must be able to operate within arenas that are quickly and constantly changing. To be able to navigate contemporary challenges and changes "out there," strangely enough you must begin "in there." *You* and your keen self-awareness are the keys to unlocking the promise of those challenges and changes. Your self-awareness will give insight into why you want to respond the way that you do. This insight may also keep you from doing something you'd later regret. Self-awareness interacts with your having and receiving information and influences how you respond. If you are conscious of your knowledge, capabilities, impulses, and mind-set, these internal factors become useful resources.

Let's assume that you have a firm grasp of knowledge from your experience and training. And we hope this book is prompting you to see the practical value of theories and self-awareness Let's spend more time discussing these three factors in detail: capabilities, mind-sets, and impulses. Although many psychological factors contribute to unlocking the hidden aspects of your potential, these internal resources tap directly into your developing expertise.

In scholarly literature, these factors are known by the terms self-efficacy (capabilities), goal orientation (mind-sets), and self-regulation (control of impulses). For this chapter, we will no doubt oversimplify what has emerged in leadership literature as aspects that are complex and difficult to discuss and research. Bear with us. First, we note that although we discuss these things independently of one another, they are interdependent and interconnected. One affects and is affected by the others. So imagine, if you will, interlocking cogs; when one turns, the whole system turns. When one stops, they all stop. One goes backward, and the entire system shifts into reverse. Although we discuss each of these separately and removed from your own psyche, we are talking about how the status of the internal factors collectively is affecting your willingness to engage with risk and responsibilities (self-efficacy), your motivation to reflect and learn (goal orientation), and your control of thoughts and behaviors (self-regulation). Your "cognitive cogs" influence your leader expertise development.

Self-Efficacy

We can't help but hear Cher as we write this: "Do you believe in life after love? I can feel something inside me say, 'I really don't think you're strong enough.'" Okay, well, this may be a bit harsh (although a catchy tune), but much of who we become depends upon our belief in—ourselves. Do you see yourself as a leader? Do you seek out leadership opportunities? How do you ride the risky line between great success and failure? Are you strong enough to be introspective, to know your strengths and what you need to change—without being overwhelmed? Do you believe in you? The lead scholar on self-efficacy, Bandura (1997), argues that "personal aspirations, outcome expectations, perceived opportunities, structures, and constraints provide an integrated view" (p. 10) of a person's perceived potential. This may be just a fancy way of saying that before you can lead others, you have to believe that you are capable of leading. The belief you have in yourself is greatly influenced by your past experiences and your observations of the performance of others (who are similar to you).

Sounds easy enough, doesn't it? But we learn the following from leadership research: (1) few people talk about beliefs in their own capabilities; (2) few people reflect upon the performance that they tug along with them from the past into the present and how it affects their belief in their ability to do the job—to resiliently overcome past hardships—and their motivation to lead; (3) and therefore few people acknowledge how they might be getting in the way of their own destiny. Self-efficacy is strengthened by taking on leadership challenges, reflecting on the performance, and being aware of vulnerabilities (Wood and Bandura, 1989). Further, self-efficacy is the belief that you have the capacity to "mobilize the physical, intellectual, and emotional resources needed to succeed" (Eden and Aviram, 1993, p. 352) in the face of these challenges. How you feel about your performance in these endeavors affects your self-efficacy and in turn influences your level of motivation to take on (or avoid) more challenges. In terms of leadership development, the more you feel capable, the stronger your self-efficacy will become and the stronger will be the orientation toward leadership that you acquire.

So explore with us for a minute. How comfortable are you with claiming leadership? Isn't it interesting how difficult it can be for some individuals to say simply, "I am a leader." Can you? Say it. Okay, now aloud—"I am a leader. I have the ability to become a good leader." Does it feel a little awkward? Did you find yourself giggling or scowling? Why do you think this might be? Are you getting in your own way?

Trust Your Resilience

So if you have taken on the mantra "I am a leader," you are ready for the next step. Take on a leadership challenge. Keep in mind, the challenges discussed throughout our book may have no clear-cut answers or responses. You may not feel fully capable of taking on such a nebulous challenge. Remember, all your experiences can provide growth opportunities for your passion and leadership abilities. Orient toward leadership, take on a challenge, and prepare for hardship. Sounds like a downer, doesn't it? Well, if it were easy, then everyone would want to lead, right? So, let's think about this differently. Why not try on, "I will do the best I can with what I know and who I am and how I can operate within the context." Believing in this will help you draw upon your knowledge and yourself and will engage your self-efficacy. Acknowledge that you have the right tools to address the challenge.

So, "hardship." We don't talk about this word very much, do we? Know yourself and prepare for things to get tough. Curious, isn't it? In leadership classes, we spend a lot of time talking about crafting collaborative visions and then "walking that talk." Know where you want to take the organization and then go there. We often forget to discuss and prepare for "the hard times." If we do discuss these challenges, they emerge in conversations about carefully crafted solutions falling short or conflict erupting among the people within the organization. But let us cut to the chase. Being an expert requires not only practicing every day but also bouncing back up and continuing to practice every day even though you feel that yesterday you were not successful. If anything, feel capable in your ability to keep going when it gets tough and to figure out how to make it better.

It is a bit of perseverance wrapped up in a whole lot of regrouping, analyzing why things did not work, fixing it, and getting back into action. You have to take on a leadership challenge and be willing not only to fail but also to learn from your mistakes and regroup to carry on. Always remember you will fall short; the real strength comes in picking up and thoughtfully pushing on. It is thinking about your performance perhaps with a new mind-set. Integrated with other factors of the self, self-efficacy—belief in your abilities and motivation to persevere through hardships and continue developing—fosters your ability to negotiate quandaries of the superintendency. Now let's turn our focus to those mind-sets.

Goal Orientation

Let's talk about mind-sets. There are two types of behavior in the world that are almost legendary. The first is that of the person who cannot hear criticism. This person's associates know to not bother pointing out any flaws or mistakes because he or she will not take it well—will become defensive or hostile. The second type is often described as "fishing for compliments." This individual will ask how she or he has done, but we know when we hear the question that our assignment is to come back with only good news, because that is really all the individual is interested in hearing. When around these two types, others become careful of what they say for fear of offending their friend, colleague, or even family member. Psychologists refer to these legendary behaviors as two kinds of feedback-seeking. Unfortunately, people who cannot hear criticism or who fish for compliments can be harming themselves, because they miss opportunities to hear feedback that might actually help them, particularly by supporting their growth.

These feedback-seeking behaviors come about when people are focused on their efforts, i.e., having a goal orientation (GO) (Cron, Slocum Jr., VandeWalle, and Fu, 2005). Interest in GO grew out of earlier research on feedback-seeking behavior. Individuals seek feedback to reduce uncertainty about what goals to pursue and the behaviors required to achieve those goals. Individuals also seek feedback about how their behaviors are being evaluated by others in order to achieve a sense of competency (VandeWalle, 2003). GO addresses this question: When you are striving to accomplish something, what do you want the outcome to be? You might think the answer to this question is simple: when you are working to accomplish something, you want to achieve the outcome. Achieving the outcome would be defined as success for you. But there are several ways to define success. Different people want different forms of outcomes.

Two Kinds of Goal Orientation

A simple model of GO (Radosevich, Vaidyanathan, Yeo, and Radosevich, 2004) posits that there are two major goal orientations: a learning goal orientation (LGO) aims to improve one's own learning, and a performance goal orientation (PGO) aims to demonstrate one's competence. The orientations are not mutually exclusive, and both can serve positive purposes. Leaders need to learn, and they need to show that they are competent. But the importance of GO rests on the possibility that excessive concentration on a performance goal might drive out interest in a learning goal and thus inhibit our development of expertise. VandeWalle (2003; Cron, Slocum Jr., VandeWalle, and Fu, 2005) posited that one's goal orientation influences one's feedback-seeking behavior, which in turn influences one's performance. VandeWalle explained that our GO is really related to our attitude toward expertise and to whether and how we think we should pursue it. Here are ways to understand these two different mind-sets:

(a) Do you think leaders are born or made? People with a PGO tend to think that leaders are born, that they just have the talent, "the right stuff." They view ability "as a fixed, inherent attribute that is difficult to develop" (VandeWalle, 2003, p. 583; Dweck, 1986; for a reader-friendly book on this topic, see Dweck, 2006). People with an LGO, on the other hand, tend to think that persistence and effort are more important than talent, that "the bars are full of incredibly talented people" (Werner, 1996, p. 113).

(b) People with a strong PGO may look askance at effort. After all, if you really had the right stuff to be a leader, you would not have to work that hard at it. Putting in a lot of effort, in the eyes of these people, only proves that you lack real talent. LGO people see attempts (and even failures) as learning and growth. Leadership development is a lifelong commitment.

(c) Now let us ask: What is your attitude toward feedback? PGO people may see feedback as a judgment of one's competence, perhaps even one's self-worth. For those with a strong LGO, however, feedback is seen as useful for correcting errors and improving competence.

(d) Finally, VandeWalle (2003) maintained that in response to failure, a PGO might lead one to "withdraw from the task, make negative ability attributions, and report decreased interest in the task" (p. 584), while an LGO could lead a person to "persist, escalate effort, [and] engage in solution-oriented self-instruction" (VandeWalle, 2003, p. 584; see also Day, Harrison and Halpin, 2009), and even to enjoy the process.

VandeWalle's (2003) descriptions have direct implications for growing in expertise as a quandary-negotiating superintendent. It is apparent in the research literature that having a variety of rich developmental leadership experiences can prepare one for future leadership roles (DeRue and Wellman, 2009; Dragoni, Tesluk, Russell, and Oh, 2009). But one's goal orientation in leadership experiences is key. The more one sees the experiences as opportunities for learning, the more one will learn from them. In fact, the more one has a GO to learn, the more leadership experiences one is likely to have, perhaps because one seeks them out (Dragoni et al., 2009). Dragoni and her colleagues argue strongly that having challenging leadership experiences is critical to growing as a leader, so her research is important for quandary negotiators. Do you see how self-efficacy might be connected here?

A Third Kind of Goal Orientation

To muddy the waters a bit, we offer another type of goal orientation, in addition to the previous two (Radosevich et al., 2004). Radosevich et al. further subdivide PGO into performance *prove* goal orientation (PPGO) and performance *avoid* goal orientation (PAGO). Persons with a strong PPGO want to *earn* external judgments of competence. Those with a strong PAGO want to *avoid* external judgments of incompetence (see also Hendricks and Payne, 2007). Now, again: it is not that any of these are necessarily good or bad. We all need to learn; we need to appear competent, at least sometimes; and we need to avoid looking incompetent. But if we are interested in gaining expertise, then we need to consider what GO theories say about the effect on our learning of the different orientations. We saw above that PGO might hinder our learning. Cron et al. wrote that PAGO has an "especially deleterious impact" (2005, p. 58) on self-regulation and other aspects of learning. It should be clear why. If we want to avoid an external judgment of incompetence, perhaps the surest way to do that is to avoid trying anything at which we might appear inept.

One of us (Gary) started studying Spanish over 40 years ago. Unfortunately, Gary's goal was often to avoid sounding like an idiot and hearing people laugh at him. The surest way to avoid having people laugh at you is *to not try* speaking a second language. But the surest way to not learn a second language is to not practice it. So, Gary missed countless opportunities to improve. This is how PAGO is theorized to work. Now, let us apply the concept to organizations troubled by a failure or a scandal. We commonly hear that they go "into damage-control mode." This is understandable. Avoidance of a perception of having failed can be a necessary tactic. But organization leadership that focuses too much of its attention on avoiding the appearance of failure is likely to be missing opportunities to learn and improve (Dragoni et al., 2009).

Where Do We Go from Here?

So, what are the takeaways from this brief introduction to GO? If you aspire to be a superintendent who thrives as a quandary negotiator, how can an understanding of GO help you? Think carefully about the whole issue of developmental experiences. It is important, if you aspire to be a better leader, to seek out developmental experiences—that is, experiences that force us "to initiate new ways of coping with problems, reveal when existing approaches are inadequate" (Dragoni et al., 2009, p. 732), and require us to perform in front of new audiences. It seems to us vitally important that we approach these developmental experiences as learning opportunities rather than as ways to prove ourselves—or worse, as hurdles that may cause us to fall on our faces. *The three factors (developmental experiences, self-efficacy, and goal orientation) go together, and you need to be alert to all of them*: a strong self-efficacy and a learning goal orientation might well lead you to seek out developmental experiences and to learn most efficiently from those experiences; the experiences are needed to put your learning goal orientation into practice and to develop your self-efficacy. A strong self-efficacy and a learning goal orientation also motivate you. After a failure, you can decide, "Well, that's it; I do not have the right stuff or the capability to be a leader." Or you could tell yourself, "Mistakes are an expected and acceptable part of the development process" (DeRue and Wellman, 2009, p. 871). "Now I know where I need to work on myself so I can approach similar situations differently, or improve my leadership capacity so as to do better next time" (DeRue and Wellman, 2009; Dweck, 1986, 2006).

If you do not have a strong self-efficacy and LGO, you need to work on yourself and seek to come to an understanding of how these two "cogs" are interconnected and of how important they are in developing your expertise. If you do not have access to developmental experiences, you should go somewhere that will give you that access. Dragoni et al. (2009) go a step further: If you are offered a new job, even a promotion, consider it carefully. Will it provide you with developmental experiences, especially as a quandary negotiator? Unless those developmental experiences will be available to contribute to your "long-term professional growth" (Dragoni et al., 2009, p. 741), that new job or promotion may not be right for you.

SELF-REGULATORY KNOWLEDGE

Consider the task of scanning a leadership article. An expert has learned how to skim pages quickly, pick out text of interest, and gloss over paragraphs and even pages that are considered unimportant for the topic being reviewed. Researchers of expertise and leader development agree that the knowledge essential in accomplishing the task of scanning the article is self-regulatory knowledge (Bereiter and Scardamalia, 1993; Day et al., 2009; Zimmerman, 2006).

Self-regulatory knowledge is self-knowledge relevant to performance in some domain. It is part of an expert's knowledge in a domain, but it is not knowledge *of* that domain. It is knowledge that works *for me*. It will not necessarily work for you.... Self-regulatory knowledge may be thought of as knowledge that controls the application of other knowledge. Thus it is often referred to as "metaknowledge" or "metacognition." (Bereiter and Scardamalia, 1993, pp. 59–60)

Scholars also agree that any two individuals are likely to differ in their self-regulatory knowledge strategies for accomplishing a task because leadership knowledge, leadership experiences, and orientation goals may be different. What one individual does to accomplish the task may not be what another does to accomplish the same task.

According to Zimmerman (2006), self-regulatory knowledge comprises three personal elements. The first of these is behavioral self-regulation knowledge, that is, knowing how to adjust what you do to accomplish a task. For example, if organizing the workday to accomplish professional reading in the morning is not yielding the time needed for reading, a shift to afternoon reading is behavioral self-regulation. The second element is environmental self-regulation knowledge, that is, knowing how to adjust the environment. While working on the reading task, if you cannot focus because the room is too cold or too hot, adjusting the thermostat or moving to a different location are environmental self-regulation strategies. The third personal element is covert self-regulation knowledge, that is, knowing how to adjust your cognitive and affective states. If your reading progress is still not moving in the right direction and the deadline for completion is rapidly approaching, a covert self-regulatory knowledge strategy would be to handle the angst from this pressure by visualizing the task completed.

Zimmerman (2006) goes on to propose that behavioral, environmental, and covert cognitive/affective "self-regulatory processes are linked to key self-motivational beliefs during three cyclical phases: forethought, performance control, and self-reflection" (p. 707, see Figure 39.2 as well). Each of these phases focuses on processes related to learning, practice, and performance. Forethought focuses on processes that precede and can enhance learning; performance control focuses on processes that improve the quality and quantity of learning; and self-reflection focuses on processes that occur after learning.

Forethought

Research has shown that experts establish more specific techniques or processes in their goal setting than nonexperts and that their decisions about how to accomplish a particular goal are more technique oriented. When working on the reading project noted earlier, given an hour, the expert might set the specific goal to scan the readings, then sort them by topic, then read the finance section first, whereas the nonexpert might intend simply to "scan articles." Task analysis by novices or nonexperts is frequently "superficial or inaccurate . . . [and] can lead to ineffective or even counterproductive efforts" (Zimmerman, 2006, p. 710).

Performance

In this phase, goals determined in the forethought phase are operationalized and, as needed, adjusted. In each instance, experts engage in these processes more regularly and successfully than do novices. A variety of strategies are used to adjust actions to achieve goals, including self-instruction, imagery, task strategies, time management, environmental structuring, and help-seeking. Self-instruction involves "talking" through negative performance and is similar to imagining or seeing oneself successfully completing a task. Task strategies include developing cognitive maps, note-taking, and mnemonics. Time management refers to purposefully budgeting the use of time to accomplish goals. The process of seeking help also fosters the development of expertise in that people, things, or models are selected to assist in learning. Environmental structuring refers to selecting or creating effective settings for learning.

As you acquire more expertise and develop as a leader, you will be able to be specific and accurate when you monitor and record your performance. You will be able to provide a full set of details about your learning—when, how long, what worked, and what did not (Zimmerman, 2006).

Self-Reflection

In this final self-regulatory phase, experts are more likely to adapt processes to accomplish the task; novices are more likely to avoid the task (Zimmerman, 2006). As an expert, you will grow in the ability to evaluate your performance in ways that help focus your actions, accuracy, and helpfulness. You will be able to compare your current efforts and outcomes against your and others' past best efforts. You will also be able to effectively compare your efforts against those of your competitors. And, you will be able to compare your performance against a national standard or record. Research has shown that when self-evaluative standards are realistic, not too high or too low, learning is enhanced (Schunk, 1983).

Self-Regulation and Leadership

The focus of self-regulation research in the leadership literature has been on adaptive self-regulation, a "social process in which leaders attempt to understand and adapt to the role and performance expectations of organizational constituents" (Sosik, Potosky, and Jung, 2002, p. 212). Through adaptive self-regulation, leaders detect discrepancies between their current behaviors and the standards held by their various constituents within the organization. They then resolve these discrepancies by managing the expectations of others through standard setting, enacting different behaviors, and self-monitoring, all regulation techniques (Tsui and Ashford, 1994).

It has also been shown that self-regulation processes are important in leader development in terms of self-regulation strength, "an individual difference variable that describes the capacity or ability needed to inhibit, override, or alter responses" (Day et al., 2009, p. 302). Current theories conceptualize self-regulatory strength as similar to a muscle (Baumeister, Heatherton, and Tice, 1994). Higher levels of self-regulatory strength appear to be conceptually related to the higher levels of self-discipline and self-control needed for effective leadership. This is linked as well to the long-term development of leaders.

SUMMARY

The overall point we make here is how the strong correlations among self-efficacy, learning goal orientation, and self-regulation influence your leader expertise and decision making. They work together, reinforcing one another (Radosevich, Vaidyanathan, Yeo, and Radosevich, 2004; Zimmerman, 2006). Although scholars do not have enough evidence to claim that one factor directly causes another, they do argue that the three are interrelated and influence leader expertise development (Day et al., 2009). Perhaps you realize now that these three factors are important for leader expertise development, and specifically for your growth as a quandary negotiator.

Keep in mind that you control these internal factors that influence your leadership expertise development. Be aware of your capabilities, the need to seek out leadership development opportunities, your orientation toward performance or growth, and your reactions to people, events, and your own development that can detract from your leadership potential. Believe in your ability to develop and strengthen these factors.

Research has shown that when one's self-efficacy beliefs—that is, beliefs in the capability to perform—are stronger, higher goals are set and the commitment to these goals is greater. Outcome expectations, or beliefs about the ends of learning, are often linked with enhanced competence in experts as well. Task interest or value increases when outcomes reflect increases in one's learning competence. And, goal orientation shifts from concentrating on achievement to concentrating on the value of the learning process. These factors are not molded easily. You must have the drive to believe in, pursue, grow, and control your leader capabilities.

Further, recognize that these factors alone do not make you an expert leader. They must be integrated with experiences and voices from the field; skills and theories acquired, often through preparation programs; and your own leadership platform. As you reflect upon your experiences with and reactions to the questions prompted by this book, consider how your knowledge and leadership platform informed your approach. As you consider decisions regarding these quandaries, draw upon this knowledge base *and then* consider how you influence your decision. What will you decide to do? How will you challenge your own capabilities, orient yourself toward growth, and regulate your behavior and thoughts to get the job done?

ADDITIONAL READING AND REFERENCES

Bandura, A. (1977). Self-efficacy: Toward a unifying theory of behavioral change. *Psychological Review*, 84(2), 191–215.

Bandura, A. (1986). *Social foundations of thought and action: A social cognitive theory*. Upper Saddle River, NJ: Prentice Hall.

Bandura, A. (1997). *Self-efficacy: The exercise of control*. New York: W. H. Freeman.

Baron, L., Morin, L., and Morin, D. (2011). Executive coaching: The effect of working alliance discrepancy on the development of coachees' self-efficacy. *Journal of Management Development*, 30(9), 847–864.

Baumeister, R. F., Heatherton, T. F., and Tice, D. M. (1994). *Losing control: How and why people fail at self-regulation*. San Diego, CA: Academic Press.

Becher, T. (1989). *Academic tribes and territories: Intellectual enquiry and the culture of disciplines*. The Society for Research into Higher Education. Milton Keynes, UK: Open University Press.

Bereiter, C., and Scardamalia, M. (1993). *Surpassing ourselves: An inquiry into the nature and implications of expertise.* Chicago: Open Court.

Cron, W. L., Slocum, J. W., Jr., VandeWalle, D., and Fu, F. Q. (2005). The role of goal orientation on negative emotions and goal setting when initial performance falls short of one's performance goal. *Human Performance,* 18(1), 55–80.

Day, D., Harrison, M. M., and Halpin, S. M. (2009). *An integrative approach to leader development: Connecting adult development, identity, and expertise.* New York: Routledge.

DeRue, D. S., and Wellman, N. (2009). Developing leaders via experience: The role of developmental challenge, learning orientation, and feedback availability. *Journal of Applied Psychology,* 94(4), 859–875.

Dragoni, L., Tesluk, P. E., Russell, J. E. A., and Oh, I. (2009). Understanding managerial development: Integrating developmental assignments, learning orientation, and access to developmental opportunities in predicting managerial competencies. *Academy of Management Journal,* 52(4), 731–743.

Dweck, C. S. (1986). Motivational processes affecting learning. *American Psychologist,* 41(10), 1040–1048.

Dweck, C. S. (2006). *Mindset: The new psychology of success.* New York: Random House.

Eden, D., and Aviram, A. (1993). Self-efficacy training to speed reemployment: Helping people to help themselves. *Journal of Applied Psychology,* 78(3), 352–360.

Ericsson, K. A., Charness, N., Feltovich, P. J., and Hoffman, R. R. (2006). *The Cambridge handbook of expertise and expert performance.* New York: Cambridge University Press.

Ericsson, K. A., Krampe, R. T., and Tesche-Romer, C. (1993). The role of deliberate practice in the acquisition of expert performance. *Psychological Review,* 100, 363–406.

Glaser, R., and Chi, M. T. H. (1988). Overview. In M. T. H. Chi, R. Glaser, and M. J. Farr (Eds.), *The nature of expertise* (pp. xv–xxviii). Hillsdale, NJ: Lawrence Erlbaum Associates.

Hannah, S. T., Avolio, B. J., Luthans, F., and Harms, P. D. (2008). Leadership efficacy: Review and future directions. *Leadership Quarterly,* 19, 669–692.

Hendricks, J. W., and Payne, S. C. (2007). Beyond the big five: Leader goal orientation as a predictor of leadership effectiveness. *Human Performance,* 20(4), 317–343.

Hyle, A. E., Ivory, G., and McClellan, R. (2010). Hidden expert knowledge: The knowledge that counts for the small school-district superintendent. *Journal of Research in Leadership Education,* 5(4), 154–178.

Johnson, E. J. (1988). Expertise and decision under uncertainty: Performance and process. In M. T. H. Chi, R. Glaser, and M. J. Farr (Eds.), *The nature of expertise* (pp. 209–228). Hillsdale, NJ: Lawrence Erlbaum Associates.

Kirschenbaum, D. S., O'Connor, E. A., and Owens, D. (1999). Positive illusions in golf: Empirical and conceptual analyses. *Journal of Applied Sport Psychology,* 11, 1–27.

Lester, P. B., Hannah, S. T., Harms, P. D., Vogelgesang, G. R., and Avolio, B. J. (2011). Mentoring impact on leader efficacy development: A field experiment. *Academy of Management Learning and Education*, 10(3), 409–429.
Radosevich, D. J., Vaidyanathan, V. T., Yeo, S., and Radosevich, D. M. (2004). Relating goal orientation to self-regulatory processes: A longitudinal field test. *Contemporary Educational Psychology*, 29(3), 207–229.
Schunk, D. H. (1983). Progress self-monitoring: Effects on children's self-efficacy and achievement. *Journal of Experimental Education*, 51, 88–105.
Sosik, J. J., Potosky, D., and Jung, D. I. (2002). Adaptive self-regulation: Meeting others' expectations of leadership and performance. *The Journal of Social Psychology*, 142(2), 211–232.
Tsui, A. S., and Ashford, S. J. (1994). Adaptive self-regulation: A process view of managerial effectiveness. *Journal of Management*, 20, 93–121.
VandeWalle, D. (2003). A goal orientation model of feedback-seeking behavior. *Human Resource Management Review*, 13, 581–604.
Werner, K. (1996). *Effortless mastery: Liberating the master musician within*. New Albany, IN: Jamey Aebersold Jazz.
Wood, R., and Bandura, A. (1989). Social cognitive theory of organizational management. *Academy of Management Review*, 14, 361–384.
Yeow, J., and Martin, R. (2013). The role of self-regulation in developing leaders: A longitudinal field experiment. *Leadership Quarterly*, 24, 625–637.
Zimmerman, B. J. (2006). Development and adaptation of expertise: The role of self-regulatory processes and beliefs. In K. A. Ericsson, N. Charness, P. J. Feltovich, and R. R. Hoffman (Eds.), *The Cambridge handbook of expertise and expert performance* (pp. 705–722). Cambridge, UK: Cambridge University Press.
Zimmerman, B. J., and Kitsantas, A. (1999). Acquiring writing revision skill: Shifting from process to outcome self-regulatory goals. *Journal of Educational Psychology*, 91, 1–10.

Appendix

Where Did We Get These Quandary Stories?

Gary Ivory and Michele Acker-Hocevar

One of the jobs of being a scholar is to be as clear as possible about where we get our ideas. People can critique our sources, question our methods, fault our logic, and disagree strongly with our conclusions. But they should not be able to criticize us for lack of transparency. It should be as clear as possible to everyone what we did and why. So, here we will explain where and how we got the anecdotes we offer as examples of quandaries.

Virtually everyone who has written for this book has participated in some way in the University Council for Educational Administration (UCEA), a consortium of approximately one hundred doctoral-granting universities, mostly from the United States. UCEA's mission is to advance "the preparation and practice of educational leaders for the benefit of schools and children" through three emphases: (1) promoting, sponsoring, and disseminating research on the essential problems of schooling and leadership practice; (2) improving the preparation and professional development of educational leaders and professors; and (3) positively influencing local, state, and national educational policy (UCEA, 2014). We do not know if our work on this book will influence policy, but we have worked hard to ensure that it complies with the first two UCEA emphases.

In the mid-1990s, in an effort to learn more about the essential problems of schooling and leadership practice, UCEA undertook a project, entitled *A Thousand Voices from the Firing Line* (Kochan,

Jackson, and Duke, 1999), to conduct one-on-one interviews with principals and superintendents to learn more about the challenges they face. After the initial phases of the project were completed, the two of us were honored to take on the project's leadership. Eventually, we renamed it "Voices from the Field: Phase 3," or simply "Voices 3," and we switched from one-on-one interviews to focus groups. A focus group is designed to be a conversation in which a moderator presents discussion prompts and a group of individuals, generally with similar backgrounds or interests, talks about them. The conversation is recorded, and a transcription is made for later analysis. As we began to design Voices 3, there was considerable discussion in UCEA at the time about a call from Joseph Murphy (2002) to redesign education leadership preparation around the three concepts of school improvement, social justice, and democratic community. After considerable discussion with colleagues (Acker-Hocevar and Ivory, 2006; Ivory and Acker-Hocevar, 2003), we decided that these were promising concepts to ask principals and superintendents to discuss in focus groups.

We designed the study in detail (Acker-Hocevar and Ivory, 2004), setting up the focus groups so that principals would meet together in focus groups with other principals and superintendents with other superintendents. We gave much thought to our focus-group interview questions. We wanted questions that would get participants talking to one another without leading them toward the kinds of answers that would be considered valid or desirable. We hoped, instead, to learn their honest opinions and perceptions. After careful study of Krueger and Casey (2000) and doing a pilot study, we finalized our list of ten discussion prompts. The ones most pertinent to this book are these three: (1) What has No Child Left Behind meant for you as a leader in education? (This was to get at their responses concerning school improvement.) (2) Superintendents talk about doing what's best for students. Tell me about your experiences with that. (To get at their perceptions regarding social justice.) (3) There is a piece of paper in front of you. Write an answer to this question and then we'll share our responses with one another: What does it mean that other people want to have a voice in decision making? (To elicit their ideas regarding democratic community.)

Then we attended meetings of UCEA, the National Council of Professors of Educational Administration, and the American Educational Research Association to call for volunteers to conduct focus groups. We trained all volunteers on the study design, either in person or via telephone. Each volunteer then invited superintendents or principals to participate.

By the end, we had conducted 14 focus groups with a total of 81 superintendents. In the focus groups, we had superintendents from New England and the Mid-Atlantic states, the Midwest, the Southeast, and the Southwest and West. We regret that we never conducted any superintendent focus groups in the Pacific Northwest. Both men and women participated. We had almost no members of ethnic minority groups among our superintendents, perhaps because there are so few ethnic minority superintendents. We transcribed the recordings and numbered all superintendents to maintain the confidentiality of the data. You can read the transcriptions on the website of Information Age Publishing: http://www.infoagepub.com/assets/files/companion_sites/snapshots_of_leadership/?q=snapshots_of_leadership.

References

Acker-Hocevar, M., and Ivory, G. (2004). *Voices from the field phase 3: Principals' and superintendents' perspectives of school improvement, social justice, and democratic community: Instructions for focus-group moderators.* Unpublished manuscript. Retrieved from http://emd.education.nmsu.edu/files/2013/07/voices-from-the-field-phase-3-principals-and-superintendents.pdf.

Acker-Hocevar, M., and Ivory, G. (2006). Update on Voices 3: Focus groups underway and plans and thoughts about the future. *UCEA Review*, 48(1), 22–24.

Ivory, G., and Acker-Hocevar, M. (2003). UCEA seeks superintendents' and principals' perspectives in "Voices 3." *UCEA Review*, 45(2), 15–17.

Kochan, F. K., Jackson, B. L., and Duke, D. L. (1999). *A thousand voices from the firing line: A study of educational leaders, their jobs, their preparation, and the problems they face.* Columbia, MO: University Council for Educational Administration.

Krueger, R. A., and Casey, M. A. (2000). *Focus groups: A practical guide for applied research* (3rd ed.). Thousand Oaks, CA: Sage.

Murphy, J. (2002). Reculturing the profession of educational leadership: New blueprints. *Educational Administration Quarterly*, 38, 176–191.

University Council for Educational Administration. (2014). *Who we are.* Retrieved from http://www.ucea.org/who-we-are/.

Notes on Contributors

Michele Acker-Hocevar, professor, coordinator of the doctoral program and graduate programs in education on the Tri-Cities campus of Washington State University, and also the coeditor of the *Journal of Research on Leadership Education* (JRLE). Her research in leadership studies brings together organizational power, structure, culture, and change that is often around poverty and English Language Learners and how policy affects leadership decision making and reform.

Thomas L. Alsbury, professor of educational leadership at Seattle Pacific University in Seattle, Washington. He is a former school teacher and administrator and currently serves as codirector of the University Council for Educational Administration (UCEA) National Center for Research on the Superintendency and District Governance. He has over 50 publications on school board and superintendent research. He received the UCEA Culbertson Award for significant contributions to education leadership research in 2008 for his book *The future of school board governance: Relevance and revelation*. His newest book, *Improving school board effectiveness: A balanced governance approach*, includes a new model for school board governance and practical tools for improving school board effectiveness.

Sharon Gieselmann, associate professor of education at the University of Evansville in Indiana. She has been an elementary school principal, a staff developer, and an elementary school teacher. Her research interests include social justice issues in public schools. She has presented her work internationally at conferences in Moscow, Russia; Paris, France; and Brighton, United Kingdom.

Adrienne E. Hyle, professor and chair of Educational Leadership and Policy Studies at the University of Texas at Arlington, Arlington, Texas. She has coauthored books that explore the socialization of women faculty (*From girls in their elements to women in science: Rethinking socialization through memory-work*), international uses of the research method memory-work (*Dissecting the mundane: International perspectives on memory-work*), and women leaders in higher education (*Women at the top: What women university and college presidents say about effective leadership*), as well as multiple book chapters and over 30 peer-reviewed journal articles.

Gary Ivory, associate professor of educational leadership and administration at New Mexico State University in Las Cruces, New Mexico. He has taught in grades five through eight and at the community college level. He has been a university department head and coordinator of research, testing, and evaluation in a district of fifty thousand students. He is coeditor with Michele Acker-Hocevar, Julia N. Ballenger, and A. William Place of *Snapshots of School Leadership in the 21st Century* (Information Age Publishing).

Chad R. Lochmiller, assistant research scientist at the Center for Evaluation and Education Policy at Indiana University. His research focuses on contemporary education policy issues, including those related to resource allocation, human resource management, and leadership development. His research has been published in the *Journal of School Leadership*, *Education Policy Analysis Archives*, the *Journal of Research on Leadership Education*, and the *Journal of Cases in Educational Leadership*.

Teena McDonald, clinical assistant professor in educational leadership, sport studies, and educational/counseling psychology at Washington State University, Tri-Cities. She works closely with professional organizations and school districts, teaches courses in the principal certification program, and is program director for the Spokane campus. She is a practitioner-scholar, and her research interests are in the areas of leadership and organizational studies including the superintendency, mindfulness, the principalship, and organizational and occupational socialization of women administrators.

Rhonda McClellan, associate professor and director of the interdisciplinary PhD in leadership program at University of Central Arkansas in Conway, Arkansas. She has taught and coordinated graduate programs in educational leadership development in New Mexico, Texas, and Arkansas. Social justice, educational leader development, and women in (education) leadership continue to be her research interests. She has publications in *Educational Administration Quarterly*, *Journal of Educational Administration*, *Journal of Higher Education*, and *Journal of Research on Leadership Education*.

Susan Printy, associate professor in the Department of Educational Administration at Michigan State University, East Lansing, Michigan. She investigates the importance of an environment in which principals and teachers share leadership and how such an environment helps schools to be effective. At the doctoral level, she teaches leadership theory and practical application; at the masters level, she teaches action research and data use.

Cristóbal Rodríguez, assistant professor in the Department of Educational Leadership and Policy in the School of Education at Howard University in Washington, DC. His research focuses on concentrated diverse demographics, particularly in the U.S./Mexico borderlands, and explores variations in policy development, implementation, and results and their influence on access throughout the educational pipeline. Dr. Rodríguez's recent work has been published in the *Journal of Latinos and Education*, the *Harvard Journal of African American Policy*, and the *Journal of Hispanic Higher Education*.

William G. Ruff, associate professor of educational leadership at Montana State University. He has published more than a dozen journal articles and book chapters addressing school leadership, social justice issues, and comprehensive school reform. Additionally, he has served as the primary investigator for a series of U.S. Department of Education grants resulting in the preparation and placement of over one hundred American Indian educational leaders serving indigenous communities at the federal, state, tribal, or local level.

Corrie Stone-Johnson, assistant professor of educational administration at the University at Buffalo, State University of New York. Over the last several years, her research has examined such topics as generations and change, relationships between school leaders and school communities, and differing concepts of professionalism. Her work is published in her field's leading journals, including *Educational Administration Quarterly*, *Education and Urban Society*, the *Journal of Educational Change*, the *International Journal of Leadership in Education*, and *Teachers and Teaching: Theory and Practice*.

Debra Touchton, associate professor of educational leadership graduate programs at Stetson University in Florida. She earned a PhD in interdisciplinary studies with a concentration in organizational development from the University of South Florida. Working in education for over 30 years, Dr. Touchton has educational and administrative experience at the school, district, regional, and state levels. Her research interests and publications are in the areas of leadership and organizational development, women in leadership, and the effects of poverty on teaching and learning. She is a former president of the Florida Association of Professors of Educational Leadership and continues to be an active member.

Kathryn S. Whitaker, professor emerita of educational leadership and policy studies at the University of Northern Colorado. Prior to serving 25 years as professor, she was a K–12 teacher, assistant principal, and principal. She has published in journals such as the *Journal of School Leadership*, the *Journal of Educational Administration*, and *Planning and Changing*. She is author or coauthor of several books and book chapters.

Index

Acker-Hocevar, Michele, 1–12, 35, 74, 79–80, 91–109, 197–99, 201
Alsbury, Thomas L., 35–50, 201
Alvesson, M., 94
Archer, J., 36
Argyris, C., 4, 42, 46

baby boomers, 94–96, 103, 108
Bandura, A., 182, 184
Barbour, J. D., 118
Baumeister, R. F., 192
Baumgardner, J., 4, 99, 108
Bennis, W., 25, 70
Bereiter, C., 179, 181, 190
Bertalanffy, L., 79
Bill and Melinda Gates Foundation, 36
Bird, J. J., 135–36
Bishop, S., 42, 59
Björk, L. G., 35–36, 50
Bohman, J., 118–19
Bolman. L. G., 58
Bredeson, P. V., 36, 41
Bridges, E., 36
Brody, R., 59
Burns, J. M., 4, 56, 69
bus drivers, 62–63

Cameron, K., 5, 154–55, 177
capabilities, 127, 135, 176, 183–84, 189, 192–93
Chambers, J. G., 134
Chapman, C., 82–83

Cohen, Samantha (pseudonym), 132, 139–42, 144–46
Cohen, W. M., 45
Collins, J., 153
Common Core, 44, 171
Competing Values Framework (CVF)
  describing quandaries with, 5, 154–55
  example, 156
  overview, 155–57
  quadrants, 155–57
  using for decision making, 172–78
complexity theory
  complex adaptive systems, 79–80
  explained, 80–82
  networked leadership, 82–83
  overview, 73–75, 85–87
  in practice, 83–85
  work of superintendents, 75–79
contextuality, 43, 45–46
control of impulses, 183
  see also self-regulation
Coogan, Nancy, 61
Creswell, J., 102
critical theory, 114, 117–21, 123–24, 126, 128
Cron, W. L., 186–88
Crowson, R., 36, 47
Cuban, L., 36

Daft, R. L., 56
Daly, A. J., 80

Day, D. V., 7, 17, 154, 187, 190, 192
De Meyer, A., 31
Deal, T. E., 58
decision-making
  example scenarios, 64–69
  mindfulness theory, 59–63
  overview, 55–56
  transformational leadership theory, 56–59
  using CVF for, 172–76
deference to authority, 62, 98
deference to expertise, 60–63, 65–66
Depres, B., 36, 51
DeRue, D. S., 187, 189
Dhiman, S., 4, 59
double-loop learning, 46–47
Dragoni, L., 187–89
Driver, M., 46
DuFour, 21, 28
Dweck, C. S., 187, 189

Eagly, A., 57–58
Earl, L., 82–83
Easton, David, 4, 132, 136–39, 147–50
Eden, D., 184
Ellerson, N. M., 133–34
Enomoto, E. K., 100
Epstein, M., 59
Erlichson, B., 134
Etzioni, A., 8–9
Evan, M. P., 83

Fahey, K. M., 83
failure
  administrators, 24, 28, 38, 46–47
  "failure traps," 46
  leadership and, 60, 126, 154, 184, 188–89
  learning goal orientation and, 187
  PAGO and, 188
  preoccupation with, 62, 65
  schools, 36, 38, 43
  students, 16, 39

feedback, 78, 167, 186–87
Feldman, M. S., 45
feminist waves and epistemology
  implications for stakeholders, 100–1
  leadership approaches, 101–2
  overview, 99–100
Ferguson, K., 100
Feuer, M. J., 120, 128
Fiol, C., 46
Firestone, W. A., 36
Follett, Mary Parker, 4, 20–32
Fullan, M., 36, 44–45, 69, 74, 83, 117
Furman, G. C., 92

Generation X, 94–97, 108
Generation Y
  see millennials
generational diversity
  baby boomers, 96
  four generations, 95–99
  Generation X, 96–97
  generational leadership approaches, 98–99
  generational leadership implications for stakeholders, 97–98
  generations and waves, 93–94
  millennials, 97
  no easy answers, 93
  exploring diversity, 94–95
  overview, 91–92
  perspectives, 92–96
  problem, 92
  veteran generation, 96–97, 103
generational theory, 4, 91–95, 109
Gieselmann, Sharon, 19–32, 179–93, 201
Gilligan, Carol, 100–1
Ginsberg, A. E., 101
Giroux, Henri, 108, 124
Glass, T., 36, 75
goal orientation
  application of, 188–89
  leadership and, 183

learning goal orientation (LGO), 186–88
  overview, 186, 192–93
  performance avoid goal orientation (PAGO), 188
  performance goal orientation (PGO), 186–88
  performance prove goal orientation (PPGO), 188
Goldring, E., 47
Graham, P., 22
Gramsci, Antonio, 118
Gravett, L., 96, 108
Great Depression, 96, 133
Grogan, M., 100, 117–18
Gronn, P., 81
Guthrie, J. W., 133

Harris, A., 83
Harrison, M. M., 7, 17, 154, 187
Hart, A. W., 36
Hartman, W., 134
Hatch, T., 75
Hauke, M., 46
Heifetz, R. A., 4
Hendricks, J. W., 188
Herbert Valley School District (pseudonym), 139–41
Hess, F. M., 42
hierarchy, 21–22, 27, 31, 99
Hierarchy Culture, 155–56, 173–76
Hightower, A., 36
Honig, M. I., 41, 43–44, 46
Hord, S., 21
Hoy, W., 46
Hyle, Adrienne E., 1–12, 201

Interstate School Leaders Licensure Consortium (ISLLC) standards
  developing formal organizations/communities and, 24
  joint work and, 44
  listed, 3–5
  organizational learning theory and, 43
  Standard 1, 3–4, 19, 32
  Standard 2, 3–4, 35
  Standard 3, 3–4, 56, 67, 73–76, 81, 83, 85–86
  Standard 4, 3–4, 91, 120
  Standard 5, 3–4, 113–16, 120–21
  Standard 6, 3–4, 131
  superintendents and, 4–5, 43, 48
Ivory, Gary, 1–12, 15–18, 35, 44, 107, 113–29, 179–93, 197–99, 202

James, William, 9
Jazzar, M., 75
Johannesen-Schmidt, M. C., 57
Johnson, A. G., 100, 108
Johnson, P. F., 4, 116–18
joint work, 43–44

Kabat-Zinn, J., 59
Katz, D., 4, 41
Katz, S., 82–83
Keedy, J., 36
Kew, K., 82–83
Kirst, M. W., 4, 44, 132, 137–38, 147, 149–50

Laible, Julie, 100, 102
Lancaster, L. C., 94–99, 108
Landrieu, M., 27
Langer, E., 58–59
Leachman, M. L., 134
leadership platforms
  overview, 15–16
  vision and, 29–31
  your cultural autobiography, 17–18
  your leadership platform, 16–17
Leithwood, K., 4, 35–36, 41–42, 46, 48, 51, 114
Levinthal, D. A., 44–45
Levitt, B., 44, 46
Lewin, R., 80
local education agencies (LEAs), 23
Lochmiller, Chad R., 131–50, 202
Lovely, S., 96–97, 109
Lunenberg, F., 8

Lyles, M., 46
Lynch, M., 24

Manifesta: Young Women, Feminism, and the Future (Baumgardner and Richards), 99
March, L. G., 43–44, 46
Marion, R., 79
Marks, H., 4, 42, 89
Marzano, R., 31, 36, 39, 58, 67
Maslow, Abraham, 11
Maxwell, J. A., 9
Mazzoni, T. L., 136
McClellan, Rhonda, 1–12, 113–29, 179–93, 202
McDonald, Teena, 55–70, 202
McGregor, D., 156
McLaughlin, M. W., 36
McNulty, B. A., 58, 67
McQuillan, P. J., 80
Miles, K., 134
millennials, 94, 97–98, 103, 108
mind-sets, 31, 96, 183, 185–87
mindfulness theory, 4, 55–56, 58–63
Miskel, C., 40
Monk, D. H., 134
Morrison, K., 80–82, 84
Murphy, Joseph, 6, 198
Murray, L. M., 135–36

No Child Left Behind (NCLB), 5, 37–40, 43, 45, 166, 170–71
Noddings, N., 101, 109

O'Day, J. A., 43, 46
Odden, A. R., 134
organizational learning theory
  characteristics, 43
  contextuality and, 45
  improvement and, 43
  overview, 42
  role theory and, 35, 37, 41
  sense-making and, 44–45
  single-loop/double-loop learning and, 46–47
  superintendents and, 44, 47–48
Orr, M., 75

parents, 20, 25–26, 55, 63, 66–67, 74, 78, 86, 97, 103–4, 106, 114, 124–25, 134–35, 137, 139, 143, 145, 160–61
Peters, T., 157
Pitner, N. J., 125
Plecki, M. L., 135–36
Prestine, N., 41, 56, 58
Printy, Susan, 4, 42, 82, 153–77, 202
prior knowledge, 43–45
promoting student success
  democratic school leadership, 121–22
  empirical approach, 116–17, 119–21
  example story, 115–16
  normative approach, 116–19
  overview, 113–15, 127–28
  questions on dealing with school board, 123
  student behavior problems, 124–27

quandaries
  contextuality and, 45
  democratic school leadership and, 121
  of developing formal organizations or communities, 24–27
  disagreement and, 19–20, 23
  examples of, 48–50, 197–99
  external accountability mandates and, 27–39
  improvement and, 43
  inclement weather, 55–56, 62
  of integration, 27–29
  leadership and, 16, 85–86, 114, 179–82, 185
  local internal interests and, 40–41
  mindfulness and, 62–63
  negotiating, 6–8, 117, 187–89, 192–93
  organizational learning theory and, 42–43

overview, 5–6
perspectives on instructional quandaries, 47–48
resources and, 39–40
student behavior problems and, 124–25
superintendents and, 35–41, 43–45, 47, 55–56, 79, 85, 120–21, 153–54
theories and, 8–11
unfunded mandates, 39–40
Quinn, Robert, 5, 154–56, 177–78

Radosevich, D. J., 186, 188, 192
Raines, C., 95–98, 109
Rainey, R., 119
resource allocation in rural school districts
  adjusting leadership in response to stakeholders, 146–47
  Easton's model and, 137–39, 147–50
  identifying assumptions about resources, 133–34
  illustrative case, 139–41
  overview, 131–33
  as political endeavor, 136
  political perspectives on fiscal leadership, 135–36
  political systems perspective, 136–37
  productively engaging stakeholders in political process, 144–46
  reacting to resource decisions and gauging community support/demands, 142–44
Richards, A., 4, 99, 108
Rodriguez, Cristóbal, 113–29, 202–3
role theory, 35, 37, 41–42, 47–48, 50
Rowe-Finkbeiner, K., 4, 99
Ruff, William G., 19–32, 203

satisficing, 114, 119–24, 126–29
Schön, D., 42, 46

Schunk, D. H., 192
Schwan, C., 36
self and leader expertise
  development of leader expertise, 182–83
  forethought, 191
  goal orientation, 186–89
  overview, 179–82, 192–93
  performance, 191
  self-efficacy, 184–85
  self-reflection, 191–92
  self-regulation and leadership, 192
  self-regulatory knowledge, 189–92
  trusting your resilience, 185
self-efficacy, 184–85, 188–89, 192–93
self-regulation
  forethought, 191
  leadership and, 183, 192
  PAGO and, 188
  self-reflection, 191–92
  self-regulatory knowledge, 189–93
Senge, P., 58, 157
sense-making, 44–45
Short, P., 36
Sidorkin, A., 95
Silins, H., 42
Simon, Herbert, 119, 129
single-loop learning, 43, 46–47
Smarter Balanced Assessment System, 44
Snyder, K. J., 4, 74, 79–80
Sommers, P., 4, 21, 99
Sosik, J. J., 192
Spillane, J. P., 75
standards
  see Interstate School Leaders Licensure Consortium (ISLLC) standards
Staufer, D., 21
Stephenson, L. E., 83
Stone-Johnson, Corrie, 4, 73–87, 203
Strauss, W., 4, 92–93, 109

superintendents
  aligning resources in order to satisfy accountability requirements, 39–40
  challenges of external accountability mandates, 38–39
  contextuality and prior knowledge, 45–46
  discussion questions, 48
  as instructional leaders, 35–36
  organizational learning theory and, 42–43
  overview, 35
  perspectives on instructional quandaries, 47–48
  positive aspects of external accountability mandates, 37–38
  quandary examples, 48–50
  responding to local internal interests, 40–41
  role theory and, 41–42
  sense-making, 44–45
  single- and double-loop learning, 46–47
  stories, 102–7
  supporting engagement in joint work, 43–44
  valuing and legitimizing improvement, 43
  voices on instructional leadership, 36–37
superintendents, framework for choosing
  Competing Values Framework (CVF), 155–57, 172–76
  examples of candidates, 163–172
  green technology companies, 158–59
  overview, 153–55
  reflection on leadership, 177
  Summerland school district, 159–63
Sutcliffe, K., 60
Systems Analysis of Political Life, A (Easton), 136

Teddlie, C., 83
testing, 22–23, 49
Thomas, J. Y., 51
Thomas, T., 59
Thousand Voices from the Firing Line, A (UCEA), 197
Touchton, Debra, 91–109, 203
transformational leadership theory
  change and, 58
  components of, 56–57
  gender and, 57–58
  mindfulness theory and, 59, 63
  overview, 56–59
Tsui, A. S., 192

UCEA Voices project, 2, 5, 11–12, 35–37, 47–48, 56, 63, 102, 120–21, 132–34, 139, 154–55, 177, 197–98
unfunded mandates, 39
Urwick, L., 24

van Engen, M., 57
VandeWalle, D., 186–87
veteran generation, 96–97, 103
vision, disagreement and opportunities for introspection about your leadership platform, 29–31
  overview, 19–20
  pitting perspectives against one another, 23–29
  quandaries of developing formal organizations/communities, 24–27
  quandaries of integration, 27–29
  theoretical framework, 20–23
Voices data
  see UCEA Voices project

Wang, C., 135–36
Waters, J., 31, 36, 39, 58, 67
Weber, Max, 4, 20–24, 26–32, 155
Weick, K., 59–60

Werner, K., 197
Whitaker, Kathryn S., 35–51, 203
Wirt, F. M., 4, 132, 137–38, 147, 149–50
Wood, R., 184

Young, M., 102

Zellermayer, M., 74, 80
Zemke, R., 95, 97–98, 109
Zimmerman, B. J., 190–92

CPSIA information can be obtained at www.ICGtesting.com
Printed in the USA
LVOW01*2034040315

429280LV00010B/329/P